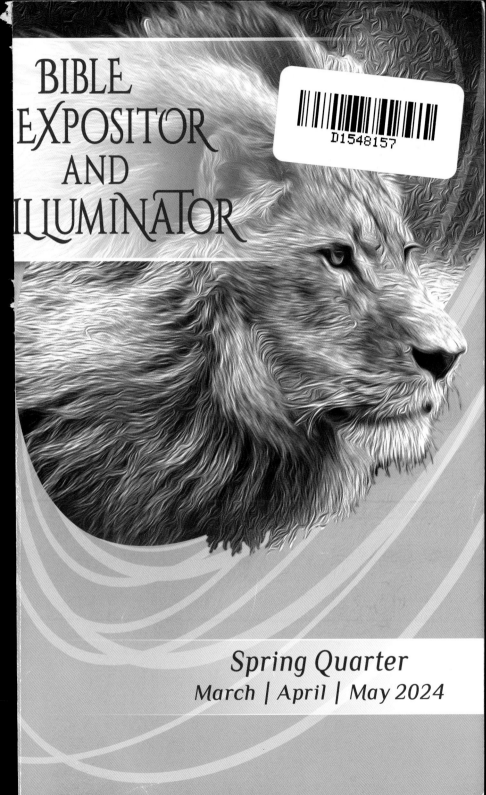

BIBLE EXPOSITOR AND ILLUMINATOR

Spring Quarter
March | April | May 2024

LifeStone

Dear Customers,

We are very excited to share with all of you that Union Gospel Press will be expanding our impact in the Great Commission. We believe God is prompting our vision to expound the passion He placed in our founder's heart, William Brunner Musselman. Mr. Musselman had a love for Christ and serving people for Christ. For over 120 years, UGP has been publishing God's truth in our Sunday school materials. With God's grace, we will continue to produce material for another 120 years.

God is convicting our hearts to come alongside our struggling churches in this nation with coaching and discipleship training services. We believe that the Great Commission involves evangelizing the lost, bringing people to saving faith in Christ, and then teaching them to obey all the commands of Jesus. We are commanded to make disciples!

With prayerful consideration, we have altered our vision and mission to include all of the elements of the Great Commission. Our new Vision: Building Christian leaders' conviction and confidence to help transform people into the image of Christ through biblical resources and real-life application training. Our new Mission: Empowering Christian disciples to make disciples.

Union Gospel Press will remain God's publishing company as a subsidiary of LifeStone Ministries. LifeStone Ministries is being created so that we can begin rolling up our sleeves and outwardly helping churches improve their disciple-making skills through coaching and training services. We will also be expanding our mission ministries to reach a global impact. We ask for your prayers as we become empty vessels to serve God.

Under the Mercy,

President & CEO
Craig Wrobleski

Vol. XCVI

No. 2

Bible Expositor and Illuminator

SPRING QUARTER

March, April, May 2024

Jesus Is God
UNIT I: Confirmed by Power over Death

UNIT II: Confirmed by Mighty Miracles

UNIT III: Confirmed by His Exaltation

Editor in Chief: James M. Leonard, Ph.D.
Managing Editor: Michelle Birtasevic
Edited and published quarterly by
LIFESTONE MINISTRIES
UNION GOSPEL PRESS DIVISION
Rev. W. B. Musselman, Founder
Price: $8.19 per quarter*
shipping and handling extra
ISBN 978-1-64495-421-8

Union Gospel Press

LOOKING AHEAD

This quarter will focus on passages that reveal Jesus' identity as God the Son. We will see that people responded in one of two ways to His claims to deity: faith or rejection. Likewise, we must take Jesus' claims seriously.

Our first unit confirms Jesus' deity by His power over death. In lesson 1, Jesus claims that anyone who abides in His word will never taste death, because He is none other than the self-existent "I AM."

In lesson 2, Jesus raises Jairus's daughter from the dead. Though many scoff at His words of assurance to this distraught father, Jairus maintains faith and thus witnesses the power of the Son of God. We next see Jesus raising His friend Lazarus from the dead (lesson 3), leading many to believe in Him but others to seek His death.

Lessons 4 and 5 focus on Jesus' crucifixion and resurrection. His resurrection confirms the authority over death that He promised to the thief on the cross: "To day shalt thou be with me in paradise" (Luke 23:43).

Our second unit confirms Jesus' deity by His miraculous works. His first miracle (lesson 6) identifies the purpose of all His miracles: to reveal His glory as God's Son and to bring about faith in Him.

In lesson 7, Jesus casts a demon out of a boy, causing the demon to cry out in anguish. This highlights the spiritual warfare that surrounded Jesus' ministry. That warfare frequently surfaced in the scribes' and Pharisees' cold rejection of Jesus, as seen in lesson 8, when they fail to recognize Him as Lord of the Sabbath.

In lesson 9, Jesus' disciples worship Him as the Son of God after seeing His power over nature. In lesson 10, He forgives the sins of a paralytic, causing the scribes to accuse Him of blasphemy. His healing of the paralytic confirms His divine authority to forgive sins.

In our final unit, Jesus' deity is confirmed by His exaltation in heaven. Even the angels worship Him (lesson 11), and lesson 12 shows that all living things will one day bow before Him. In lesson 13, we have the promise that He is coming back soon to set all things right.

Do you believe that Jesus is not only a good teacher, but also the Lord of the universe? When He returns, will He find faith on the earth? May this study encourage you to submit your whole life to Him, for He is worthy of nothing less.

—*Matthew Robinson*

PLEASE NOTE: Fundamental, sound doctrine is the objective of LifeStone Ministries, Union Gospel Press Division. The writers are prayerfully selected for their Bible knowledge and yieldedness to the Spirit of Truth, each writing in his own style as enlightened by the Holy Spirit. At best we know in part only. "They received the word with all readiness of mind, and searched the scriptures daily, whether those things were so" (Acts 17:11).

EDITORIALS

Jesus, Our Great God

GLENN WEAVER

How do we identify a great man in our culture? Some great men wear fine clothes and fill prestigious office positions. Other great men gather large crowds of people and give moving speeches. And others hit home runs, win races, or lead their teams to victory. In earlier times some kings even claimed to be gods, but they died like everyone else.

Jesus is the greatest man who ever lived. He demonstrated His greatness in ways that only He could. He claimed to be God, but He did not simply make the claim; He revealed the truth of His claim in multiple ways.

In John 8:31-59, Jesus spoke to a crowd about His identity. He claimed that God was His Father, that God sent Him, and that He was an eyewitness to His Father's heavenly works. He also asserted that He existed before Abraham (vs. 58). Jesus even called Himself "I am," appropriating for Himself the divine Name (cf. Ex. 3:14)! The crowd's response to these claims was to pick up stones to kill Him for blasphemy.

Physicians are great people who heal the sick, but Jesus' greatness goes beyond the abilities of any doctor. Luke 8:40-56 records two miracles of healing that support Jesus' claim to deity. Jairus's daughter was dying. Her father begged Jesus to come to his house and heal her. When Jesus arrived, the girl had already died, but this was no obstacle for Him. He took her by the hand and raised her from the dead.

On His way to Jairus's house, Jesus was delayed by a sick woman. Physicians had been unable to heal her despite their repeated attempts (Luke 8:43). Still, she had faith that Jesus could heal her. She touched the edge of His garment, and she was healed!

Jesus claimed authority to forgive sin. Some men brought their paralyzed friend to Jesus for healing (Mark 2:1-12). Jesus declared the man's sins forgiven, prompting religious teachers to object on the basis that only God could forgive sin. Then, to substantiate His authority to forgive sin, Jesus dramatically healed the paralytic.

Mary and Martha also were convinced of Jesus' power. Their brother, Lazarus, had been dead for four days. Jesus demonstrated His power over death by calling for Lazarus to come out of the tomb. Lazarus arose from the dead and walked out of the tomb in obedience to Jesus' voice. Lazarus's death and resurrection revealed God's glory (John 11:40).

Not only did Jesus have power over death when other people died, but He had power over His own death. While He was dying on the cross, the crowd taunted Him, saying that if He was who He claimed to be, He should save Himself (Luke 23:35). When Jesus died, many supernatural things happened. For example, the sun was darkened, even though it was still day (vs. 45).

The greatest miracle was yet to come. Having been buried, he was raised to life. The disciples were confronted with the risen Christ, and they were convinced that Jesus did indeed have power over death.

Jesus also has power over natural forces such as the wind and water. In Matthew 14:22-33, Jesus came walking on the water to his disciples as their boat was tossed about on the stormy sea. Je-

(Editorials continued on page 186)

SCRIPTURE LESSON TEXT

JOHN 8:31 Then said Jesus to those Jews which believed on him, If ye continue in my word, *then* are ye my disciples indeed;

32 And ye shall know the truth, and the truth shall make you free.

33 They answered him, We be Abraham's seed, and were never in bondage to any man: how sayest thou, Ye shall be made free?

34 Jesus answered them, Verily, verily, I say unto you, Whosoever committeth sin is the servant of sin.

35 And the servant abideth not in the house for ever: *but* the Son abideth ever.

36 If the Son therefore shall make you free, ye shall be free indeed.

37 I know that ye are Abraham's seed; but ye seek to kill me, because my word hath no place in you.

38 I speak that which I have seen with my Father: and ye do that which ye have seen with your father.

48 Then answered the Jews, and said unto him, Say we not well that thou art a Samaritan, and hast a devil?

49 Jesus answered, I have not a devil; but I honour my Father, and ye do dishonour me.

50 And I seek not mine own glory: there is one that seeketh and judgeth.

51 Verily, verily, I say unto you, If a man keep my saying, he shall never see death.

52 Then said the Jews unto him, Now we know that thou hast a devil. Abraham is dead, and the prophets; and thou sayest, If a man keep my saying, he shall never taste of death.

53 Art thou greater than our father Abraham, which is dead? and the prophets are dead: whom makest thou thyself?

54 Jesus answered, If I honour myself, my honour is nothing: it is my Father that honoureth me; of whom ye say, that he is your God:

55 Yet ye have not known him; but I know him: and if I should say, I know him not, I shall be a liar like unto you: but I know him, and keep his saying.

56 Your father Abraham rejoiced to see my day: and he saw *it,* and was glad.

58 Jesus said unto them, Verily, verily, I say unto you, Before Abraham was, I am.

59 Then took they up stones to cast at him: but Jesus hid himself, and went out of the temple, going through the midst of them, and so passed by.

NOTES

Jesus' Claim to Deity

Lesson Text: John 8:31-38, 48-56, 58-59

Related Scriptures: Deuteronomy 13:6-11; Romans 6:15-23;
I John 2:1-6, 22-25; II John 1:9-11

TIME: A.D. 29   PLACE: Jerusalem

GOLDEN TEXT—"If ye continue in my word, then are ye my disciples indeed; and ye shall know the truth, and the truth shall make you free" (John 8:31-32).

Introduction

In this present age, the truth is not always well received. Even though people raise their right hands and swear on oath to tell nothing but the truth, many lie anyway. Corporate scandals seem to occur regularly, and some of the highest executives have been convicted for falsifying records. It is now commonplace for people to lie about anything and everything.

Dishonesty is by no means something new to our society. History is filled with lies. Sadly, lying goes along quite naturally with a secular society, for there is no accepted standard of truth by which people live, only each individual's preference. In contrast, the child of God knows God's revealed truth. That is the only standard by which people can rightly measure themselves.

LESSON OUTLINE

I. **NEEDING TRUTH—**
   John 8:31-38

II. **CONFRONTING ACCUSATIONS—**
    John 8:48-53

III. **HONORING CHRIST—**
     John 8:54-56, 58-59

Exposition: Verse by Verse

NEEDING TRUTH

JOHN 8:31 Then said Jesus to those Jews which believed on him, If ye continue in my word, then are ye my disciples indeed;

32 And ye shall know the truth, and the truth shall make you free.

33 They answered him, We be Abraham's seed, and were never in bondage to any man: how sayest thou, Ye shall be made free?

34 Jesus answered them, Verily, verily, I say unto you, Whosoever committeth sin is the servant of sin.

35 And the servant abideth not in the house for ever: but the Son abideth ever.

36 If the Son therefore shall make you free, ye shall be free indeed.

37 I know that ye are Abraham's seed; but ye seek to kill me, because my word hath no place in you.

38 I speak that which I have seen with my Father: and ye do that which ye have seen with your father.

The freedom of abiding (John 8:31-33). Verse 30 says that as Jesus spoke, "many believed on him." He then addressed those believers, telling them how to live out their faith as His disciples. {To be disciples, Jesus told them they needed to abide in His word, seeking to live according to His teachings (vs. 31).}**Q1** The same is true today. Anyone who abides in Jesus by faith will not remain unchanged but will be transformed by the Holy Spirit (Rom. 12:2).

{To continue in Jesus' word means to stay—to remain, or abide—in it. That is, a person who hears Jesus' teachings will then endeavor to live by them.}**Q2** Jesus' word is truth to be lived; it is not merely academic information. As someone lives by the teachings of Jesus, he will experience a spiritual freedom never known before. If we only make a mental commitment to the teachings of Jesus but never obey them in our actions, we need to examine whether our faith is genuine (cf. Jas. 1:22).

Genuine salvation results in a clean heart and a new person (cf. Acts 15:9; II Cor. 5:17) The inner freedom that comes from knowing Jesus Christ as personal Saviour cannot be understood by those who have never experienced it. At least some of the Jews listening to Jesus could not comprehend what He had just said. {Their response was that they had not been in bondage and thus had no need for the freedom Jesus offered.}**Q3** They felt that their physical descent from Abraham secured their right relationship with God.

The slavery of sin (John 8:34-36). The Jews' claim that they had never been in bondage to anyone was not accurate, for their ancestors had been slaves in Egypt and Babylon. Furthermore, at that very time, they were under the control of the Roman Empire. Since that was not the kind of slavery Jesus had in mind, He did not correct these historical inaccuracies. He was speaking of spiritual slavery rather than physical slavery.

Jesus was speaking of the kind of freedom that comes to people when sin no longer has power over them. {Sin in a person's life is like a taskmaster who makes cruel demands. A person living apart from God does not have the spiritual strength to live apart from sin and is therefore a slave to it.}**Q4** Only Christ can set us free from that bondage.

The apostle Paul explained that those who offer themselves to sin are actually slaves to sin. He writes, "But now being made free from sin, and become servants to God, ye have your fruit unto holiness, and the end everlasting life. For the wages of sin is death; but the gift of God is eternal life through Jesus Christ our Lord" (Rom. 6:22-23). To be free from the wages of sin is a wonderful deliverance!

Slaves never had permanent residence with their masters. They could be sold to someone else at any given moment. Sons, on the other hand, had a permanent home with their parents. Jesus Christ frees us from slavery to sin and gives us a permanent relationship with Him and His Father.

The result of unbelief (John 8:37-38). The Jews had pointedly reminded Jesus of their descent from Abraham, believing that this status automatically put them into a right relationship with God (vs. 33). Here Jesus reminded them that He was well aware of their genealogy. {Abraham, however, was known for having faith in God, and these Jews obviously did not have that faith.}Q5 This was proved by the fact that they wanted to kill Jesus. They were Abraham's physical descendants, but they were not his spiritual descendants.

The reason these Jews wanted to kill Jesus was that His word was not in them; that is, they were spiritually blind and did not recognize Jesus as the Messiah. Furthermore, in wanting to kill Him, these Jews revealed that they were following someone other than God, for such desires come from Satan. They had set themselves up in total contrast with Jesus. He pointed this out by saying that He was speaking what He had seen with His Father, while they were doing what they had seen with their father (vs. 38).

We know Jesus was referring to God as His Father, but who did He refer to as their father? They immediately claimed again that Abraham was their father (vs. 39), but Jesus responded that if that were so, they would live like Abraham. After some more dialogue, Jesus pointedly said, "Ye are of your father the devil, and the lusts of your father ye will do. He was a murderer from the beginning, and abode not in the truth, because there is no truth in him" (vs. 44).

CONFRONTING ACCUSATIONS

48 Then answered the Jews, and said unto him, Say we not well that thou art a Samaritan, and hast a devil?

49 Jesus answered, I have not a devil; but I honour my Father, and ye do dishonour me.

50 And I seek not mine own glory: there is one that seeketh and judgeth.

51 Verily, verily, I say unto you, If a man keep my saying, he shall never see death.

52 Then said the Jews unto him, Now we know that thou hast a devil. Abraham is dead, and the prophets; and thou sayest, If a man keep my saying, he shall never taste of death.

53 Art thou greater than our father Abraham, which is dead? and the prophets are dead: whom makest thou thyself?

Conflict (John 8:48-49). When Jesus once again told the unbelieving Jews they were not hearing God's word because they did not belong to Him (vs. 47), they snapped back, "Say we not well that thou art a Samaritan, and hast a devil?" (vs. 48). Have you ever noticed that when people cannot respond with an intelligent argument to refute what has been said, they often resort to name-calling? That is what the Jews did here. {Since they had no effective response to what Jesus was saying, they reacted bitterly, calling Him a "Samaritan" and demon possessed. In doing so, they were essentially saying that Jesus' description of their own spiritual state actually applied to Him. He had said they were not true children of Abraham but instead were of the devil. Their response was to ascribe to Jesus their own guilt.}Q6

To call a Jewish person a Samaritan was to deny them their full Jewishness. When Assyria defeated the northern kingdom of Israel in 722 B.C., Assyria sent people from other nations to occupy Samaria, the capital of Israel (II Kgs. 17:24). The first-century Samaritans were the likely descendants of those foreign peoples who intermingled with the remaining Israelites, contrary to Mosaic Law. As a result, the Jews of Jesus' day despised them as impure half-breeds. By calling Jesus a Samaritan, they were claiming that He was not a true child of Abraham--and that He certainly was not the Messiah.

Confidence (John 8:50-51). Jesus did not respond to the first accusation. He knew that the Samaritans were just as valuable in God's eyes as anyone else; so He let that accusation go without a response. To call Him demon possessed, however, was a matter of grave dishonor.

He was not about to be associated with the devil in any way, for His intent was to honor His Father. He was not seeking glory for Himself; instead, He said, "There is one that seeketh and judgeth" (vs. 50)." This was a reference to His Father, who seeks Jesus' glory and judges those who dishonor Him.

In spite of the bitter attack against Him, Jesus did not respond in kind. Instead, He referred once again to the mutual glory He had with His Father, thus continuing to present the truth. If anyone in the crowd wanted to avoid the judgment of God, they needed to listen to His words and obey them. By saying "Verily, verily" (vs. 51), Jesus assured them that what He was about to say was a certain and trustworthy statement. Their obedient faith in His word would not only free them from the power of sin but also assure them of eternal life.

{When Jesus said that those keeping His word would never see death, He was referring to spiritual death, not physical death.}[Q7] Clearly, we all die physically. Only the generation living at the time of Christ's return will escape physical death. But all who abide in Jesus by faith will always remain alive with Him, even though they die (cf. 11:25). At the moment of physical death, their souls will be with Him in heaven, and at His return, they will receive resurrected bodies in the new heavens and new earth.

Confrontation (John 8:52-53). All this was just too much for these unbelieving Jews to accept. In their minds, they now knew for certain that Jesus was demon possessed! How could He say there was a way to escape death? Did He consider Himself to be greater than Abraham and all those who died before? How preposterous! Who did He think He was? Such a claim asserted He was more than merely a man. He was calling Himself equal with God; so He had to be insane!

When we listen to the reasoning of these Jews, it may shock us that anyone could so blatantly deny the Lord as He stood right in front of them. The fact, however, is that this is the same kind of blindness we see in the world all around us today.

HONORING CHRIST

54 Jesus answered, If I honour myself, my honour is nothing: it is my Father that honoureth me; of whom ye say, that he is your God:

55 Yet ye have not known him; but I know him: and if I should say, I know him not, I shall be a liar like unto you: but I know him, and keep his saying.

56 Your father Abraham rejoiced to see my day: and he saw it, and was glad.

58 Jesus said unto them, Verily, verily, I say unto you, Before Abraham was, I am.

59 Then took they up stones to cast at him: but Jesus hid himself, and went out of the temple, going through the midst of them, and so passed by.

Honored by God (John 8:54-56). As His questioners became bolder, Jesus responded more boldly. In response to their question about who He made Himself out to be, {Jesus simply said that if He tried to honor Himself, it would mean nothing. He was not trying to honor Himself; He was being honored by God, His Father. Jesus was indicating that no matter what the Jews thought of Him, He did not have to vindicate Himself. His Father would do the vindicating. To vindicate Himself meant nothing; vindication from God meant much.}[Q8]

The crux of the exchange was that Jesus knew God, and these Jews did not: "Ye have not known him; but I know him" (vs. 55). Previously, Jesus had told His disciples that those who would abide in His word would "know the truth" (vs. 32). Now, we see the reverse of that principle at work. The Jews' disbelief in Jesus' word meant that they did not know God.

Jesus then made two more points. First, He stated that if He said He did not know God, He would be a liar just like them. Just as the unbelieving Jews, as children of the devil, were unable to tell the truth (vs. 44), so Jesus, as the perfect Son of God, was unable to tell a lie. Everything Jesus says is truth.

Second, He said that Abraham had rejoiced to see His coming (vs. 56). That must have been astounding to His opponents. In making this claim, Jesus indicated that the very Old Testament saint to whom these Jews were appealing had anticipated His coming through faith in the promises God gave him.

Dishonored by men (John 8:58-59). As we would expect, the Jews haughtily asked Jesus whether He had ever seen Abraham, since He was not even fifty years old (vs. 57). In response, Jesus assured them of the truth: He had existed before Abraham. In saying "Before Abraham was, I am" (vs. 58), He was not merely claiming to exist before Abraham. He was appropriating to Himself nothing less than the divine Name, for God's name (Yahweh) was revealed as "I AM THAT I AM" (Ex. 3:14). Jesus' use of "I am" was therefore a most certain claim to deity.

The Jews immediately understood what Jesus was claiming. In response, they picked up stones in order to stone Him to death. {They believed He had just committed blasphemy by claiming equality with God,}**Q9** and under the Mosaic Law, blasphemers were to be put to death (Lev. 24:16). Somehow Jesus walked through their midst, calmly left the temple, and hid Himself from them. He was delivered from danger by His Heavenly Father.

We should examine carefully Jesus' claim of deity and its implications for our lives. Either what He said is truth, or He was self-deceived and had the mind of a madman. {Likewise, we have two options: honor Him as Lord, or reject Him as a blasphemer. There is no middle ground.}**Q10**

Scripture is consistent in presenting Jesus as the Son of God and as God Himself. Since He is divine, He alone has the power to set us free from the slavery of sin. Those who have received Him and live by His words understand this truth.

—Keith E. Eggert.

QUESTIONS

1. What did Jesus identify as the mark of a true disciple?
2. What did Jesus mean when He told the Jews to continue in His word (John 8:31)?
3. How did they react regarding Jesus' offer of freedom?
4. What does sin do to a person who is living apart from God?
5. What contrast did Jesus draw between Abraham and the Jews who opposed Him?
6. What two accusations did the Jews fling at Jesus, and why did they do so?
7. What did Jesus mean about never seeing death?
8. Why did Jesus say He was not seeking His own glory?
9. What was the conclusion the Jews came to about Jesus' claim of deity?
10. What are our only two options in responding to Jesus' claim to deity?

—Keith E. Eggert.

Preparing to Teach the Lesson

The lessons this quarter establish Scripture's teaching that Jesus is God. Our first unit focuses on Christ's power over death, in demonstration of His deity. This week's lesson focuses on Christ's offer of eternal life and freedom from sin for all who abide in His word.

TODAY'S AIM

Facts: to explore passages from John 8 that reveal Jesus' ability to liberate from sin.

Principle: to affirm that true liberty is possible through Christ.

Application: to challenge Christians to live out the freedom that their relationship with Christ has made possible.

INTRODUCING THE LESSON

"Freedom" is a beautiful word that can be applied in many contexts. To prisoners, freedom means release from confinement. To revolutionaries, freedom means independence from the domination of a tyrannical power. To a debtor, freedom means release from a financial obligation. The word "freedom" has also become a patriotic slogan associated with representative government.

The concept of freedom, however, has a far deeper meaning for the Christian. Christian liberty is not merely the release from political tyranny, foreign occupation, or the burden of debt. Christ came to set us free from sin and its consequences, leading us into eternal life. This lesson deals with that kind of freedom.

DEVELOPING THE LESSON

1. Freedom defined (John 8:31-38). Some claim to be Jesus' disciples, but their lives do not bear it out. The lesson text indicates that some Jews professed belief in Jesus. Jesus taught them that a test of true discipleship was continuity. Believers will ultimately "continue" in Jesus' word (vs. 31), bearing the spiritual fruit along the way. To illustrate this point further, refer to I John 2:19, and to Jesus' parable of the sower (Matt. 13:1-9; 18-23).

Discuss what it means to "continue in my word" (John 8:31). Refer to Acts 2:42, which tells us that the early Christians continued to devote themselves to the apostles' doctrine. Continuing in Jesus' word involves both hearing and obeying.

Moving to John 8:32, focus on two words: "truth" and "free." What truth makes one free? In what sense can one be liberated by this truth? Accepting Jesus for who He is amounts to receiving the truth. Read 14:6. Jesus is the truth that liberates from the penalty and power of sin.

Jesus' listeners misunderstood the freedom that He was talking about. Their statement about always having been free was totally inaccurate. As "Abraham's seed" (8:33) they had been in bondage to the Egyptians, Babylonians, Greeks, and Romans. Use this to illustrate to the class that slaves to sin seldom realize that they are in bondage.

How is John 8:34 crucial to Jesus' message of freedom? People need to realize that, apart from Christ, they are slaves in sin. Ironically, those who claim to be the most liberated are often the most enslaved.

Discuss Jesus' logic in verses 34-35. Note that true liberation from sin is linked to the Son (vs. 36). Relate this to 3:16.

Discuss the irony in 8:36-38. The people who had Abraham's genes did not have Abraham's saving faith.

2. Identity defended (John 8:48-56). Jesus' detractors charged Him with being a Samaritan and demon possessed. Discuss what Jesus' response in verses 49-50 tells us about His identity. How does what Jesus says about the Father seeking His glory compare with Isaiah 48:11?

Move on to consider John 8:51-56. Note that the discussion intensified as Jesus linked eternal life to the keeping of His word. What made Jesus' antagonists angry? Clearly, He was coming to the encounter from an entirely different perspective from theirs. Explain this difference in perspective by reading I Corinthians 2:14. As Jesus' representatives, we are often misunderstood.

Abraham's name occurs numerous times in John 8. It occurs three times in verses 51-56. Why was Jesus' reference to Abraham so offensive to those Jews who were debating Him? Jesus was a young man living in the first century A.D. Abraham, the revered patriarch of the Jews, had lived about two thousand years before. In their eyes, Jesus' claim that Abraham rejoiced to see His day was both arrogant and preposterous.

What other sayings of Jesus in this passage offended and incensed the Jews? Jesus called them liars and denied that they knew God as they claimed. It is obvious that Jesus was not attempting to be diplomatic!

3. Deity declared (John 8:58-59). Read also verse 57 for continuity and context. Note the tense of the verb "to be" in verse 58. Refer the class to Moses' encounter with God at the burning bush (Ex. 3:13-14), where God identified Himself as "I AM." Jesus did not simply claim to predate Abraham. Rather, He identified Himself in the same terms that God had used with Moses. Whoever the great "I AM" is, Jesus is also. This is one of the greatest evidences of Christ's deity in Scripture.

The response of Jesus' enemies was immediate and violent. How does this response reinforce that Jesus' statement was a claim to deity? Obviously, those who had been debating with Jesus knew exactly what His choice of words implied. In their minds, He had committed the ultimate blasphemy by identifying Himself with God.

ILLUSTRATING THE LESSON

When sinners come to Jesus, they are set free from the shackles of sin.

FREE INDEED!

SIN

JESUS HAS DEFEATED SIN

CONCLUDING THE LESSON

The lesson began with certain Jews who professed belief in Christ. As Jesus told them of the truth that could set them free, it became clear that they had not experienced the freedom of which Jesus spoke. As Jesus revealed more, the crowd, previously sympathetic, turned ugly. When Jesus identified Himself clearly as God, they tried to kill Him.

Some imagine that freedom is freedom to sin. Those who accept Jesus, however, are set free from the slavery of sin. Those the Son sets free are free indeed!

ANTICIPATING THE NEXT LESSON

In the next lesson we will see the power of Jesus on display as He raises a young girl from the dead.

—Bruce A. Tanner.

PRACTICAL POINTS

1. True freedom comes only from surrender to God (John 8:31-32).
2. We are not always good judges of our own spiritual condition (vss. 33-36).
3. Our actions reveal our true spiritual heritage (John 8:37-38; cf. Matt. 7:15-20).
4. We should not be surprised when unbelievers draw wrong conclusions about us due to their spiritual blindness.
5. People are often quick to reject the gospel even without understanding it (vss. 51-53).
6. Self-honor is no honor at all (vss. 54-56).
7. When we tell people the truth about who Jesus is, we can expect some antagonistic responses.

—Ralph Woodworth.

RESEARCH AND DISCUSSION

1. Why is it difficult for us to recognize when we are in bondage to sin?
2. Are there terms you use without thinking that might denigrate other people or groups (John 8:48)?
3. Why do some people falsely claim to serve a God they do not even know (John 8:54-55; cf. Matt. 6:2; 23:5)?
4. How could Jesus say that Abraham had seen His day (John 8:56)?
5. How should this impact the way we read the Old Testament (cf. 5:45-47)?
6. What other instances do you remember in which Jesus used the phrase "I am" (8:58)?

—Ralph Woodworth.

ILLUSTRATED HIGH POINTS

The truth shall make you free (John 8:32)

When God gave the gift of salvation, He did not send a booklet of complicated instructions. He did not send an angel to interpret. He simply sent His Son.

The Son . . . shall make you free (vs. 36)

Do you remember Thomas after the resurrection? He said that he would not believe unless he could see the nail prints in the Lord's hands, put his finger in those prints, and thrust his hand into the Lord's wounded side.

When Jesus appeared again, He summoned Thomas to come and do what he needed to do in order to believe. Thomas's response was, "My Lord and my God" (John 20:28). All his doubts were answered.

So it is with us, for Jesus blessed those who believe in Him even though they have not seen Him the way Thomas saw Him. Our freedom is secured when we acknowledge Jesus for who He is.

Before Abraham was, I am (vs. 58)

One journalist, William Allen White, wrote this about his first meeting with Theodore Roosevelt in 1897: "I had never known such a man as he and never shall again. In the hour or two we spent that day at lunch, he poured into my heart such vision, such ideals, such hopes, such a new attitude toward life and patriotism as I had never dreamed men had. After that, I was his man."

In Christ we have more than a charismatic personality. We have the eternal Lord of the universe. How much more, then, does He have the power to change us and claim us as His own?

—Ted Simonson.

Golden Text Illuminated

"If ye continue in my word, then are ye my disciples indeed; and ye shall know the truth, and the truth shall make you free" (John 8:31-32).

Young people want to be free from parents. Workers want to be free from bosses. Prisoners want to be free from incarceration. Citizens want to be free from dictatorial despots. Addicts want to be free from habits. Freedom is defined many different ways according to one's situation.

There is another kind of freedom, however, and it is a freedom we all need, for the ailment is universal. Each of us is addicted to sin. Each is born with a sin nature, which manifests itself early in life. Even after we receive Christ, the remnant of indwelling sin—our "flesh"—often holds sway over us (Rom. 7:21-25).

In this week's golden text, Jesus reveals how to be free from the bent to sin and from sin's eternal penalty. It begins with faith in Him—but not just an intellectual nod in His direction. It is a commitment. That this is true is seen in His statement that one must "continue" in His word.

To continue in His word is to abide there, to be at home with His teachings and have them be the guiding principles of one's life. The concept Jesus conveys here is expanded later in His teaching on the vine and the branches (John 15). To abide in His word, of course, requires a relationship with Jesus. There needs to be a growing relationship and familiarity with the Lord and a sincere desire to hear and heed Him. Accordingly, one must become a disciple.

Discipleship is what the Lord wants in each one who comes to Him. The Great Commission (Matt. 28:19-20) tells us He wants more than just converts; He wants disciples. Continuing to hear His Word and then making it the foundation for life is proof of one's faith.

When Jesus spoke about continuing in his word as the way to know truth, He most likely had a double meaning in mind. He Himself is truth (John 14:6), and so is the word He spoke (17:17). The more one hears the Word of God, the better one knows the Lord. The better one knows the Lord, the easier it is to understand the Word. It is to such a person that freedom—the most important kind of freedom—comes.

The truth that is in Christ Jesus and in His Word is more powerful and life-giving than anything else. By coming to Christ in humble submission and entering into the kind of relationship He wants with us, we are set free from the chains that bind us to sin. Those who have experienced this release know full well the power of the Lord and the freedom He offers.

Genuine disciples of Jesus desire that others will surrender their lives at the Cross so that they too can be free from sin and become devoted to Christ and His Word.

The question we are confronted with today is where we are in terms of our relationship with Christ. Have we accepted His word as true but stopped short of a personal relationship with Him? Is He simply "fire insurance" to us, or is He our Saviour or is He Saviour and Lord? How well do we know Him? How deep into His Word have we gone?

May all of us search our hearts and answer truthfully such questions. May no one dismiss the matter as being of little or no importance.

—Darrell W. McKay.

Heart of the Lesson

This week's lesson focuses on Jesus' ability to bring people out of slavery to sin into the freedom of eternal life.

Various leaders have fought for freedom in many things, such as freedom of speech, freedom to vote, freedom to organize, and so forth. However, the greatest freedom available to mankind is found only in Jesus Christ. Jesus sets us free, and in His sovereignty He supports and sustains us with His power and love.

Christians are set free from the penalty of sin by Jesus. We, as believers, are enlightened by His truth. It is truth that makes the believer free. Jesus said, "I am the way, the truth, and the life" (John 14:6). His Word is truth (17:17). We must continue in the Word of the Lord (8:31). Sadly, not all who profess faith continue in His Word.

1. Jesus' power over sin (John 8:31-38). Jesus had been teaching in the temple. Some of the Jews believed Him, but not all of them did. The unbelieving Jews thought they were free because they were the descendants of Abraham. They did not grasp what Jesus meant about bondage. Sinners are enslaved by sin; therefore, they are in bondage. In other words, they are servants of sin. Jesus' mission on earth was to save people from sin.

Everyone is born in sin and needs deliverance. Freedom from sin can come only by Jesus Christ (Acts 4:12). It does not come by heritage. When we are free from sin (no longer servants to sin), we become servants of righteousness (Rom. 6:18). We begin to do what is right and continue to do so.

Salvation is offered to everyone. But to receive it, a person must believe in Jesus Christ, receiving Him as Saviour.

2. Jesus' power over death (John 8:48-56). Jesus has all power, including power over death. He offers eternal life to all who will accept Him as Lord and Saviour. Jesus said that if we keep His word, we will never see death. Some of the Jews who heard Him speaking thought He was speaking only about natural death, which occurs when breath leaves the body. They knew Abraham and other prophets had died. How could Jesus keep others from dying?

They did not realize that the eternal life Jesus offered was much greater than a mere avoidance of natural death. The life He gives us has implications both now and after death. As soon as we receive Him by faith, we are no longer dead in our sins but are partakers of new life (Eph. 2:5). At the same time, we are assured that not even death can take away our everlasting life in Christ (John 11:25; Rom. 8:38-39). When we die in the body, our souls will immediately be in His presence. And at the last day, we will receive resurrected, glorified bodies.

3. Jesus' eternal power (John 8:58-59). It is apparent that the Jews became more angry as their conversation with Jesus continued. Jesus proclaimed that He existed before Abraham. Thus, He openly declared His divinity. In proclaiming His preexistence, He also referred to Himself as "I Am." This is the same name God used to reveal Himself when He spoke to Moses concerning the Israelites.

Jesus is God. John's statement about Jesus in the beginning of his Gospel was proved to be true. Jesus was in the beginning and created all things (1:1-3).

The Jews who confronted Jesus refused to accept Him. They saw Him as a blasphemer. According to the Law, blasphemers were to be stoned (Lev. 24:16). They picked up rocks to stone Jesus, but He slipped away.

—*Arletta Merritts.*

World Missions

Some years ago a missionary from Brazil said that in his area a religious leader had gone around giving guns to the indigenous people and telling them to fight for their land. Things got heated as some of them began taking him up on his offer.

We cannot overlook the oppression that many people groups have endured in the past and continue to endure today, but we also must realize that true freedom and liberation is not found in guns. True freedom is found in the gospel. Even in a worthy cause, the result of war is death. But the gospel brings freedom from fear of death. It brings freedom from all kinds of addictions. It brings freedom from the constant urge to get even with other tribes for real or imagined wrongs.

The missionary brings freedom to the people through the gospel message. This freedom is first and foremost a freedom from sin and its power. But it also entails freedom from all kinds of cultural and religious rules that are taken away in Christ. Former Hindus are able to eat beef, former Muslims pork; others find similar dietary restrictions lifted in Christ. Taboos and superstitions about travel at night, birthing rituals, clothing, planting, animal husbandry, and a host of other things are lifted.

Compulsory giving to shrines is gone. Bodily mutilation, such as the cutting off of fingers to show grief and the piercings and bindings of feet and heads, is left in the past.

Society is changed. In a tribe where men were the only ones allowed to use the family ax, after the missionary came, the women also could now share in the work of chopping wood. Anthropologists criticized the missionary for effecting this cultural change, but the people were happier. An anthropologist might study the poverty and cultural disadvantages of a people, but he will not necessarily try to bring about a change to that people's situation. In fact, there are some who *prefer* no change so that they can study the culture more easily. They merely observe people like lab specimens. In response to this mindset, one shaman said, "Do they think that when the bugs bite us, it doesn't hurt?"

In contrast, the missionary always brings an opportunity for change, because the glorious freedom of the gospel transforms both individual lives and societies as a whole. The children are healthier, the family home is more comfortable, and the village is safer. Theft and violence decrease. Killings through tribal warfare decrease. The population grows.

The missionary starts schools so that people can learn not only about the Bible, but also about the nature of the world around them. The people learn to read and interact with the traders on an equal basis. One trader in South America had virtually enslaved the people by giving them goods on credit at an inflated price with the understanding that they would bring him certain produce from their jungle area. Of course, it was never enough to cover their purchases. They were always in debt. The missionary helped them break free; the trader was very angry.

There will always be those who malign the gospel by misrepresenting it, but we should never be in doubt that it is an agent of liberating change. The missionary starts schools so that people can break out of their ignorance. They learn not only about the Bible, but also about the nature of the world around them. Science and Scripture go together. God wants to set His creatures free.

—Philip J. Lesko.

The Jewish Aspect

The setting of John 8 is the temple in Jerusalem during a time when the Romans were despised and thoughts of revolting against them were common. Jesus came into that setting with some provocative teachings about His identity and mission.

In response to Jesus' offer to make them free, the revolutionary-minded Jews responded that they were not slaves. Their answer in verse 33 is similar to some other words that would be spoken a generation later. Eleazar, a Jewish revolutionary leader, inspired the survivors at Masada who were being besieged by a Roman legion. Josephus recorded his words: "Long ago we determined to be slaves to neither the Romans nor anyone else, save God" (Brown, *The Anchor Bible: John,* Doubleday).

The Jewish audience that was hearing Jesus' words was potentially violent; yet He spoke without fear. If it had been God's time for it, Jesus would have died during this encounter, for His words led the crowd to try to stone Him (vs. 59). What finally led them to such violence? Jesus said to them, "Before Abraham was, I am" (vs. 58).

There could be no doubt that this was a claim that He was God. First of all, Jesus spoke of existing prior to Abraham, and no one alive in His day could claim that. Even more significantly Jesus used the words "I am" to refer to Himself.

There is a parallel expression to "I am" used in a special way for God Himself. In Exodus 3:14 God explained who He is, saying, "I AM THAT I AM." A similar idea is expressed in Deuteronomy 32:39: "I, even I, am he, and there is no god with me." Because of who God is, He brings all blessings to His people (cf. Isa. 43:25).

By the time of Jesus, the Exodus 3 passage was rightly taken to indicate a special title for God, a special way of speaking about Him. In a number of Jewish texts, such as the Greek translation of the Old Testament, "I am" is used as a title for God. The Greek translation of Isaiah 43:25, for example, essentially says, "I am I-AM that blotteth out thy transgressions" (Brown).

Jesus knew what He was doing and made His claim to be God at the perfect time. The people of Israel were fervently celebrating the Feast of Tabernacles at the temple (cf. John 7:2). On that very day, Rabbi Judah recorded in the Mishnah, priests would circle the altar in a great ceremony, shouting, "I-AM, save us we pray! I-AM, save us we pray!" (Mishnah Sukkah 4:5, Neusner, ed., *The Talmud of Babylonia,* Scholars Press).

As the people called upon the God of Israel to save them, shouting "I-AM, save us, we pray," Jesus said, "Before Abraham was, I am" (John 8:58). His claim could not have come at a more volatile time. It was appalling for those Jews who did not yet see who Jesus really is. His claim to divinity came at a time when none could miss the significance of His statement, though many would not believe.

When the Jews around Him picked up stones, they no doubt had in mind Leviticus 24:16: "And he that blasphemeth the name of the Lord, he shall surely be put to death, and all the congregation shall certainly stone him." It is difficult to believe that someone standing right in front of you is God!

The deity of Jesus is still difficult for Jewish people to accept today. As in His own time, the identity of Messiah becomes clear only as we believe in His power.

—*Derek Leman.*

Guiding the Superintendent

Wherever and whenever Jesus Christ made a claim about Himself, it created a crisis. People were forced to make a choice, either for Him or against Him. One thing was clear: There could be no middle ground.

This quarter we will be looking at statements and actions of Jesus that revealed His identity. The conclusions always point to the same reality: He is truly God and truly man in one person. In this week's text Jesus Christ made two great claims: He is the truth, and He is the life. To believe Jesus Christ is both of these is to be set free.

DEVOTIONAL OUTLINE

1. I am the Truth (John 8:31-38). Jesus said that those who believed in Him would be set free. Many times people fear the truth. Often great effort is expended to make sure people do not hear the truth. However, once a person encounters Jesus Christ, he has encountered truth. This is liberating when accepted by faith.

Christ's claim greatly annoyed the Pharisees. How dare He say they were not free? They ignored their captivity under Rome and, even worse, their enslavement to sin and self.

The Jews of Jesus' day considered their souls safe and secure with God simply because they were Abraham's descendants.

They could have been set free from their sin by believing that all truth is to be found in Jesus Christ, but this is just the opposite of what the Jews of Jesus' day believed. They believed that freedom was to be found in a family tree.

2. I am the Life (John 8:48-56). It was hard enough for the Pharisees to accept Jesus' claim of being truth. Now He claimed that those who believe in Him will "never see death" (vs. 51).

His enemies had enough. They concluded that Jesus had a demon. After all, Abraham and the prophets had been dead for many years. How could Jesus give eternal life when not even those giants of the faith had avoided death?

To this Jesus responded with another claim—that He had a unique relationship with God. He knew God, and they did not. The basis for this claim was that the Father honored Him. His most amazing claim was that Abraham looked forward to the time when He would come to earth.

3. I am the Lord (John 8:58-59). For these Jewish leaders it was one thing for Jesus to claim to be truth and life but quite another to claim to be God Himself.

By saying, "Before Abraham was, I am" (vs. 58), Jesus was claiming not only to be eternal but also to be the Lord of the Old Testament. Many times in the Old Testament God referred to Himself as "I Am."

Jesus' opponents went ballistic. To them this was pure blasphemy; thus, they tried to kill Him. They had made their choice.

Like the people of Jesus' day, people today must make a choice about Him. Only in Jesus Christ can they find truth and life (that is, freedom).

AGE-GROUP EMPHASES

Children: Even at a young age, children struggle under enslavement to sin. Explain to them how believing in Jesus can free them.

Youths: Have your students contrast Jesus' claims to truth with popular, modern-day beliefs and culture.

Adults: Challenge your students to consider what impact these claims of Jesus have had on them.

—*Martin R. Dahlquist.*

SCRIPTURE LESSON TEXT

LUKE 8:40 And it came to pass, that, when Jesus was returned, the people *gladly* received him: for they were all waiting for him.

41 And, behold, there came a man named Jairus, and he was a ruler of the synagogue: and he fell down at Jesus' feet, and besought him that he would come into his house:

42 For he had one only daughter, about twelve years of age, and she lay a dying. But as he went the people thronged him.

43 And a woman having an issue of blood twelve years, which had spent all her living upon physicians, neither could be healed of any,

44 Came behind *him,* and touched the border of his garment: and immediately her issue of blood stanched.

45 And Jesus said, Who touched me? When all denied, Peter and they that were with him said, Master, the multitude throng thee and press *thee,* and sayest thou, Who touched me?

46 And Jesus said, Somebody hath touched me: for I perceive that virtue is gone out of me.

47 And when the woman saw that she was not hid, she came trembling, and falling down before him, she declared unto him before all the people for what cause she had touched him, and how she was healed immediately.

48 And he said unto her, Daughter, be of good comfort: thy faith hath made thee whole; go in peace.

49 While he yet spake, there cometh one from the ruler of the synagogue's *house,* saying to him, Thy daughter is dead; trouble not the Master.

50 But when Jesus heard *it,* he answered him, saying, Fear not: believe only, and she shall be made whole.

51 And when he came into the house, he suffered no man to go in, save Peter, and James, and John, and the father and the mother of the maiden.

52 And all wept, and bewailed her: but he said, Weep not; she is not dead, but sleepeth.

53 And they laughed him to scorn, knowing that she was dead.

54 And he put them all out, and took her by the hand, and called, saying, Maid, arise.

55 And her spirit came again, and she arose straightway: and he commanded to give her meat.

56 And her parents were astonished: but he charged them that they should tell no man what was done.

NOTES

overview

Jairus's Daughter and the Bleeding Woman

Lesson Text: Luke 8:40-56

Related Scriptures: Matthew 9:18-26; Mark 5:22-43;
Leviticus 15:25-30; Numbers 19:11-22

TIME: A.D. 28   PLACE: Capernaum

GOLDEN TEXT—"But when Jesus heard it, he answered him, saying, Fear not: believe only, and she shall be made whole" (Luke 8:50).

Introduction

God allows us an opportunity to smile even in the face of hurtful events. E. Edward Tornow once wrote in the *Christian Reader* about an experience he had as the soloist in a church service.

"While a student . . . I served as choir director and radio soloist for one of the local churches. One Sunday during our live broadcast, I faced the ultimate test of keeping my composure when the pastor announced my solo: 'Mr. Tornow will now sing the old Swedish hymn, "Children of the Heavenly Father," in memory of Gust Johnson, who died at the request of his wife on January 18.' Fortunately, the accompanist came to my rescue by playing a long introduction—enough time for me to stop laughing."

Jesus surely had a sense of humor, but even more, He has a deep sense of compassion for those who are hurting.

LESSON OUTLINE

I. **A WOMAN HEALED—** Luke 8: 40-44

II. **WORDS OF HOPE—** Luke 8: 45-50

III. **A GIRL RAISED—** Luke 8:51-56

Exposition: Verse by Verse

A WOMAN HEALED

LUKE 8:40 And it came to pass, that, when Jesus was returned, the people gladly received him: for they were all waiting for him.

41 And, behold, there came a man named Jairus, and he was a ruler of the synagogue: and he fell down at Jesus' feet, and besought him that he would come into his house:

42 For he had one only daughter, about twelve years of age, and she lay a dying. But as he went the people thronged him.

43 And a woman having an issue of blood twelve years, which had spent all her living upon physicians, neither could be healed of any,

44 Came behind him, and touched the border of his garment: and immediately her issue of blood stanched.

A multitude's welcome (Luke 8:40). Jesus' most recent ministry had been in the "country of the Gadarenes," which was located on the southeastern side of the Sea of Galilee (vss. 26-39). This was part of the Decapolis, one of the five major regions of New Testament Israel. While there, Jesus cast a legion of demons out of a man and sent them into a herd of swine, which then perished by running off a steep place into the lake. This caused the people there to ask Him to leave because of the fear His miracle instilled in them.

After getting into a boat and traveling across the Sea of Galilee, Jesus arrived in Capernaum, located at the northwest corner of the sea. {Because of the effective ministry He had already done there, the people eagerly welcomed Him back. A large crowd had gathered, waiting for His arrival.}[Q1] We are not told how they knew He was coming, but apparently the word got around rapidly so that He was greeted by a multitude.

Jairus's request (Luke 8:41-42a). It was right after Jesus arrived that Jairus appeared, specifically seeking Jesus. He was a ruler of the synagogue, probably meaning he arranged the services, conducted the meetings, and was responsible for the care of the building. He was also responsible for supervising the teaching that went on there. The fact that a ruler of the synagogue was seeking out Jesus gives evidence that at least some Jews had accepted Him. Jairus had heard and believed that Jesus had the power to help him.

{When Jairus found Jesus, he fell at His feet and begged Him to come to his house. It was in an attitude of submission and desperation that he came. His daughter was dying, and he knew of no other place to find help.}[Q2] The last time Jesus had been in Capernaum, a Roman centurion's servant had been sick and about to die (Luke 7:2). At that time the centurion had sent elders of the Jews to appeal to Jesus for help (vs. 3). Is it possible Jairus had been one of the elders? If so, he would have had personal knowledge about Jesus and what He could do.

Jairus certainly faced a hopeless situation. He had just this one daughter, and she was on her deathbed. Whenever a child dies, it is a heartbreaking situation. This is the kind of pain that makes us realize our only help is in God, for in spite of all the well-meaning condolences of other people, the pain is so deep that it goes beyond human touch. We do not know what Jairus might have seen and heard about Jesus, but he was right in realizing that Jesus was the only one who could help.

A woman's touch (Luke 8:42b-44). "Christ responded to his plea and began to move toward Jairus' home. Jairus' petition indicated faith in the person of Christ, and now that faith was put to a test. Since his daughter was dying, it seemed imperative that they move to his home with utmost haste; but the procession was interrupted as Jesus responded to another's need" (Pentecost, *The Words and Works of Jesus Christ,* Zondervan). Jairus's anxiety was certainly high, and his faith was real, but how strong was it?

The multitude that was waiting for Jesus when He arrived in Capernaum now thronged Him, moving along with Him as He headed toward Jairus's home. The word translated "thronged" in verse 42 has the connotation "to press upon" or "choke." The people were thronging around Jesus so heavily that He was almost choked off from being able to move at all. It was a matter of simply getting one foot in front of the other, probably at no more than a snail's pace.

{In the midst of this, a woman who had been suffering with hemorrhaging for twelve years came up behind Jesus and touched the border of His garment.}^Q3 Mark 5:26 says she had suffered much at the hands of physicians, but instead of getting better, she had continued to get worse. She had spent all her money on medical care without finding a cure, but the moment she touched Jesus' garment, she was immediately and completely healed. What even doctors had been unable to do in twelve years, Jesus did instantaneously just by a touch.

WORDS OF HOPE

45 And Jesus said, Who touched me? When all denied, Peter and they that were with him said, Master, the multitude throng thee and press thee, and sayest thou, Who touched me?

46 And Jesus said, Somebody hath touched me: for I perceive that virtue is gone out of me.

47 And when the woman saw that she was not hid, she came trembling, and falling down before him, she declared unto him before all the people for what cause she had touched him, and how she was healed immediately.

48 And he said unto her, Daughter, be of good comfort: thy faith hath made thee whole; go in peace.

49 While he yet spake, there cometh one from the ruler of the synagogue's house, saying to him, Thy daughter is dead; trouble not the Master.

50 But when Jesus heard it, he answered him, saying, Fear not: believe only, and she shall be made whole.

Jesus' question (Luke 8:45-46). A touch on a garment's hem seems like a very insignificant act. It was, however, the act of a subject kneeling before the King, showing her desire and willingness to be loyal and submissive. It was an act of hope based on what she had heard about this man, now being accepted by many as the Messiah. She knew the man she reached toward had a royal authority that had been granted from heaven. In a single act of desperation, she reached out, touched the garment's hem, and was healed.

{Surely such a simple act would be completely unnoticed by the Rabbi. It is doubtful anyone was more surprised than she when He suddenly stopped and asked, "Who touched me?" (vs. 45).}^Q4 There was something in the authority of that question that caused everyone nearby to deny being the one who had touched Him. Finally, Peter, incredulous over the idea, pointed out that in such a throng many were touching Him. Why would He ask such a foolish question?

Jesus then said, "Somebody hath touched me: for I perceive that virtue is gone out of me" (vs. 46). The word translated as "virtue" refers to "force" or "power."

Jesus' commendation (Luke 8:47-48). It was obvious to the healed woman that there was no hiding truth from this man. Perhaps He looked in her direction as He spoke, for she "saw that she was not hid." (vs. 47). With great fear and physical trembling, she came forward and fell prostrate at His feet. We can almost hear the tremor in her voice as she humbly explained what she had done and why. Included in her explanation was the fact that she had immediately been healed and made whole when she touched Jesus' garment.

In all that thronging mass of people, Jesus had recognized a single touch of faith different from all the accidental touches. {It was this faith, not the action itself, to which Jesus responded.}^Q5 Jesus did not ask who touched Him for His own benefit but for the benefit of the woman, to give her the opportunity to express her faith before all the people. It was, after all, her faith that had healed her, because it had led her to seek out Jesus for healing. She now gave testimony of that faith before the thronging masses of people. Jesus' response was one of commendation, for she had done well.

This woman's hemorrhaging had made her ceremonially unclean, according to Leviticus 15:25-30. That meant everything she contacted became unclean also. No doubt, it had been a terrible stigma with which to live for twelve years. But when she touched Jesus, she did not make Jesus unclean; Jesus made her clean. When she fell before Him, Jesus tenderly called her "Daughter" (Luke 8:48) and assured her that she could go away happy and with peace in her heart. Her faith had made her whole. Her hope in Him had resulted in her healing.

Jesus' encouragement (Luke 8:49-50). In the meantime, while all this was going on, Jairus waited for Jesus to continue His journey to his home. This must have been an agonizing time for him, because time was surely of the essence if his daughter was to be saved from death. Soon the word came. {Even as Jesus talked with the healed woman, a messenger brought the news to Jairus that it was too late. His daughter had died, and there was no need for to bother Jesus any longer.}[Q6] Jesus was apparently standing close to Jairus, for He heard the bad news.

{He spoke to Jairus instantly and calmly: "Fear not: believe only, and she shall be made whole" (vs. 50).}[Q7] Jairus had heard many things about Jesus, but at this moment his faith was being tested to the limit.

A GIRL RAISED

51 And when he came into the house, he suffered no man to go in, save Peter, and James, and John, **and the father and the mother of the maiden.**

52 And all wept, and bewailed her: but he said, Weep not; she is not dead, but sleepeth.

53 And they laughed him to scorn, knowing that she was dead.

54 And he put them all out, and took her by the hand, and called, saying, Maid, arise.

55 And her spirit came again, and she arose straightway: and he commanded to give her meat.

56 And her parents were astonished: but he charged them that they should tell no man what was done.

The scene at the house (Luke 8:51-52). Once again a test of faith was successfully passed. Every indication is that Jairus believed Jesus' words of encouragement. The journey continued until they arrived at his house, where the mourners were already present, weeping with sorrow over the little girl's death. Only a small group of people was going to be allowed to be with Jesus as He did what He was about to do. They were the apostles Peter, James, and John, and the girl's parents. The others would have to wait outside.

{On the way to Jairus's house, Jesus had demonstrated His authority over disease. Now He was about to demonstrate His authority over death.}[Q8] His disciples were learning all the time as they accompanied Him. Peter, James, and John had already witnessed His power over death once (Luke 7:11-15), and now they were about to witness it again. These three would eventually become important leaders for the believers after Jesus' death, resurrection, and return to heaven. This was a special teaching time for them and one that would positively affect their future ministries.

Jesus again spoke calmly: "Weep not; she is not dead, but sleepeth" (8:52). Clearly the girl was dead, but her condition was like sleep in that it was temporary, as was the case with Lazarus, whom Jesus also described as sleeping before He raised him from the dead (John 11:11-14). Jairus's heart must have leaped with joy and hope all over again. His flickering faith continued to burn as he waited and watched to see what would happen.

The private scene with the girl (Luke 8:53-54). Most of the other people present did not have the faith Jairus did. They had all seen the girl's body and knew very well that she was dead. {Thinking Jesus' words about her sleeping were spoken in ignorance, they laughed at Him derisively.}^Q9 Such a response might indicate that this was a group of "professional" mourners. There was no hope as far as they were concerned, and they were totally unaffected by Jesus' calming words.

Jesus, unmoved by the response of these mourners, proceeded to usher them out of the house. For people, death is an irreversible condition. For God, nothing is irreversible, and He can overcome death simply by speaking a word (John 5:25).

By raising Jairus's daughter physically from the dead, Jesus foreshadowed what is to come on the last day. This was not difficult for Jesus because He is the Giver of Life. {To Him death is no more difficult to overcome than sleep. He could restore life as easily as He could awaken someone.}^Q10

The scene with the parents (Luke 8:55-56). The little girl's spirit had gone from her body, but it returned now at Jesus' command for her to arise. She got up immediately, revealing that there were no lingering symptoms from her experience. She was immediately alive and completely well. Jesus said they should give her something to eat, probably because of her hunger following the time of illness.

The parents were "astonished" (vs. 56). The word indicates that they were beside themselves with amazement. What had just happened was far beyond their greatest hopes. They had hoped Jesus could keep their daughter alive. Far better than that, they had seen Him raise her from the dead and make her perfectly well again.

Jesus did not want to be known for His miracles alone, which is probably why He told the parents not to tell people about what had happened. He had a message of salvation for the Jews, but He knew they would be distracted from the message if they only came to Him to see the wonders He could do. Thus, He preferred not to publicize this miracle.

—*Keith E. Eggert.*

QUESTIONS

1. Why was the crowd so eager to meet Jesus when He arrived in Capernaum?

2. What individual sought out Jesus, and why was he looking for Him so desperately?

3. What happened to interrupt Jesus' journey to Jairus's house?

4. Why was it so surprising that Jesus asked who had touched Him?

5. What was it about the woman that caused Jesus to respond to her?

6. What message came to Jairus as Jesus was talking with the woman He had healed?

7. How did Jesus respond to the bad news about Jairus's daughter?

8. Over what two areas did Jesus demonstrate His authority here?

9. How did the people respond when Jesus said the girl was asleep?

10. Why is it significant that Jesus refers to death as "sleep"?

—*Keith E. Eggert.*

Preparing to Teach the Lesson

Our lesson this week shows us how Jesus has authority even over death and so offers us hope in any and every situation.

TODAY'S AIM

Facts: to show how Jesus offered hope to Jairus and the woman with the hemorrhage of blood.

Principle: to show that faith in Jesus is the only way to have true hope in the face of difficulties and death.

Application: to encourage students to see difficult situations as opportunities to trust in Jesus and see Him work.

INTRODUCING THE LESSON

George Mueller was an ordinary man with great faith in God. He was able to start an orphanage without a penny in hand simply because he had a very strong faith in a wonder-working God. God provided the daily needs of hundreds of orphan children in response to Mueller's prayers. We dare not underestimate what God can do when we trust Him fully in seemingly hopeless situations.

DEVELOPING THE LESSON

1. Jairus's daughter dying (Luke 8:40-42). People in desperate need sought out Jesus. They knew that He would have the answer. The crowds who were waiting for Jesus received Him with open arms. It was at this time that Jairus, a leader of the local synagogue, came forward to meet Him and to beg Him to come heal his daughter, who was dying. She was his only daughter and was just twelve years old. The situation was desperate, and Jesus was his only hope. The people were watching to see what Jesus would do.

2. Faith in a hopeless situation (Luke 8:43-48). While Jairus was pleading for Jesus to come to his daughter's aid, a woman in the crowd was wrestling with her own need, but she had faith in the power of Jesus to heal. She had heard about Jesus, and we can assume that she had probably seen the miracles that Jesus did since He had done them publicly in Capernaum before (7:1-23). She had a severe problem of hemorrhaging that had lasted for twelve long years. She had spent all her earnings on doctors but could get no relief from her bleeding. Now she came up behind Jesus and touched His robe, believing in her heart that a touch was enough to heal her.

The "border of his garment" (vs. 44) may refer to tassels that reminded Jewish people to keep the commandments of God (cf. Num. 15:37-41). When the woman touched Jesus' robe, she was instantly healed. The miracle she had waited so long for had happened.

Jesus felt it too, even though the crowd was pressing all around Him. He asked, "Who touched me?" (Luke 8:45). The disciples responded with disbelief that Jesus would ask such a question when the crowd was all around them. Jesus pointed out that this was a special touch, a touch of faith that had caused power to go out from Him.

Discuss with your students this "touch of faith." What can we learn from this woman's daring act? Note that in Jewish society, women did not touch men they did not know, especially in public.

The woman came forward when she knew that she was found out. She trembled in fear and fell to her knees before all those people. She explained how she had touched Jesus in faith and was healed immediately. Jesus responded, calling her "Daughter" (vs. 48), a term of endearment. He then sent her away in peace, commending her strong faith, which had caused her to seek Him out so that He might heal her.

Encourage the class to talk about how we trust God today. Can we express our faith as this woman did? Although faith does not guarantee that we will receive exactly what we ask for since we often do not know what is best to ask (Rom. 8:26), God wants us to ask of Him confidently, knowing that His answer will always be good for us (Matt. 7:7-11).

3. Hope in the face of death (Luke 8:49-50). While Jesus was still talking to the woman, a messenger came with some bad news. Jairus's daughter was dead, and there was no need to trouble the Master now. It was too late.

Talk with your students about times when they have received bad news and their situation seemed absolutely hopeless and beyond repair. Our lesson shows us that Jesus works in just such situations. Reflect on the times when God has answered in hopeless situations.

4. Hope and rejoicing (Luke 8:51-56). When Jesus and the crowds arrived at Jairus's house, Jesus took only Peter, James, John, and the girl's parents into the room where the dead girl lay. He drove out those who were mourning. In that culture it was common to make a display of mourning. It indicated grieving for the dead and therefore respect for them. Sometimes, as is suggested by this passage, mourners were hired to do just that.

Jesus said that the girl was just sleeping and not dead, and the mourners laughed at Him. Discuss in your class the possibility that in our lack of faith, we sometimes scorn what God may have for us.

Jesus then took the child by the hand and raised her up to life, telling her to get up. Then He told the parents to give her something to eat. It is possible that the instruction to give her something to eat was to confirm that she was indeed

alive. You may remember that Jesus asked for something to eat when He appeared to His frightened disciples on the evening of the day He rose from the dead (Luke 24:35-43).

The parents were amazed, but Jesus told them not to tell anyone what had happened. If we experience God's gracious work in our lives, we normally want to tell everyone about it. However, Jesus often told people to keep His work secret until after His resurrection (cf. Matt. 17:9). Everything would be disclosed at the right time in God's plan.

ILLUSTRATING THE LESSON

Jesus offers us hope in our desperate situations. He only calls on us to have faith in Him.

CONCLUDING THE LESSON

Our lesson this week has shown us how Jesus intervenes in hopeless situations. He offers us hope and healing. We are called to trust Him, even when things seem impossible.

ANTICIPATING THE NEXT LESSON

Next week we will again encounter Jesus' power over death, this time in His friend Lazarus.

—*A. Koshy Muthalaly.*

PRACTICAL POINTS

1. Our needs should drive us continually to Jesus (Luke 8:40-42).
2. The Lord knows and cares for each one of us (vss. 43-45).
3. Faith in the Lord is well placed and will always be rewarded (vss. 46-48).
4. Faith is a powerful antidote for fear (vss. 49-50).
5. In Christ one can find hope in any situation (vss. 51-52).
6. The faithless forfeit the right to see God's works (vss. 53-54).
7. The Lord is greater than any problem we might face (vss. 55-56).

—Jarl K. Waggoner.

RESEARCH AND DISCUSSION

1. What evidences of Jairus's faith in Christ can you find in Luke 8:41-42 and 49-56?
2. What obstacles or discouragements to faith are illustrated in this lesson?
3. What does the role of faith in this lesson imply about its role in salvation (vss. 48, 50)?
4. In what ways are Jesus' humanity and deity both revealed in His dealings with Jairus and the woman?
5. What similarities and differences can you find between the raising of Jairus's daughter and the other times Jesus raised the dead (cf. Luke 7:11-17; John 11:1-46)? What was Jesus' purpose in each case?
6. Does Jesus' command to remain silent about His work ever apply to us today (Luke 8:56; cf. Matt. 17:9; 28:19-20)?

—Jarl k. Waggoner.

ILLUSTRATED HIGH POINTS

Thy faith hath made thee whole (Luke 8:48)

One of the great ministries of Christ was healing the sick. But how does God's power to heal apply to us today? One answer is found in James 5:13-16.

An example of God's immediate healing occurred after a physician declared that it was uncertain whether a very young child was going to survive his illness. Arrangements were made with the church elders to have an anointing service at the request of the boy's father. Prayer was made before the men went to the hospital for the service. When they arrived, the child was found to be very much better.

The service was conducted anyway, for it was evident that their faith had been honored by the Lord. Credit must not be given to the elders, but their obedience to the Word of God was efficacious with the Lord. The use of the oil in the ceremony was according to the scriptural injunction and had only symbolic importance.

Fear not; believe only (vs. 50)

Many illustrations could be given about the Lord's miraculous healing power. They prove that we have a compassionate God who can touch people of all ages.

However, in stressful times, when healing is needed, we must learn to accept the fact that God does not always heal immediately. In some cases He waits to answer, and in others the person is healed by passing into the presence of Christ if he or she is a true believer in Him. That constitutes the greatest deliverance of all.

Let us have peace in our hearts when God's timing in healing is not immediate.

—P. Fredrick Fogle.

Golden Text Illuminated

"But when Jesus heard it, he answered him, saying, Fear not: believe only, and she shall be made whole" (Luke 8:50).

Death is the inescapable end for every human being on this earth. Christians and non-Christians alike must face this last enemy. And that is a fearful thing. But this text encourages us that death will not have the last word and our fear can be conquered, because Jesus has power over death for all who believe in Him.

Before Jairus even had time to respond to the report that his daughter was dead (vs. 49), Jesus commanded him not to be afraid. What gave Jesus the authority to give such a command? What kind of way was this to comfort a grieving father—instructing him how he should respond to such devastating news? Jesus had the authority to command Jairus not to fear because Jesus also has authority over death itself.

It was His power that brought all life into being out of nothing (Gen. 1:1; John 1:3); it is His power that breathes life into people who are dead in their sins (Eph. 2:5); and it is His power that will raise our perishable bodies from the dead to become imperishable (I Cor. 15:42). He crushed sin, death, and Satan underfoot through His death and resurrection, and He is in the process of crushing these same enemies under the feet of every believer as well (Rom. 16:20).

If Jesus did not have such power, then we would be right to be afraid when we think about our impending death. But as it is, the Father has given Jesus all dominion and authority, in heaven and on earth (Eph. 1:20–22), and nothing can stop the Good Shepherd from guiding His sheep safely through the valley of the shadow of death (Ps. 23:4).

The account goes on to tell us that Jesus went to Jairus's house and raised his daughter from the dead, simply by speaking to her (Luke 8:54–55). In doing so, He gave a foretaste of what it will be like at His return. He will speak, and the dead will be raised, and death will be swallowed up in victory (I Cor. 15:52–54).

Knowing the power of Jesus, we have every reason to cast off all fear of death. But don't miss the other part of Jesus' command to Jairus. Not only does He command Jairus *not* to fear, but He also commands him to *believe*. There is something that should replace our fear, and that is faith. As the apostle John tells us, our faith in Christ is the victory that overcomes the world (I John 5:4).

Yet, when we read what happened after Jesus' command to Jairus, it is surprising that the text says nothing about whether or not Jairus believed. This seems to be intentional. Scripture says nothing about Jairus's belief because the most important aspect of his faith was not the faith itself, but the *object* of his faith. Faith is not a *thing* that has power in itself. Jesus is the one who has power, and when our trust is directed toward Him, that is when the enemies of God have no power over us.

Does the thought of death make you fearful? There is only one remedy for that fear: faith in Christ. The more you look with trust upon Him, the more you will know the power of His resurrection. Do not fear; only believe, and have confidence that Christ will raise you up just as He did the daughter of Jairus.

—*Matthew Robinson.*

Heart of the Lesson

It has been said that every person has a disability. There are obvious ones, such as blindness or lameness, as well as internal ones, such as cancer or heart disease. Many people are emotionally disabled because of a traumatic experience in their lives.

But there is one disability that everyone has. Every person is born spiritually disabled. That is, he has sin in his life. No one comes into or lives in this world without sin, and it is only through Jesus that people have hope for healing from this spiritual disease. In this week's lesson we see how Jesus healed people physically, which points us to His even greater spiritual healing.

1. Jairus's faith (Luke 8:40-42). A man named Jairus hurried to Jesus and fell down at His feet. Because he was a ruler in the synagogue, Jairus was a prominent man in his town. It was probably his responsibility to make arrangements for the Sabbath: selecting who would teach, lead in prayer, and read Scripture. When Jairus prostrated himself at Jesus' feet, he was showing utter humility. What would cause such an honored man to act this way?

Jairus's beloved twelve-year-old daughter lay at home, dying. Jairus must have heard of Jesus' miracles and believed Jesus could heal his daughter. He had faith in Jesus.

2. Ailing woman's faith (Luke 8:43-48). Amid the crowds of people, Jesus felt someone touch Him. He asked His disciples who it was. They did not understand His question, for everyone was touching Jesus!

Jesus insisted that this touch was unusual, for He had felt power go out from Him. Jesus' words forced the woman who had touched Him to come forward and speak to Him. This woman had been suffering from hemorrhaging for twelve years. She had sought all possible medical help to no avail. The Law declared a woman with this type of malady to be ceremonially unclean (Lev. 15:25-30). This meant she was not able to take part in temple worship. No doubt she felt ostracized and alone.

This woman thought that if she could just touch Jesus' robe, she would be healed and could go on her way without bothering Him. She was miraculously healed, but Jesus did not want her to go away quietly.

When the woman fearfully came forward, Jesus comforted her. "Thy faith hath made thee whole" (vs. 48). It was not His robe that healed her but Jesus Himself, and it was her faith that brought her to Jesus.

3. Faith rewarded (Luke 8:49-56). While this drama went on, a messenger from Jairus's house came and told the sad news—Jairus's daughter had died; there was no need to trouble Jesus anymore.

Jesus disagreed. He told Jairus to believe, and his daughter would be made well. As they hurried along to the house, Jairus's thoughts must have been a jumble. Was it possible? Healing was one thing, but could Jesus bring the dead back to life?

Arriving at the house, Jesus took Peter, James, and John, along with the parents, into the girl's room. Not making a big show of it, Jesus quietly told her to arise. Amazingly, the girl sat up, fully alive! Imagine how thrilled Jairus was to have his daughter restored to life. Jairus's faith was rewarded.

Just as Jesus healed the physical disabilities of people who had faith in Him, so He heals our spiritual disability by our faith in Him, forgiving and breaking the power of sin.

— Judy Carlsen.

World Missions

Jeff was dejected. He wandered around Los Angeles International Airport, longing for a familiar face. He longed to see the indigenous believers he had come to know and love, but his successful ministry had been cut short by civil war in Central America. The indigenous people had scattered as their villages dissolved into a no-man's-land.

There was a steady chorus of strange tongues and dialects in the great transient hub that is known to most as LAX. Suddenly, Jeff heard it—a few words emanating from the concourse crowd in the tribal dialect he had come to know as well as his own language!

Jeff pushed his way through knots of travelers until he found a small group of Central Americans, looking out of place in their ill-fitting American clothes, chattering away in their own language. An American who spoke their language was as much a marvel to them as they were a godsend to Jeff. Jeff soon learned that there were two enclaves of the tribe in the United States, one in Texas and one in Florida. Jeff spent the following years traveling between the two groups, winning the people from his beloved tribe to faith in Christ.

Jeff's experience underlines the alarming statistic that over twenty-six million people worldwide are refugees. Two-thirds of the world's refugees are from Syria, Venezuela, Afghanistan, South Sudan, or Myanmar. Nearly half of refugee children are unable to attend school (UNHCR, "Refugee Statistics," unrefugees.org).

Jesus' compassion for the sick and needy in this week's lesson should compel us to minister to refugees, who often lack basic needs. We have an opportunity to reach out to a vast, largely untouched population to bring hope for healing, both physical and spiritual.

Unfortunately, for mission strategists seeking ways to meet the refugee challenge, there are few options available. Many host countries forbid access to the displaced or are hostile to the gospel. Most Palestinian refugees, for example, are displaced in lands closed to missionaries.

Tibetan refugees have remained stateless in India since 1959. They too are in a country that discourages evangelism (Dayton and Wilson, eds., *The Refugees Among Us,* MARC).

While some countries make it difficult to reach refugees with the gospel, let's not forget that there are also many refugees in the United States. In our home-to-home visitation ministry years ago, we met a young woman who is a refugee from Cambodia. She made it to the United States through Thailand after fleeing a widening war and genocide in her homeland.

In a Thai displaced persons camp, missionaries reached the young Buddhist girl for Christ. In this country, she identified with a local church and became an active witness for the Lord.

Her real burden is for the growing number of Cambodians who have found their way to America. In our city, all of these Cambodians are Buddhists. She prays for them and witnesses to them faithfully, and she has the tools to reach them. We also went to their homes and left literature even though our efforts were limited by language and cultural barriers.

Opportunities to minister to refugees abound. Let's not overlook this largely unreached demographic. The body of Christ in this country has plenty of missions work to do right on our doorstep.

—*Lyle P. Murphy.*

The Jewish Aspect

When the woman with the issue of blood approached Jesus, she timidly touched the border of His garment. The border was a significant part of the man's garment in Israel.

Soon after delivering Israel from Egyptian bondage, God gave specific instructions about the way the Hebrews' robes were to be made. They were to include "fringes in the borders" (Num. 15:38), and upon this fringe they were to place a "ribband of blue."

Verses 37-41 are recited every week in Jewish synagogues as part of the Shema reading, which takes its name from the first verse of the recitation (Deut. 6:4) and means "Hear."

The Hebrew word for the fringe is *tzitzit.* In Jesus' day it was worn on each of the four corners of the robe.

Since robes are no longer fashionable, today the *tzitzit* are sewn onto a tallith, or prayer shawl. The tallith may be either a large shawl worn on the outside or a small garment worn under the clothing. The tallith can be of any color, but it must have four corners with a *tzitzit* on each corner.

The modern *tzitzit* itself must be white. Originally, one strand of the *tzitzit* was to be blue. The white symbolized purity, and the blue symbolized the blue of God's heaven. The modern Israeli flag derives its blue and white colors from the *tzitzit.*

Each *tzitzit* begins with four strands. One strand is longer than the others. Through a series of wrappings and knots, each *tzitzit* ends up with five double knots that separate four wrappings of the strands. The first wrapping is wrapped seven times, the second eight, the third eleven, and the fourth thirteen times.

Gematria is a Jewish method of interpretation in which the numerical values of letters are studied to uncover hidden meanings. When some Jewish scholars added the number of the wrappings in the *tzitzit,* they concluded that the Hebrew phrase "God is One" was contained in the *tzitzit.* This phrase is the heart of the Shema, which God instructed the Israelites to keep close to their hearts and minds (Deut. 6:4-9). The *tzitzit* was thus the holiest portion of a Jewish man's clothing.

Some have even attempted to use *Gematria* to decipher the number of the beast (man), "six hundred three-score and six," in Revelation 13. Caution is in order in such matters.

The woman in Luke 8 had an issue of blood. According to Leviticus, she would have been in a continuously ceremonially unclean condition for the entire twelve years of her illness (15:25-30). According to Haggai 2:11-13, if something ceremonially unclean touches something clean, that which is clean becomes contaminated and unclean.

Having had her condition for twelve years, the woman would have known all too well that she was unclean. In spite of this, she ventured forth and touched the *tzitzit* of Jesus' robe.

In the unique case of Jesus, He did not become contaminated at the touch of the unclean woman. Instead, His power healed the woman and cleansed her.

Jesus' subsequent visit to the young girl bore an additional connection to the Levitical laws of uncleanness. The high priest was forbidden to come into contact with a dead body (Lev. 21:10-11). As the ultimate High Priest (Heb. 4:14), Jesus purified the unclean.

—*Carter Corbrey.*

Guiding the Superintendent

In our two lessons so far, we have seen the authority Jesus has over death and how that authority displays His deity. Today's text also emphasizes another theme—faith. This emphasis on faith should give us hope, not only that we will be resurrected on the last day but also that God delights in displaying His power through the faith of His people.

In this week's lesson text, Luke recorded two intertwined events that dealt with physical healing. Even as we occupy ourselves with the emphasis on healing, let us not overlook the impact of personal faith in both events.

DEVOTIONAL OUTLINE

1. A desperate plea for a daughter's healing (Luke 8:40-42). Jesus' compassionate and miraculous ministry to people in need continued to astound those who followed Him. As a result, word spread concerning the mighty acts that He had accomplished; thus, "people gladly received him: for they were all waiting for him" (vs. 40).

A leader of the local synagogue named Jairus was among those who were awaiting the Lord's return from the other side of the Sea of Galilee. When he saw Jesus, Jairus humbled himself and pleaded with the Lord for his twelve-year-old daughter, who was on the verge of death.

2. The healing of a woman (Luke 8:43-48). While they were traveling to Jairus's home, a woman who had struggled with a physical malady for twelve years pushed through the throng and touched Jesus' garment from behind. She was immediately healed.

Jesus knew that healing power had gone out from Him. He asked, "Who touched me?" (vs. 45). The woman fearfully approached the Lord and publicly declared what had happened to her. Jesus approved of her confession of faith and sent her away with His blessing.

3. The raising of a daughter (Luke 8:49-56). As the Lord pronounced His blessing on the woman, word came that Jairus's daughter had died. Jesus confidently told Jairus that there was no need to fear, that faith would result in her healing.

When the Lord arrived at Jairus's home, He told the mourners to leave. He assured them that the girl was not dead but sleeping. Jesus then allowed a few special people to enter with Him.

The Lord then commanded Jairus's daughter, saying, "Maid, arise" (vs. 54). Immediately the girl got up and received something to eat. Her parents were overwhelmed but were told by Jesus that they were to tell no one what had occurred.

AGE-GROUP EMPHASES

Children: Children naturally want to please people, such as their parents and teachers. Have your teachers use this week's lesson text to teach their students that they can please God by trusting in Him as their Heavenly Father.

Youths: Young people often respond willingly to a dare. In doing so, they often exhibit unusual courage. Encourage your teachers to use this week's lesson text to challenge their students to demonstrate boldness in faith as they serve the Lord, perhaps in some new or unexpected way.

Adults: Those who have served the Lord for many years should know the importance of faith. Still, some may have forgotten that God delights in responding to faith. Encourage your adults to joyfully and thankfully receive God's blessed approval as they continue to display faith in Him.

—*Thomas R. Chmura.*

SCRIPTURE LESSON TEXT

JOHN 11:38 Jesus therefore again groaning in himself cometh to the grave. It was a cave, and a stone lay upon it.

39 Jesus said, Take ye away the stone. Martha, the sister of him that was dead, saith unto him, Lord, by this time he stinketh: for he hath been *dead* four days.

40 Jesus saith unto her, Said I not unto thee, that, if thou wouldest believe, thou shouldest see the glory of God?

41 Then they took away the stone *from the place* where the dead was laid. And Jesus lifted up *his* eyes, and said, Father, I thank thee that thou hast heard me.

42 And I knew that thou hearest me always: but because of the people which stand by I said *it,* that they may believe that thou hast sent me.

43 And when he thus had spoken, he cried with a loud voice, Lazarus, come forth.

44 And he that was dead came forth, bound hand and foot with graveclothes: and his face was bound about with a napkin. Jesus saith unto them, Loose him, and let him go.

NOTES

* There was no resurrection for Lazarus. He was raised from the dead Lazarus had to die again

* Dismiss the fear of death

* John emphasis Jesus diety

* Season - Life
* Purpose - Time

The Raising of Lazarus

Lesson Text: John 11:38-44

Related Scriptures: John 11:1-37; Luke 10:38-42; John 12:1-11

TIME: A.D. 30   PLACE: Bethany

GOLDEN TEXT—"When he thus had spoken, he cried with a loud voice, Lazarus, come forth. And he that was dead came forth, bound hand and foot with graveclothes" (John 11:43-44).

Introduction

It is easy to recognize the Lord's presence in the pleasant experiences of life. Jesus' presence blesses our weddings, births, baptisms, graduations, holidays, and other joyful occasions.

But it is more difficult to recognize His presence in the hardships of life. Is He really there when we suffer financial reverses, natural disasters, automobile accidents, or lawsuits? Does He care when our children are sick and tottering on the brink of death? Where is He when families split apart, when we lose our jobs, or when we contract incurable diseases?

Job's experience teaches us that we may never know why God allows us to suffer. But it also shows that He goes with us through the suffering. Jesus' ministry also reveals that He cared for people in their times of deepest need. This week's lesson takes us to one of His most spectacular miracles—when He confronted death and overcame it by His divine power.

LESSON OUTLINE

I. THE GRAVE APPROACHED—John 11:38-40

II. THE PRAYER OFFERED—John 11:41-42

III. THE DEAD CALLED FORTH—John 11:43-44

Exposition: Verse by Verse

THE GRAVE APPROACHED

JOHN 11:38 Jesus therefore again groaning in himself cometh to the grave. It was a cave, and a stone lay upon it.

39 Jesus said, Take ye away the stone. Martha, the sister of him that was dead, saith unto him, Lord, by this time he stinketh: for he hath been dead four days.

40 Jesus saith unto her, Said I not unto thee, that, if thou wouldest believe, thou shouldest see the glory of God?

From our human point of view, the resurrection of Lazarus should not have been necessary. His sisters, Martha and Mary, had informed Jesus that their brother was sick (vss. 1-3). {Jesus could have gone immediately to Bethany and healed him, or if time was too short, He could have healed him from a distance, as He had the nobleman's son (4:46-54).}^Q1 Yet, in spite of His love for Lazarus and his sisters, He purposely delayed going to them, allowing Lazarus to die (11:5-6).

Jesus' command (John 11:38-39a). Jesus' delay, however, did not mean he was indifferent to Lazarus's need, for as He approached the grave, He was "groaning in himself." The word for "groaning" means "deeply moved." It occurs in only three passages outside the two in this chapter (cf. vs. 33). In two of them (Matt. 9:30; Mark 1:43), it describes Jesus' stern warning for persons He healed to be quiet about their healing. In the third (Mark 14:5), it refers to the disciples' angry scolding of Mary for wasting her perfume.

Thus, the verb describing Jesus' reaction when He came to Lazarus's tomb speaks more of indignation than of sorrow. {It was not anger against the mourners present; it was anger against Satan and the terrible tragedy he had brought upon the human race through sin.}^Q2 This, of course, was combined with genuine sorrow, for Jesus grieved with the sisters and their friends and wept (John 11:35). The onlookers interpreted His tears as a sign of His deep love for Lazarus (vs. 36).

The grave in which Lazarus lay was a cave with a stone covering the entrance. Sometimes natural caves were used as tombs; more often, artificial tombs were created by hewing out limestone rock. Because of the rocky hills around Jerusalem, many such man-made tombs were found there. Some of these were hewed out horizontally; others were cut downward with steps leading down into the tomb.

Inside the grave there were often a number of shelves or niches for all the members of a family, and sometimes there was more than one chamber. To keep predatory animals from entering, a large stone was placed across the entrance, either vertically or horizontally.

{The fact that Lazarus was buried in such a tomb shows that his family was not poor.}^Q3 Their affluence may also be deduced from the many mourners from Jerusalem who joined them (John 11:19, 31, 33, 45) and the costly perfume Mary later used to anoint Jesus (12:3). This underscores a solemn truth—death has no respect for social class. It is a fate that finally comes to all.

But in this case, the death would not be final. Jesus would confront it with divine power. So He ordered that the stone be removed. He directed this to those who were present nearby, for it was no small task to remove the heavy stone. There were many bystanders who could have assisted in doing this.

We can well imagine some hesitation in complying, however, for opening a tomb brought the risk of ritual defilement by contact with the dead. Adding to this hesitation was the question of why Jesus would want the stone removed. What possible purpose would it serve? The crowd had no expectation that a resurrection was about to take place.

It is worthy of note that Jesus did not remove the stone Himself. {He assigned to the people around Him a task that they could do and reserved for Himself only what they could not.}[Q4] In His first miracle (2:1-11), He had done something similar. Though He could have created wine out of nothing, He had instructed the servants to fill the jars with water, which He then turned into wine. Likewise, in this instance, though Jesus had the power to simply command the stone to move, He let others move it, preparing the way for what only He could do.

Martha's objection (John 11:39b). To Martha, Lazarus's sister, the thought of removing the stone from the grave was utterly repulsive. "Lord," she said, "by this time he stinketh: for he hath been dead four days." Whatever Jesus had in mind, she wanted to spare Lazarus and his family the indignity of disturbing his decomposing body. The smell of death could only add to the abhorrence of their situation. Under normal circumstances, she would have been right; the warm climate would have done its nasty work.

But had not Martha already expressed faith that God would answer any request Jesus made (vs. 22)? And had not Jesus assured her that her brother would rise again (vs. 23)? Yes, indeed, but even then her faith struggled to reach the conclusion that his resurrection was imminent. {She preferred to think it would be "at the last day" (vs. 24). Even after Jesus reminded her that He was the Resurrection and the Life (vs. 25), she seemed not to apply that truth to the present need.}[Q5] So at the grave, her faith faltered.

Jesus' reassurance (John 11:40). Jesus responded to Martha's doubts with a mild rebuke that at the same time reassured her of the outcome. "Said I not unto thee," asked Jesus, "that, if thou wouldest believe, thou shouldest see the glory of God?" We do not find these exact words in His earlier conversation with her (vss. 21-27), but

they were the essence of what He had told her. In addition, when the sisters had first notified Him of Lazarus's sickness, He had said that this illness was "not unto death, but for the glory of God" (vs. 4).

That manifestation of God's glory would come through Jesus' power to raise Lazarus from the dead, but only by faith would Martha be able to see that glory. This is still the key for us to see God's glory manifested in our midst. His power is always more than sufficient, but too often our lack of faith keeps us from seeing it displayed (cf. Mark 6:1-6; 9:17-19).

Early in his Gospel, John declared, "We beheld his glory, the glory as of the only begotten of the Father" (1:14). Thereafter, he cited numerous examples of the manifestation of Christ's glory. Jesus began to manifest that glory with His first sign in Cana (2:11), and each subsequent sign revealed more. And now He displayed it in the most remarkable way of all—by overcoming the decay of death. It would be a foretaste of both His and His people's bodily glorification (cf. John 17:5; I Cor. 15:42-43; I Pet. 1:21).

THE PRAYER OFFERED

41 Then they took away the stone from the place where the dead was laid. And Jesus lifted up his eyes, and said, Father, I thank thee that thou hast heard me.

42 And I knew that thou hearest me always: but because of the people which stand by I said it, that they may believe that thou hast sent me.

Removal of the stone (John 11:41a). Martha was apparently persuaded by Jesus' response that the stone had to be removed from the tomb for her to see the glory of God manifested. So the bystanders obeyed Jesus' directions and took it away. It is doubtful that anyone present (except perhaps

Mary, whose thoughts we are not told) expected Jesus to actually restore Lazarus to life.

Jesus' prayer (John 11:41*b***-42).** Jesus therefore preceded His miracle with a prayer to His Father—not so much for His own sake as for that of the bystanders. He did not petition His Father to raise Lazarus; He merely thanked Him that He had already heard His petition. His will was so unified with His Father's that He already knew what the Father wanted Him to do at Lazarus's tomb.

Jesus alluded to His unity with the Father when He said, "And I knew that thou hearest me always" (vs. 42). The communion of minds and wills in the Father and the Son showed itself in the Son's obedience to the Father and the Father's witness to the Son's divine identity and mission (cf. 5:18-37; 8:17- 18; 10:30, 36-38). A part of this witness was the Son's ability to give life (5:21, 24-26). So Jesus prayed with confidence at the tomb.

{But the real reason for this prayer was for the benefit of the people standing by. Jesus desired that they believe that God had sent Him.}[Q6] Thus, His prayer was audible and public. The crowd knew that He was addressing His Father, and when the miracle was performed, they would attribute it to Him. They would also see Jesus as God's obedient Son, not calling attention to Himself but to the One who had sent Him.

{Did the miracle that followed actually arouse faith in those who saw it? As with all miracles, the results were mixed.}[Q7] The faith of the two sisters and of Jesus' disciples obviously was strengthened. In addition, many of the friends present trusted Him (11:45). From them the news spread quickly to many more, who, upon seeing Lazarus alive (12:9), placed their faith in Jesus. This miracle was a major reason for the

huge crowds at the time of the triumphal entry (vss. 17-18).

{But other witnesses of the sign went to the Pharisees and reported what had happened (11:46). Then the Pharisees, in desperation, sought to kill Jesus (vss. 47-53).}[Q8] They even tried to put Lazarus to death in order to destroy the evidence for the miracle (12:10). So the same supernatural work that softened some hearts and led to Jesus' triumphal entry into Jerusalem hardened others to murderous rage and led to His death.

THE DEAD CALLED FORTH

43 And when he thus had spoken, he cried with a loud voice, Lazarus, come forth.

44 And he that was dead came forth, bound hand and foot with graveclothes: and his face was bound about with a napkin. Jesus saith unto them, Loose him, and let him go.

Jesus' command (John 11:43). Jesus turned from addressing His Father and stating the reason for His impending action to addressing the dead man. He "cried with a loud voice, Lazarus, come forth." It was not His usual practice to speak loudly. In fact, He fulfilled Isaiah's prophecy that He would "not strive, nor cry; neither shall any man hear his voice in the streets" (Matt. 12:19). One of the few other times He cried out in a loud voice was on the cross, just before He yielded His spirit to the Father (Luke 23:46).

We have reason to believe that cry from the cross was the victorious shout "It is finished"! (cf. John 19:30). His cry at Lazarus's tomb also signified a victory—victory over death and the one who had the power of death, Satan (cf. Heb. 2:14-15).

{Jesus had earlier foretold a day when all who were in graves would hear His voice and come forth (John 5:28-29). His call to Lazarus was a foreshadowing of that final resurrection (cf. I Thess. 4:16).}[Q9] The duration of bodily decomposition, whether four days, as in the case of Lazarus, or thousands of years, makes no difference to Him. It is the power of His word that restores life, just as the divine word brought life in the original Creation (cf. John 1:1-4; 5:21; 11:25).

The dead man's response (John 11:44). Jesus' crisp command brought an immediate response. To the amazement of everyone, Lazarus came out of the grave! This was the third recorded time Jesus restored the dead to life. He brought back the daughter of Jairus shortly after she had died (Mark 5:35-42). The young man from Nain was being carried to the cemetery on the day of his death (Luke 7:11-16). In those two cases, some might have argued that they had merely been unconscious. But in Lazarus's case, there could be no mistake. He was in the tomb four days!

In fact, he came forth with the graveclothes on (John 11:44). The Jews did not embalm bodies as the Egyptians did, but they did wash and anoint the body and wrap it with strips of cloth. The face was wrapped with a separate cloth (cf. 19:39-40; 20:3-7). Lazarus appeared at the entrance of the tomb still bound by these graveclothes.

Some believe it took a separate miracle for Lazarus to reach the entrance still bound. But that was not necessary, since the wrappings were not tied so tightly as to keep him from moving. Still, he would have had to hobble to the opening. His appearance was certainly incongruous—a living man wearing graveclothes!

{Jesus, however, soon remedied this matter: He ordered the bystanders to unwrap him and let him go.}[Q10] This would not only release Lazarus to live a normal life but also provide proof that it was a real body and not an apparition. Jesus had directed others to remove the stone; now He likewise had them free Lazarus. He did what only He could do in raising him but let others do what they were capable of doing (cf. Mark 5:43).

This marvelous account reveals the extent of Jesus' divine power. As "the resurrection, and the life" (John 11:25), He overcomes the power of man's last enemy—death (I Cor. 15:26, 53-57). But it also reveals His compassion for those suffering grief. To be sure, He could prevent death from occurring, but in His infinite wisdom and love, He uses it to bring even greater blessing to those willing to trust Him.

—*Robert E. Wenger.*

QUESTIONS

1. From a human perspective, why does Lazarus's death seem unnecessary?

2. Why was Jesus angry as He approached the grave of Lazarus?

3. What does the description of Lazarus's tomb reveal about his family's social status?

4. Why did Jesus ask others to remove the stone from the tomb?

5. Did Martha believe Jesus would raise Lazarus? Explain.

6. Why did Jesus pray before raising Lazarus?

7. Did the resurrection of Lazarus fulfill Jesus' desire to arouse faith in the onlookers? Explain.

8. How did this miracle help lead to the crucifixion of Jesus?

9. What was foreshadowed by Jesus' call for Lazarus to come out?

10. What still had to be done for Lazarus after he was raised?

—*Robert E. Wenger.*

Preparing to Teach the Lesson

It is always helpful to intently read all the background verses before studying and teaching the Scripture lesson. In this case, we learn that the Lord Jesus had a deep personal interest in and affection for the three siblings in the story. Yet, in His own assessment of the situation, Lazarus's death was intended to glorify God. Do the best you can to help your students see that life's circumstances are rarely what they seem to be and that God can be glorified out of even the most dire events. While it is often hard to discern this in our own personal stories, it is clearly stated here that the story of Lazarus and his two sisters was recorded to show us this truth.

TODAY'S AIM

Facts: to see how Jesus is glorified through the raising of Lazarus from the dead.

Principle: to understand that the glory of God is central in every aspect of life, even in the most difficult trials.

Application: to trust God is working in every situation for His glory and our good.

INTRODUCING THE LESSON

Begin the lesson by reading both the background verses and the lesson text aloud. There may be some who have never heard this story. It appears only in the Gospel of John, exemplifying the theme of Jesus as the revelation of God's glory: "And the Word was made flesh, and dwelt among us, (and we beheld his glory, the glory as of the only begotten of the Father,) full of grace and truth" (1:14).

The glory of God could well be taken as the theme of the entire Bible. This theme is so big and broad that it can be overlooked in all the details of the many stories in which it is worked out. This lesson is a perfect opportunity to draw attention to that broad perspective and show how the raising of Lazarus is a perfect illustration of the Bible's main theme.

DEVELOPING THE LESSON

1. The grave of Lazarus (John 11:38-41a). After Jesus heard that Lazarus was ill, He deliberately delayed His journey to Bethany. By the time He arrived, Lazarus had been buried for four days. Lazarus's body would not have been embalmed, and in the Near East's heat, it would have decomposed rapidly. The Lord Jesus was known for His great compassion, and Lazarus was His friend. That made it difficult for Mary and Martha to understand why it took Him so long to arrive. From our background verses, we get the complaint from both sisters, "Lord, if thou hadst been here, my brother had not died" (vss. 21, 32). The Lord Jesus had already healed many people of all kinds of diseases, and certainly He could have prevented Lazarus's death, but He had chosen not to.

We may not know the reason for a specific incident in our lives, but we know for certain that God loves us and cares about every minute detail of our lives. He does not allow things to happen to us randomly. He designs every day of our lives according to His sovereign will and for the greatest spiritual good.

Consider Joseph in the Old Testament. He suffered at the hands of his brothers, but God intended it for the good of Joseph and of the whole land (Gen. 50:20). He has laid out His plan for each detail of our lives. It is our part to react to Him with faith, love, and gratitude, no matter our circumstances. We are included in His vast, eternal plan to show forth the glory of His grace and love. What an unspeakable privilege!

2. Communication with the Father (John 11:41b-42). This is a rare glimpse into the working relationship between the Lord Jesus and His Heavenly Father. We know that the Father, Son, and Holy Spirit are one, a Triunity. Their communication is instant, perfect, and eternal. As the incarnate Son, Jesus communicated perfectly with the Father through prayer. We know that prayer was a necessary component of His earthly life, as He often withdrew from the crowds to speak with His Father (Mark 1:35; Luke 5:16; 6:12). In this text, however, He prayed not for His own benefit but so that those present would understand what He was about to do.

In our background Scripture, the Lord Jesus had said to Martha, "I am the resurrection, and the life: he that believeth in me, though he were dead, yet shall he live: and whosoever liveth and believeth in me shall never die. Believest thou this?" (John 11:25-26). When He asked to have the stone removed from the grave, Martha objected because the body would be decomposed and have a foul odor. The Lord Jesus replied that if she would believe, she would see the glory of God. He did not say, "If you believe, Lazarus will be raised from the dead." God was to be glorified by this incident, regardless of Martha's response. All of us, like Lazarus, will eventually face death. Even Lazarus presumably died again and is buried until the resurrection on the last day. But this text teaches us that even in our deaths, God will be glorified. Our part is to believe.

3. The restoration of Lazarus to life (John 11:43-44). We know from John 1, Colossians 1, and Hebrews 1 that the Lord Jesus is the Creator of everything, including life itself. As the Author of Life, He had the authority to raise people from the dead. Just as His voice brought all things into being out of nothing (John 1:1-3), so His voice brings the dead to life. He spoke, and Lazarus came forth.

Lazarus was wrapped and bound all around with cloth, making his appearance from the cave all the more stunning. The Lord Jesus gave a practical order to unwrap and free Lazarus.

ILLUSTRATING THE LESSON

May God be glorified in our lives.

CONCLUDING THE LESSON

It is often hard to see how God is working in the difficult parts of our lives, but Jesus shows us that even death can be used for God's glory and the strengthening of our faith. As we encounter trials, let's remember that it is especially in these times that the glory of Jesus can shine through us, as it did through Lazarus.

ANTICIPATING THE NEXT LESSON

Even at His own death, Jesus remained in authority. Our next lesson will focus on the crucifixion of Jesus and His words of hope to the thief on the cross.

—Brian D. Doud.

PRACTICAL POINTS

1. Like Jesus, we should have a holy displeasure at the destruction brought on by sin (John 11:38).
2. God has a purpose even when His ways don't make sense to us (vs. 39; cf. vs. 4).
3. We will see God's glory when we believe Jesus (vs. 40).
4. Publicly thanking God for answered prayers and blessings can help others believe (vss. 41-42).
5. Our resurrection at the last day is certain because even death has to obey the voice of Jesus (vss. 43-44; cf. 5:25-29).

—Barbara A. Edwards.

RESEARCH AND DISCUSSION

1. What does the comment that Jesus was "groaning in himself" (John 11:38) indicate about His mindset?
2. When Jesus told Martha that she would "see the glory of God" (vs. 40), was this a reference to His own glory, the Father's glory, or both (cf. vs. 4)?
3. Some have claimed that Jesus' miracles do not prove His deity, since others have also worked miracles. How does the account of John 11 help us respond to that claim?
4. Has there been a time in your life when you did not understand what God was doing, but later you saw how it worked out for His glory?
5. Lazarus responded to Jesus' call immediately. How does this relate to God calling sinners to salvation (cf. Eph. 2:1-5)?

—Barbara A. Edwards.

ILLUSTRATED HIGH POINTS

Groaning in himself (John 11:38)

Even though Jesus is fully God (Matt. 1:23), as a man He is able to experience every sinless human emotion. John 11:35 and 38 show how deeply He feels the same kind of sorrows that we do. His love and grief for His friend Lazarus overwhelmed Him. Frederick Whitfield, in the well-known hymn "Oh, How I Love Jesus," expressed Jesus' empathy beautifully:

> It tells of One whose loving heart
> Can feel my deepest woe,
> Who in each sorrow bears a part
> That none can bear below.

If thou wouldest believe (vs. 40)

An elderly preacher I knew used to tell stories of his boyhood days in the wilderness of Arkansas. At night, the cries of bobcats, panthers, and wolves sent chills up and down his back. However, when his father held his hand, he knew that he was safe and secure from all that was lurking in the darkness.

As God's children, we may fear and become distressed about the evil around us. Thankfully, we can believe and hold on to God's unchanging hand.

Lazarus, come forth (vs. 43)

While John 11:35 and 38 show Jesus displaying painful emotions, verse 43 reminds us of His absolute power.

Throughout the New Testament, we see the divine power of Jesus. In the wilderness He hungered as a man (Matt. 4:2); yet He later took a boy's lunch and fed more than five thousand (14:15-21). He is clearly God.

As God, He still intervenes in people's lives today. Though He died as a man on the cross, His resurrection validates His divinity.

—James O. Baker.

Golden Text Illuminated

"When he thus had spoken, he cried with a loud voice, Lazarus, come forth. And he that was dead came forth, bound hand and foot with graveclothes" (John 11:43-44).

I recently attended a sobering funeral. It was for a younger member of my church, a man in his early twenties. Though I did not know him well, I was acquainted with his parents.

As people filed into the church, I was struck by how very loved this young man was. People in cowboy garb packed the sanctuary and overflowed into the foyer. Every folding chair was set out; people stood in the vestibule and spilled into the halls. Although the church was large, it could hardly contain all the mourners.

The family walked up the aisle and was seated. First came the extended family: uncles, aunts, cousins—all stepping grimly past. Next came the siblings: older brothers with grief-stricken faces, a younger sister weeping profusely.

I turned my head and watched as his mother passed my seat and entered the sanctuary. But it was the last two people to enter who made my eyes water, for standing at the back of the foyer was the young man's father, carefully pushing a wheelchair. Seated in that wheelchair with a cast on her leg was the young man's fiancée, head down and eyes averted. I later learned that she had been driving the car when the accident occurred. She had watched her future groom expire.

During the service, many tears were shed as various people stepped forward to talk about this vibrant young life. A friend recalled his love of cars. Another person told the story of his proposal to his high school sweetheart. Someone else mentioned cowboy boots and plaid shirts. Memories were brought forth—a final tribute to someone who had touched so many lives.

As the day progressed, the mood changed. While it was still a day of mourning, I began to see signs of hope. Smiles were appearing on faces at the reception as people fondly told humorous stories about the deceased. I began to hear laughter ringing out from different groups around the room.

The most profound moment for me, however, happened when I was conversing with his mother. I will not soon forget her words. As I filed in front of her to share my condolences, I instead found myself being consoled by her. When I began to express my sympathy for her loss, she stopped me. "We are rejoicing right now," she said. "With God's strength, I can handle this. I know he is in the arms of our Saviour. He is happy, and I know I will see him again someday soon."

That is the reassurance we can cling to when we experience the loss of another believer. We may miss that person dearly and wonder how his homegoing fits into God's plan. We may even feel cheated. But we need not give in to those feelings. Paul clearly told us this: "For if we believe that Jesus died and rose again, even so them also which sleep in Jesus will God bring with him" (I Thess. 4:14).

As believers, we know that our loved ones in Christ are not eternally lost to us. Even in the midst of heartache, we do not have to despair. It will be only a short interlude until we meet them again in glory. Someday, we shall all be resurrected and worship our Lord together. What a day that will be!

—*Jennifer Lautermilch*

Heart of the Lesson

On a frigid, overcast day, I stood at my grandfather's graveside for the first time. A mound still rose above the buried casket; the earth had yet to settle. The few trees in the cemetery waved their skeletal limbs above the dry, yellowed grass. The bleakness, the cold, and the tombstone all spoke about the finality of death.

Jesus' close friends, Mary and Martha, were feeling the finality of death when Jesus neared their home in Bethany. Their brother Lazarus, whom He loved, had died four days earlier. Knowing of His ability to heal, the sisters had sent word to Jesus when Lazarus had fallen sick.

But Jesus had delayed coming, and Lazarus died. Martha met Jesus outside of town, and at His request, the people who had come to comfort the sisters led Him to Lazarus's burial place.

1. Jesus visits Lazarus's grave (John 11:38-40). As Jesus neared the cave where Lazarus lay, He felt deep emotion—He groaned within Himself. He felt empathy with the sisters; He already had wept with them. He knew that even after the miracle He was about to perform, some would not believe. Perhaps He felt anger over death, which was not part of God's original Creation.

Jesus asked the onlookers to remove the stone. Following Jewish custom, professional mourners and friends accompanied Mary and Martha for several days following the death. Plenty of people were present to roll away the huge stone that covered the entrance to the cave.

Martha, always practical, protested removing the stone. Four days had passed since her brother's death. In Israel's hot climate, his body would have begun to decompose and produce an unbearable stench.

The four days were significant. One Jewish midrash, which likely reflects first-century Jewish thought, teaches that a dead person's soul hovers over the body for three days (Lev. Rabbah 18.1), making it remotely possible for the body to be resuscitated during that time. But at day four, with the body's decomposition progressing, any such hope would have disappeared. The timing told Martha that no hope remained to resuscitate Lazarus.

Jesus gently reminded Martha of His words when they had first met that day: if she would believe, she would see God's glory. The number of days Lazarus had been dead did not affect that promise.

2. Jesus thanks His Father (John 11:41-42). Onlookers rolled away the stone. Then Jesus raised His eyes toward heaven and prayed. He prayed aloud for the benefit of those listening. He wanted those listening to believe that the Father had sent Him.

3. Jesus raises the dead (John 11:43-44). Jesus' words, "Lazarus, come forth," show that Jesus can bring life out of death simply by commanding it to be so.

Lazarus probably hobbled out of the cave. The graveclothes—strips of linen wrapped around his body—would have made walking difficult. Jesus told the onlookers to loosen the strips and free him.

The raising of Lazarus was Jesus' last public miracle recorded in the book of John. The story is a reminder that as we mourn our loved ones, Jesus knows our pain and cares about us.

More important, Jesus is the Resurrection and the Life. He conquered death and has power over it. His resurrection is the guarantee that if we place our faith in Him, we have eternal life.

—*Ann Staatz.*

World Missions

"And he that was dead came forth" (John 11:44). If I were asked to choose two words from this text that convey the greatest amount of comfort and hope, I would choose "was dead." This phrase indicates that a renewal has taken place, resurrecting something that had died. Lazarus was dead. His physical functions had ceased, and life had left his body. When we see this happen, we say the person is dead. This involves the assumption that the person will stay dead, with no allowance for the possibility of a return to physical, earthly life.

But with two words from the Master Jesus, "Come forth" (vs. 43), what was believed to be Lazarus's permanent condition changed immediately. The man who was dead came alive again with one command from the Son of God.

Today God sends people throughout the world with the same goal, spiritually speaking, that Jesus had when He stood outside Lazarus's tomb—to bring the dead to life. According to the Scriptures, all who have not received Jesus as Saviour are spiritually dead. "And you hath he quickened, who were dead in trespasses and sins" (Eph. 2:1). Once a person receives Jesus as his Saviour, eternal life fills the place where death from sin had been.

The light of God's life shines brightest in the darkest places. Missionaries across the world know well the opposition they face as they preach and teach the life-giving gospel of Jesus Christ. Some missionaries have worked in villages and areas of cities known for their occult involvement, such as the practice of voodoo and other forms of witchcraft. Others encounter organized New Age or humanistic practitioners. Many others accept the call to enter areas of religious antagonism where there are threats of violence or terror. These relentless individuals and groups have a common goal—to preach the gospel to those who are dead in their sins.

Instead of showing up at Lazarus's tomb, missionaries meet lifeless people on the streets, in homes, in schools, and in makeshift church buildings. Rather than "Come forth," their invitation is "Come to Jesus." Those who respond to the life-giving message are not wearing graveclothes but blue jeans, dresses, T-shirts, and business suits. Nevertheless, the spiritual life the Holy Spirit injects into the human spirit at redemption is as real and powerful as the surge of energy that stood Lazarus up on his feet inside the tomb.

Romans 4:17 tells us that God brings the dead to life. Missionaries witness this process each time they lead a person to Christ. Sometimes they see physical evidence of new life—a bright smile or a hug. Signs of joy often accompany the introduction of a new life, such as singing or words of thankfulness.

Imagine the scene outside Lazarus's grave as he emerged alive. Gasps of surprise and eruptions of praise probably filled the air. Heaven too joins in the rejoicing when a person comes from the death of sin to the eternal life found only in Christ (Luke 15:7). The angels celebrate when a person becomes born again to a life that will have no end.

Though the job of missionaries is often challenging and even dangerous, it is rewarding as they see their labor result in eternal life for those they serve.

—*Beverly Medley Jones.*

The Jewish Aspect

A modern funeral service often takes place several days after a person has died. Distant family members are given time to travel. The common practice of embalming a body makes such delay possible. But funerals conducted in New Testament times were governed by different circumstances.

Ancient cultures typically announced a person's death with loud wails. At the time of the Exodus, "there was a great cry in Egypt; for there was not a house where there was not one dead" (Ex. 12:30). Nearly fifteen hundred years later, that same custom was practiced in the days of Jesus. Musicians were often added, especially flute players, as seen at the death of Jairus's daughter (Matt. 9:23; Mark 5:38).

Burials in Jesus' time took place within a few hours of death. People assisting with the burial washed the body and then rubbed it with various oils, as demonstrated at the death of Dorcas (Acts 9:37). Bodies of wealthy people were also anointed with expensive perfumes to mask the smell of decay.

The body was wrapped in long strips of linen cloth (Matt. 27:59), beginning with the hands and feet and ending with the head. As the body was wrapped with the cloth, fragrant spices were placed between the cloth and the body. At the death of Jesus, His body was anointed with "a mixture of myrrh and aloes, about an hundred pound weight" (John 19:39)—that is, about seventy of our contemporary pounds, an extravagant amount.

After a body had been properly prepared and the family and friends gathered, it was carried through town on a bier, a sort of funeral stretcher. Sometimes a large number of people from the town followed along in the procession (Luke 7:12). The funeral procession ended at the grave site. Burial places were commonly outside the town. Poor people would typically dig a simple grave in the ground. Wealthy individuals often used caves, either natural or man-made, as burial sites. These caves often had several niches to accommodate multiple bodies.

An indication that the family of Lazarus was well-to-do is the fact that he was buried in a cave with a stone rolled in front of the opening (John 11:38-39). Joseph of Arimathea, also a wealthy man, placed the body of Jesus in a cave tomb that he had recently "hewn out in the rock" (Matt. 27:60).

The area around the entrance to a tomb was frequently whitewashed as a notice to people that a decaying body was inside. Coming near a dead body defiled a Jewish person, interfering with worship at the temple. This is the context for Jesus' words to the hypocritical Pharisees: "for ye are like unto whited sepulchres, which indeed appear beautiful outward, but are within full of dead men's bones, and of all uncleanness" (Matt. 23:27).

When death occurred in a Jewish house, everything in the house was unclean for a week (Num. 19:14). As a result, no food could be prepared in it. Neighbors brought the bereaved family food to eat (a custom still observed in our day). Unless they were dependent on daily wages, family members did not work for a week after the funeral. The full time for mourning extended for a month after the death, after which the family resumed life. They knew that death was an inevitable part of their lives. This would continue until that great day when death will be "swallowed up in victory" (I Cor. 15:54).

—R. Larry Overstreet.

Guiding the Superintendent

In the Gospel of John, we read that Jesus made several rather strong claims. Among these claims are "I am the light of the world" (8:12), "I am the bread of life" (6:35), and "I am the good shepherd" (10:11). But the claim He made in 11:25 is perhaps the most audacious of all: "I am . . . the life." This was an assertion that at some time He would have to prove. With the raising of His friend Lazarus, Jesus made good on this claim.

In the Gospel accounts of Jesus' miracles, believing is often a prominent theme. In today's text we see that Jesus raised Lazarus from the dead for two reasons: to glorify God and to lead people to believe in Him so they would see that glory.

DEVOTIONAL OUTLINE

1. Believing is seeing (John 11:38-40). In John 2, Jesus amazed everyone at the wedding in Cana by performing the first of His miracles, turning ordinary water into wine. In doing this, He had a specific purpose. God would be glorified, and people would believe in Him (vs. 11).

In John 11, He worked another miracle for the same purpose—"for the glory of God" (vs. 4) and "that they may believe that thou hast sent me" (vs. 42).

As one might expect, the scene was filled with emotion. For a while, Jesus joined them in their grief (vs. 35). Then He approached the tomb and ordered that the gravestone be removed. Martha immediately objected. After all, Lazarus had been dead several days and was starting to decompose.

To this Jesus responded, "If thou wouldest believe, thou shouldest see the glory of God" (vs. 40; cf. 2:11). What encouragement from the Master—He

calls all who are totally bewildered by life to faith first and then sight!

2. Believing is the goal (John 11:41-42). As the stone was being removed, Jesus looked up and uttered a prayer—not a prayer for resurrection but a prayer of thanksgiving, for He already knew what God the Father would do.

Jesus had been called to the home of His dear friends. Mary and Martha were concerned about their very sick brother, Lazarus (cf. John 11:3). Jesus did not arrive until it was too late to help. Lazarus had already died.

The raising of His dear friend was not simply for Lazarus's benefit. It had the much broader focus of leading people to belief in Jesus and glorifying the Father.

3. Believing is the result (John 11:43-44). Oh, the drama! One wonders who was most surprised—Lazarus, his sisters, or the crowd. With a loud voice, Jesus commanded Lazarus to come out of the tomb. Those around were then told to loosen his graveclothes. Mission accomplished! John tells the readers in the next verse (vs. 45) that many of the people did, indeed, believe in Jesus.

AGE-GROUP EMPHASES

Children: By their very nature, children tend to believe anything an adult says. This lesson can help them understand that a believer's faith is based only on what Jesus says.

Youths: This lesson will help teens grasp a very important concept of the Christian faith: believing enables seeing.

Adults: Use the points of the devotional outline to help adults understand the purpose of Jesus' miracles.

—Martin R. Dahlquist.

SCRIPTURE LESSON TEXT

LUKE 23:33 And when they were come to the place, which is called Calvary, there they crucified him, and the malefactors, one on the right hand, and the other on the left.

34 Then said Jesus, Father, forgive them; for they know not what they do. And they parted his raiment, and cast lots.

35 And the people stood beholding. And the rulers also with them derided *him,* saying, He saved others; let him save himself, if he be Christ, the chosen of God.

36 And the soldiers also mocked him, coming to him, and offering him vinegar,

37 And saying, If thou be the king of the Jews, save thyself.

38 And a superscription also was written over him in letters of Greek, and Latin, and Hebrew, THIS IS THE KING OF THE JEWS.

39 And one of the malefactors which were hanged railed on him, saying, If thou be Christ, save thyself and us.

40 But the other answering rebuked him, saying, Dost not thou fear God, seeing thou art in the same condemnation?

41 And we indeed justly; for we receive the due reward of our deeds: but this man hath done nothing amiss.

42 And he said unto Jesus, Lord, remember me when thou comest into thy kingdom.

43 And Jesus said unto him, Verily I say unto thee, To day shalt thou be with me in paradise.

44 And it was about the sixth hour, and there was a darkness over all the earth until the ninth hour.

45 And the sun was darkened, and the veil of the temple was rent in the midst.

46 And when Jesus had cried with a loud voice, he said, Father, into thy hands I commend my spirit: and having said thus, he gave up the ghost.

47 Now when the centurion saw what was done, he glorified God, saying, Certainly this was a righteous man.

48 And all the people that came together to that sight, beholding the things which were done, smote their breasts, and returned.

49 And all his acquaintance, and the women that followed him from Galilee, stood afar off, beholding these things.

NOTES

The Crucifixion of Jesus

Lesson Text: Luke 23:33-49

Related Scriptures: Luke 23:26-32; Matthew 27:11-26; John 10:11-18

TIME: A.D. 30   PLACE: Calvary

GOLDEN TEXT—"And Jesus said unto him, Verily I say unto thee, To day shalt thou be with me in paradise" (Luke 23:43).

Introduction

When Jesus was crucified, His suffering and death on the cross prompted a wide range of responses. The Jewish rulers mocked Jesus. The soldiers divided His garments, casting lots to determine who would get to keep each portion.

The two criminals who were crucified on either side of Jesus had contrasting responses. One of them joined the chorus that was abusing the Lord. The other criminal, however, admitted his own guilt and Jesus' innocence.

As Jesus hung on the cross, the whole land became dark for three hours. The temple veil leading to the Holy of Holies was torn in two as Jesus surrendered His spirit to God the Father. As he saw all of this, the Roman centurion became convinced that Jesus was indeed innocent. The crowd also recognized that something dreadful had occurred. At a distance stood Jesus' longtime followers, not comprehending what they had witnessed.

LESSON OUTLINE

I. **MOCKING RESPONSE BY THE CROWD**—Luke 23:33-38

II. **MIXED RESPONSE BY THE CRIMINALS**—Luke 23:39-43

III. **MOVING RESPONSE BY THE CENTURION**—Luke 23:44-49

Exposition: Verse by Verse

MOCKING RESPONSE BY THE CROWD

LUKE 23:33 And when they were come to the place, which is called Calvary, there they crucified him, and the malefactors, one on the right hand, and the other on the left.

34 Then said Jesus, Father, forgive them; for they know not what they do. And they parted his raiment, and cast lots.

35 And the people stood beholding. And the rulers also with them derided him, saying, He saved others; let him save himself, if he be Christ, the chosen of God.

36 And the soldiers also mocked him, coming to him, and offering him vinegar,

37 And saying, If thou be the king of the Jews, save thyself.

38 And a superscription also was written over him in letters of Greek, and Latin, and Hebrew, THIS IS THE KING OF THE JEWS.

Dividing His garments (Luke 23:33-34). After a long night that saw His arrest, trials, beating, and sentencing to death, Jesus was led to the site of crucifixion, a place called Calvary. The Aramaic name for the place was "Golgotha" (Mark 15:22). Both names mean "skull." It may have gotten this name because the hill looked like a head jutting out of the ground. At this place outside of the wall of Jerusalem, Jesus was crucified. Two condemned criminals were also executed on either side of Him.

Even when He was being terribly mistreated, Jesus reached out to forgive others. He cried, "Father, forgive them; for they know not what they do" (Luke 23:34). {Jesus had taught His disciples to love their enemies and to pray for those who treated them badly (6:27-28). In the most severe conditions, Jesus practiced what He had preached to the disciples, for He asked the Father to forgive those who had placed Him on the cross.}[Q1]

While Jesus was exposed to public ridicule, the Roman soldiers callously disregarded Him. As He died for their sins, they gambled to see who would get His clothes. Little did they realize who He was and what He was doing for them. For the soldiers, this was just another routine execution that gave them the opportunity to get a new piece of clothing for themselves.

Deriding His claims (Luke 23:35). A curious crowd gathered to watch the crucifixion, but they said nothing, at least initially. The Jewish leaders, however, started to mock Jesus.

Jesus had claimed to be the Messiah, but the rulers treated that idea as a joke. Jesus did not fit their notion of a conquering, royal Messiah. Even though He was at that very moment fulfilling Isaiah's prophecy of the Suffering Servant of God (chap. 53), they did not grasp what was happening.

{In a mocking tone the rulers urged Jesus to save Himself if He was really the Messiah.}[Q2] They had no idea what they were suggesting. In order to save the world, Jesus could not choose to save Himself by coming down off the cross. He was dying this awful death because that was God's plan of salvation at work.

Devaluing His status (Luke 23:36-37). {The soldiers had already demonstrated their disregard for Jesus by casting lots for His clothing. After they heard the Jewish leaders mocking Him, they joined in the ridicule, jeering and scoffing at Him.}[Q3]

As Jesus started to get parched in the sun, the soldiers dipped a sponge into sour wine and offered it to Him. Without realizing it, by doing so they fulfilled the ancient prophecy of Psalm 69:21: "They gave me also gall for my meat; and in my thirst they gave me vinegar to drink." This was not an act of kindness but rather a rude insult. Like the Jewish leaders, the soldiers threw one of Jesus' claims in His face. They challenged the King of the Jews to save Himself.

Defining His royalty (Luke 23:38). The soldiers probably got the inspiration for their ridicule from a sign that Pilate had placed above Jesus. Often the cross bore a notice indicating the crime that had been committed by the one being executed. Pilate placed above Jesus the claim that He had made. The superscription said, "THIS IS THE KING OF THE JEWS."

Pilate intended this as a mockery of both Jesus and the Jewish people. What Pilate did not realize was that what he intended as ridicule was in reality the truth. {He had spoken far more truthfully than he imagined or intended. God used Pilate's superscription to indicate to all who saw it that Jesus was indeed the King of the Jews.}^{Q4} Just as Caesar Augustus was God's tool to assure that Jesus was born in Bethlehem (Luke 2:1-7), so Pilate was God's means to testify to the world about Jesus' true rank.

MIXED RESPONSE BY THE CRIMINALS

39 And one of the malefactors which were hanged railed on him, saying, If thou be Christ, save thyself and us.

40 But the other answering rebuked him, saying, Dost not thou fear God, seeing thou art in the same condemnation?

41 And we indeed justly; for we receive the due reward of our deeds: but this man hath done nothing amiss.

42 And he said unto Jesus, Lord, remember me when thou comest into thy kingdom.

43 And Jesus said unto him, Verily I say unto thee, To day shalt thou be with me in paradise.

Abusive charge (Luke 23:39). One might suppose that the sight of Jesus hanging on the cross would prompt compassion in all those who saw Him. That, however, was not the case. As Jesus suffered pain while dying as God's perfect Substitute for sinners, He received no appreciation or even tenderness from many of the people assembled there. {The derision of the Jewish rulers was joined by the mockery of the soldiers. As Jesus died for the whole world, it seemed that most of the world was aligned against Him. Soon a third voice was added to the choir of ridicule. One of the criminals picked up the scornful words of the rulers and the soldiers.}^{Q5} He started railing at Jesus, saying, "If thou be Christ, save thyself and us." He knew from the intensity of his own pain what Jesus must have been enduring, and yet he only added to the ridicule. Like the rest, this criminal was blind to the fact that it was only through Jesus' death that anyone could truly be saved.

Admission of guilt (Luke 23:40-41). Hanging on the other side of Jesus, the second criminal responded in a very different way. He had heard the same jeers directed at Jesus, he had seen the callous disregard of the soldiers, and he was probably aware of the miscarriage of justice that had put Jesus on the cross. The other criminal's angry words to Jesus were the last straw for him.

No doubt with substantial effort, this man rebuked the other criminal. How could he add to the torment Jesus was experiencing by ridiculing Him? Did he not realize that Jesus was feeling the same torturous pain of crucifixion that was wracking his own body? Had he no reverence for God, that he would speak to an innocent, dying man in such harsh tones?

The second criminal then made an amazing statement. He acknowledged that the two of them were guilty of their crimes. The punishment they were enduring was exactly what their sin had earned. By contrast, Jesus had done nothing wrong. He was an innocent person dying between genuine criminals.

At that awful scene at Calvary, the crowd watched silently. The ridicule began with the Jewish rulers, spread to the Roman soldiers, and eventually included the jeering words of a convicted criminal. The first voice to speak up for Jesus was another guilty man, who saw what the others refused to admit. Jesus alone was innocent. In human terms, it was a colossal injustice, but in God's plan it was amazing grace.

Acceptance by Jesus (Luke 23:42-43). The second criminal turned to Jesus and uttered the familiar cry of the psalmists: "Lord, remember me" (vs. 42). The psalmists often appealed to the Lord to remember them. It was a plea for Him to intervene and deliver them from their predicaments (cf. Ps. 89:50; 106:4; 132:1). In the same way, the criminal asked Jesus to save him even as he was slowly succumbing to death on the cross.

The criminal's prayer to Jesus was a courageous request of faith: "Lord, remember me when thou comest into thy kingdom" (Luke 23:42). Of all the people at Calvary, he was the first to speak of Jesus as the King that He claimed to be. He asked to be included in the kingdom that Jesus would rule.

Jesus' reply must have brought incalculable comfort to the criminal in his waning hours. {Jesus told him that he would be with Him in paradise.}[Q6] Better than that, they would be there on that very day. {The criminal might have been thinking of the kingdom to come at the end of time, but Jesus assured him that he would be in paradise in a matter of a few hours.}[Q7]

In Jewish thought, paradise was the place of the future bliss of God's people. They pictured it as being like Eden, a place in which the righteous rest after death. In the New Testament, paradise is equated with heaven (II Cor. 12:4; Rev. 2:7). Those who trust Jesus Christ as their Saviour will, upon death, be absent from the body and immediately present with the Lord. That is the paradise that will be enjoyed by all those who die in Christ.

MOVING RESPONSE BY THE CENTURION

44 And it was about the sixth hour, and there was a darkness over all the earth until the ninth hour.

45 And the sun was darkened, and the veil of the temple was rent in the midst.

46 And when Jesus had cried with a loud voice, he said, Father, into thy hands I commend my spirit: and having said thus, he gave up the ghost.

47 Now when the centurion saw what was done, he glorified God, saying, Certainly this was a righteous man.

48 And all the people that came together to that sight, beholding the things which were done, smote their breasts, and returned.

49 And all his acquaintance, and the women that followed him from Galilee, stood afar off, beholding these things.

Powerful signs (Luke 23:44-45). As the hour of noon arrived, God Himself spoke in a silent but powerful voice. For the next three hours a supernatural darkness enveloped all the land. Some have suggested that this was a solar eclipse, but that could not have been the case. Eclipses of the sun at most produce only a few minutes of total darkness. In addition, solar eclipses must occur at the new moon, and Passover was at the full moon. This darkness was a special act of God.

In the Old Testament, darkness often indicated divine judgment (cf. Joel 2:10, 30-31; Amos 8:9; Zeph. 1:15). As Jesus suffered on the cross in the profound darkness, God's judgment was poured out on sin. Jesus was bearing the guilt of the world on Himself. He was made "sin for us" (II Cor. 5:21), and He received the judgment that we deserved (I Pet. 2:24).

{After the three hours of darkness and at the time of Jesus' death (cf. Matt. 27:50-51; Mark 15:37-38), the massive temple veil was torn in two.}[Q8] This veil covered the entrance to the Holy of Holies, which was the site of God's presence (cf. Ex. 25:22; 26:33-34; I Kgs. 8:6). {When the veil was torn in two, it symbolized that the way was opened to direct access to God for all, not just for the high priest.}[Q9] Because of the death of Christ, Christians can now approach God boldly and come directly into His presence (Heb. 4:14-16).

Public commitment (Luke 23:46). At about the ninth hour, or 3:00 P.M., Jesus called out to His Father one final time. Throughout His whole life, He had done as the Father directed. In the Garden of Gethsemane He had surrendered to the will of the Father, saying, "Not my will, but thine, be done" (22:42).

The Jews frequently used Psalm 31 as an evening prayer. Drawing upon verse 5 of that psalm, Jesus called out, "Father, into thy hands I commend my spirit" (Luke 23:46). With those words on His lips, Jesus breathed His last breath. He had finished the work He had come to do. By His death, the incarnate Son of God had purchased salvation for all who believe in Him.

Perceptive conclusion (Luke 23:47). The centurion who commanded the Roman soldiers most likely had seen many crucifixions. Throughout the day he had heard the ridicule directed at Jesus. He had waited throughout the three hours of supernatural darkness. He had heard Jesus' gracious response to the repentant criminal and His final words to God the Father.

As the centurion witnessed all of this, he was deeply moved. He took in the whole situation and concluded that Jesus was a righteous man. He had no doubt in his mind that Jesus was innocent of the crimes of which He had been accused.

In the parallel account in Mark, the centurion stated, "Truly this man was the Son of God" (15:39). Jesus was indeed who He claimed to be. Ironically, the superscription was accurate. He was truly the King of the Jews. Despite the taunts and mocking, Jesus was the Messiah who came to save others.

Personal reactions (Luke 23:48-49). For the most part, the assembled crowd watched without speaking. Their eyes were transfixed by the horrible spectacle they saw.

As Jesus died, the crowd sensed that something awful had happened. {They smote their breasts in the typical sign of mourning.}[Q10] They were not necessarily expressing repentance by doing this, but they were demonstrating that grief had seized their hearts.

Far back in the crowd stood those who had followed Jesus from Galilee to Jerusalem. Their Master was now dead, and they did not know what the future held. They watched with heavy hearts, wondering what would come next.

—Daniel J. Estes.

QUESTIONS

1. How did Jesus practice what He preached even when hanging on the cross?
2. How did the Jewish rulers mock Jesus' claim that He was the promised Messiah?
3. How did the soldiers evidence their disregard for Jesus?
4. How did Pilate speak more truthfully than he intended about Jesus?
5. What people ridiculed Jesus at the cross?
6. How did Jesus extend God's grace to the second criminal?
7. What hope did Jesus' reply bring to the repentant criminal?
8. What miracle did God perform as Jesus hung on the cross?
9. What did the tearing of the veil symbolize?
10. How did the crowd that witnessed these events respond?

—Daniel J. Estes.

Preparing to Teach the Lesson

The significance of Christ's crucifixion cannot be overstated. Jesus, the Son of God, died on the cross for our sins. This week's lesson gives your class an opportunity to ponder this great event.

TODAY'S AIM

Facts: to review Christ's crucifixion and the events that accompanied it.

Principle: to recognize the crucifixion of Christ as the historical fact on which our faith is built.

Application: to respond to Jesus' substitutionary death with repentance and faith in Him.

INTRODUCING THE LESSON

When Jason was a teenager, he decided to build a small log cabin in the woods. With the help of several young friends, Jason cut down trees and notched logs. At the end of the summer, Jason's rustic little cabin was completed. A small wood stove, two cots, and a discarded chair added to the decor.

But there was one major problem with Jason's cabin. The poplar logs were laid on bare soil. In a few years, the bottom logs on which the whole cabin rested had turned to mush. Without a solid foundation, Jason's rustic cabin could not survive.

Our faith rests on a solid foundation—the atoning death of the Lord Jesus Christ. Apart from His crucifixion, there could be no true Christian faith. Jesus died on the cross for us. This lesson brings us back to our spiritual foundation.

DEVELOPING THE LESSON

1. The act of crucifixion (Luke 23:33). This one verse answers three questions: Where? What? and Who? Be prepared to give your students some facts re-

garding the location of Calvary. "Sites of the crucifixion have been proposed on every side of Jerusalem" (Lockyer, ed., *Nelson's Illustrated Bible Dictionary,* Thomas Nelson). The destruction of ancient Jerusalem in A.D. 70 complicates the task of identifying the actual site. The two locations suggested most often are one near the Church of the Holy Sepulchre and a place known as Gordon's Calvary, northeast of the Damascus Gate.

Review briefly the history and mechanics of crucifixion. The Romans had borrowed this practice from the Phoenicians. It caused the condemned to suffer greatly before death came. Cruel public executions were supposed to deter others from committing crimes against Rome.

Jesus was crucified with two "malefactors" (vs. 33), or evildoers. These will be dealt with later in the lesson.

2. Jesus on the cross (Luke 23:34-38). Accounts from the other Gospel writers add richness of detail to the narrative (cf. Matt. 27:32-56; Mark 15:20-41; John 19:16-37). Focus on the following, respectively: Jesus, the people, the Jewish leaders, and the soldiers. What was the attitude of each? At the time of His death, Jesus was concerned for others, praying for their forgiveness. What must the people have been feeling? Discuss the attitude of the leaders and soldiers, respectively.

Luke 23:38 tells of the sign that was posted identifying Jesus as the King of the Jews. Read Mark 15:2 and John 19:19-22.

3. Companions in crucifixion (Luke 23:39-43). Who were the "malefactors"? Matthew 27:38 identifies the two men as "thieves." "The persons mentioned in the Gospels were, no doubt, men who had taken up arms on a principle of resistance to Roman oppression, and especially to the payment of tribute money" (Unger, *Unger's Bible Dictionary,* Moody).

It seems incredible that one dying man would have the energy and inclination to hurl abuse at another. Refer to Jeremiah 17:9, which describes the heart of man. Many who have lived apart from God choose to die apart from Him also.

What aspects of the second malefactor's words showed his genuine faith? He indicated that he feared God. He accepted responsibility for his wrongdoing. He acknowledged the righteousness of Jesus and expressed belief in Him as the Messiah. Besides this, he also called out to Jesus for salvation.

Jesus responded to the man's repentance and faith in Him. Jesus anticipated being in paradise that very day. Read II Corinthians 5:8, which tells us that for a believer, to be absent from the body is to be present with the Lord.

4. Jesus' death (Luke 23:44-49). The "sixth hour" was noon. As Jesus hung on the cross, darkness engulfed the land from noon until three o'clock. Describe the nature and function of the veil of the temple. The veil was of heavy fabric. It separated the Holy of Holies, which signified the dwelling place of God, from the holy place. Search online for a floor plan of the temple to show the class where the veil was located. The veil barred the way from God's presence. Discuss the symbolic significance of the torn veil.

Read Luke 24:46 and then John 10:17-18 to the class. Jesus gave up His life voluntarily. He was not a victim of anyone.

Refer back to Luke 23:35, which states that the people "stood beholding." Notice the change by verse 48 (cf. 18:13). Smiting the breast signified mourning or grief.

The women and those whom Jesus knew stood and watched. Discuss what they must have been feeling and thinking by this time. Shock, fear, numbness, and disbelief might all be used to describe their state.

ILLUSTRATING THE LESSON

Three crosses on a hill provide an appropriate backdrop for this lesson on Jesus' crucifixion.

JESUS' CRUCIFIXION

PROOF THAT JESUS IS RISEN

CONCLUDING THE LESSON

Jesus was led off to Calvary to be crucified. As He hung on the cross, He prayed for the forgiveness of those who had put Him there. As He was dying, the sky turned dark, the religious leaders scoffed, the soldiers gambled, and the crowd watched. When Jesus released His spirit, the veil in the temple ripped. Even the callous Roman centurion concluded that Jesus was a righteous man.

In our time the cross is a religious symbol. Even non-Christians wear crosses as jewelry. For Jesus, the cross was the instrument of death. He allowed Himself to die there to pay the penalty for our sins. Urge any unsaved students to believe in Christ today.

ANTICIPATING THE NEXT LESSON

Jesus rose triumphant over death. In the next lesson we will study the account of His resurrection in Luke 24.

—*Bruce A. Tanner.*

PRACTICAL POINTS

1. One's commitment to godly principles is revealed in times of greatest personal agony (Luke 23:33-34).
2. Man's idea of salvation often differs from the true salvation God offers (vs. 35).
3. Many mocked Christ, which means many will mock His disciples as well (Luke 23:36-37; cf. John 15:20).
4. Instead of standing up for those who are being derided, people tend to join in the attack (vss. 38-39).
5. God is looking for the person who stands up for what is right (vss. 40-43).
6. We have access to the Father through Jesus' blood (vss. 44-46).
7. When we acknowledge the Lord publicly, many unbelievers will have cause to want o seek Him (vss. 47-49).

—Steven D. Pyle.

RESEARCH AND DISCUSSION

1. What makes it so difficult for us to forgive those who have wronged us? How should Jesus' crucifixion affect that?
2. What does it tell us about the human heart that so many mocked and derided the incarnate God (Luke 23:35-37; cf. Rom. 3:10-16)?
3. What part can believers play in helping unbelievers see themselves as sinners and God as righteous (vss. 40-42)?
4. What kinds of reactions should people have after a believer dies?

—Steven D. Pyle.

ILLUSTRATED HIGH POINTS

There they crucified him (Luke 23:33)

A Christian family was traveling along a major highway when all of a sudden three large crosses on a hill came into view. The conversation of the family immediately turned to the crucifixion of Jesus. The three children, ages twelve, ten, and eight, were filled with questions.

"I feel sorry for Jesus," said eight year-old Joan. "He suffered a lot on the cross."

"Yes, He did," answered her father.

"Did He have to die like that, Dad?" asked ten-year-old Tim. "Was there another way that He could save us?"

"He had to shed His blood," answered their father. "It was His Father's way to provide eternal life for us. The cross was necessary for our salvation."

Lord, remember me (vs. 42)

A pastor was explaining that many professing Christians trust in their religious practices instead of in Jesus Himself.

"Some of the most difficult people to reach for Christ are those who are steeped in their religion," he told the congregation.

The pastor then related an experience he had with Jim, who lived on the next street. "Jim was very religious. He grew up memorizing prayers. He always carried a religious charm with him.

"One day Jim fell off a ladder and was not expected to live. I heard about the accident and rushed to the hospital. All of Jim's confidence in his religious practices was gone. He realized he had nothing that guaranteed him heaven. In his weakness, Jim humbly prayed and asked Jesus to save him. Jim recovered and became a strong witness for the Lord."

—V. Ben Kendrick.

Golden Text Illuminated

"And Jesus said unto him, Verily I say unto thee, To day shalt thou be with me in paradise" (Luke 23:43).

Here we have Jesus' response to the thief on the cross after the thief expresses faith in Him (vs. 42). It is an amazing statement because, by his own admission, the thief has lived a life worthy of condemnation up to that very moment, just hours before his death (vs. 41). Yet Jesus does not hesitate to tell this sinner that he will be "in paradise" that very day.

The term "paradise" is used in the New Testament to refer to heaven as a renewed Garden of Eden (Rev. 2:7). Here it simply refers to the heavenly presence of God (cf. II Cor. 12:4).

This promise of Jesus assures us that our eternal state does not depend on anything we do for the Lord, but only on simple faith in the gracious salvation Christ has provided through His death and resurrection. The thief had done no good in his life, yet when he believed, Jesus assured him of eternal life.

At first, we may wonder why Jesus says the thief will be with Him "today." Didn't Jesus remain in the grave for the next three days? How could the thief have been with Him in heaven the same day Jesus was crucified?

To answer that question, we need to know whether Jesus was still under the Father's wrath while in the tomb. The context (vs. 46) makes clear that God's wrath was completely satisfied at the cross. So while the body of Jesus lay in the grave, His soul was in communion with the Father in heaven.

We can see this from the text's parallel with Exodus 10 through 12. Three hours before Jesus' death, darkness encompassed the whole land (Luke 23:44). This should lead our minds back to the ninth plague, when the Lord caused darkness to cover the whole land of Egypt for three days (Ex. 10:22). This darkness was immediately followed by the death of all the firstborn of Egypt, with the exception of those whose doorpost was painted with the blood of the Passover lamb (11—12).

In the same way, the darkness on Calvary was immediately followed by the death of God's firstborn, who is Himself our Passover Lamb (I Cor. 5:7). At that very moment, the curtain of the temple was torn (Luke 23:45), indicating that the breach between God and man had been bridged. Jesus' work was complete. The wrath of God had been turned aside by the Lamb of God, just as it had been at the first Passover.

This gives us great assurance when we think about our own death. Although our bodies will not be resurrected until Christ's second coming (I Cor. 15:52), our souls will be with Christ immediately. Just as Jesus was in the presence of His Father even as His body lay in the grave, and just as the thief was in the presence of Jesus immediately after he died, so we will not be separated from Christ for even an instant after death. As Paul tells us, nothing—not even death—can separate us from the love of God that is in Christ Jesus (Rom. 8:38–39). Although death is our enemy (I Cor. 15:26), it has been turned into *gain* for us, because it means going to be in the presence of Christ (Phil. 1:21).

What a glorious thought, that Christ has transformed death into life, so that at the very moment we die, we will be nearer to Him than we ever were on this earth.

—*Matthew Robinson.*

Heart of the Lesson

This week's lesson focuses on an incident both horrifically tragic and eternally wonderful at the same time. In it one sees the gross depravity of man as well as the glorious grace of God. The incident is the crucifixion of Christ. Several points to ponder emerge from the text.

1. The heinous crime (Luke 23:33). Nothing in all mankind's history reveals the wicked heart of man so clearly as the crucifixion of Christ. Crucifixion was the worst kind of death man could impose upon anyone, and it was the kind of death man chose to do away with the God who created him and loved him.

There is something very perverse in this event. Man offered his worst to the God who offered His best. It should give us pause to consider how we treat God's grace. We were not there to participate in crucifying Christ, but we often live as though His death were of no great import.

2. The honorable prayer (Luke 23:34). With ten little words, Jesus demonstrated what He meant when He told His disciples to forgive seventy times seven times (Matt. 18:22). He showed no anger and no hostility toward His enemies. He just uttered a humble word of prayer that the Father would not hold this great sin against them.

How ashamed does this make some of us, if not all of us, as we think of how we have responded in act, thought, or word toward those who have wronged us in some way?

3. The continued mocking (Luke 23:35-39). The unspeakable injustice toward the incarnate Saviour did not cease when the last nail was driven through His body. It continued verbally. The religious rulers were joined in disrespectful taunting by the soldiers and by one of those crucified with Jesus.

How easy it is to join in with others who are for or against something without really thinking things through! There is safety in numbers, and things we might otherwise not do by ourselves we find ourselves doing when others take the lead. We need to guard ourselves from getting caught up in such mob mentality.

4. The heavenly promise (Luke 23:40-43). Not everyone present railed against Jesus. One thief was repentant of his deeds and by faith asked to be remembered by Jesus in His kingdom. His words of contrition found mercy and salvation in the heart of God. That very day his prayer was answered not only in word but also in experience.

If we followed the crowd, we would never be saved, for the crowd is against Jesus and will not turn to Him in repentance and faith. Salvation requires a bold yet humble step of reliance.

5. The holy moment (Luke 23:44-49). There was something so moving about Christ's death that it deeply affected some who stood nearby. The centurion as well as the crowd began to think differently when they saw the signs that accompanied Jesus' death and the way He responded to the injustice. Since that time, people of all kinds and in every place have also been touched by the life of Christ.

As the church is faithful in continuing to tell and retell others about Christ, hearts continue to be convicted. Such conviction combined with faith leads to salvation.

—*Darrell W. McKay.*

World Missions

Ludwig Nommensen had been crippled as a boy when a horse and cart knocked him down in a cobbled street of the little northern German island where he lived. No one believed he would ever walk normally again.

The village schoolmaster came almost daily to help Ludwig with his reading and imparted to the boy his own faith in Christ. While he was convalescing, Ludwig listened as his friend told him about faraway places where primitive peoples lived—people who had never had the opportunity to hear the good news of Jesus. The boy asked the Lord to heal his legs so that he could take the gospel to those distant lands.

One day a new doctor came to the village, took an interest in Ludwig, and began to treat his crippled legs. In a short time, the boy was walking normally.

After that, Ludwig milked cows, cleaned stables, swept the schoolhouse, and did anything that would help him raise money in order to attend the missionary school. Although he was twenty-seven before he completed his education, he was appointed as a missionary to Sumatra in the East Indies to work among the cannibals.

Almost thirty years earlier, two American missionaries had been killed and eaten by these people, but Ludwig was undaunted. Had not the Saviour laid down His life to save him from sin? Should he not be willing to lay down his life so that the cannibals might know this same great God?

Ludwig arrived in Sumatra in 1863 and decided to live in the Silindung Valley among the Toba Batak tribe. Many of the chiefs, however, were against his coming. When he tried to build a house, they tore it down. "We will cut off your legs and throw you into the river!" they warned.

Ludwig persisted, however, and finally completed his house. He was not trained in medicine, but he was able to dress the spear and bullet wounds the natives frequently received in their wars with other tribes. Ludwig interceded with the government when foreign landlords threatened to take over tribal lands.

Once, a group of unfriendly chiefs stirred up a movement against Ludwig and sent out invitations to a feast of sacrifice to the spirits. On the day of the feast, more than a thousand cannibals arrived with spears, guns, and knives.

Ludwig walked into the center of the large crowd. "I ask you all to lay aside your weapons of war!" he cried in a loud voice. The armed men were stunned by his courage as the missionary quietly walked among them, collecting weapons.

The witch doctor's voice rang out, saying, "I shall not accept an ox as sacrifice unless you sacrifice a human too!" Ludwig raised his hand. "Quiet!" he commanded. Straight toward the witch doctor he walked. The tribal religious leader fell to the ground in fear. Ludwig turned to the crowd and began telling them about the God who loved them so much that He sent His Son to die to pay the penalty for all the evil anyone had committed.

Within a month of this event, a message was on its way back to Germany: "Send more missionaries! All in the Silindung Valley are ready to hear the gospel!"

A strong Christian church emerged in Sumatra. When Ludwig died at the age of 84, more than forty thousand came to the funeral to honor the Christian who had so fearlessly risked his life to tell them about the Saviour's sacrificial death (Millen, ed., *Missionary Hero Stories*, Friendship).

—*Ted Simonson.*

The Jewish Aspect

The rabbi paced up and down in obvious agitation. The anteroom of the city hall was half filled with people, some there to appeal tax bills and some to complain about municipal services. The rabbi was there to testify in favor of a proposed city ordinance restricting home-to-home evangelistic visitation. I was there to testify on the same resolution.

I knew the rabbi by sight from visits to his synagogue. He did not know me. The township had a large Jewish population, perhaps as many as half of the residents. I knew the rabbi would urge passage of the restrictive legislation because he did not want Jews to learn about Jesus or to receive Christian literature. As a home missionary, I was there to testify against the proposal.

The long wait for the city clerk to call for the hearing on the bill proved too much for the rabbi. He left in evident disgust. No one else appeared in favor of the legislation. I testified that Christian evangelism never involves selling or soliciting funds from local residents. Christians call simply to make the saving work of Jesus Christ known to all men. The city council recognized that the bill was probably unconstitutional and soundly defeated the measure.

This rabbi's interest in restricting evangelism is not really surprising. Jewish authorities stand to lose support when people (especially Jews) hear the testimony of the Messiah Jesus, particularly the good news of His death, burial, and resurrection. Their fear that we are agents of anti-Semitism is understandable in light of centuries of violence at the hands of those who have called themselves Christians. It is hard for them to understand that we come to them in love, with a loving message.

The Jewish people do not appreciate being reminded of the death of Jesus and the first-century Jews' part in bringing it about. Often they emphasize that crucifixion was not a Jewish form of punishment; the Romans killed Jesus.

While Peter did not ignore the Jews' responsibility in the death of Jesus, he lessened their culpability: "Now, brethren, I [know] that through ignorance ye did it, as did also your rulers" (Acts 3:17). What many Jewish people do not understand and what Christians have often overlooked is that both Jews and Gentiles had a part in killing Jesus (4:27). Although it does not take away anyone's responsibility for the awful deed, the event had been ordained by God. Jews and Gentiles met to do whatever God's hand and His purpose determined to be done (vs. 28).

On one occasion, I was welcomed into a beautiful, upscale Jewish home. The conversation was lighthearted, with occasional ripples of laughter. I felt genuinely welcome until I mentioned Jesus the Messiah. A chill passed through the room. The host told me gently but firmly that I must never mention "that man" in their home.

For many Jews that is the way it will be until the return of the Messiah: "One shall say unto him, What are these wounds in thine hands? Then he shall answer, Those with which I was wounded in the house of my friends" (Zech. 13:6). What a gracious answer from our loving Lord! Zechariah also tells us that the Jewish people will finally realize the great sin of rejecting the Messiah. Mourning will be followed by cleansing (12:11—13:2).

As we look for the Messiah's coming, we must continue to take the Word of truth to the Jewish people. They can and must be reached while there is time.

—Lyle P. Murphy.

Guiding the Superintendent

The crucifixion is at the very center of the Christian religion. Without the cross there is no salvation (Gal. 6:14). Even though Christ's death was part of God's plan (Acts 2:23), this does not diminish the tragedy of the events that unfolded surrounding Christ's crucifixion.

DEVOTIONAL OUTLINE

1. Redeemer (Luke 23:33-38). Roman justice was swift and cruel. Numerous crimes were punishable by crucifixion, which was designed to strike fear into any would-be criminals. That day, two thieves were crucified alongside Jesus. Bible students have debated just who Jesus was praying for when He said, "Father, forgive them." In all likelihood, He was praying for those who were responsible for His death. Indeed, all of us are guilty!

The enemies of Christ recognized that He had saved others (vs. 35). Jesus had saved people from crippling diseases, demon possession, blindness, death, and the inevitable consequences of sin. Could He not now save Himself? Joining in this mockery were the soldiers, who offered Him vinegar (cf. John 19:29) to quench His thirst. If He was really the King of the Jews (the Messiah), surely He could save Himself from such a terrible fate as this. But had He saved Himself, He could not have saved us!

2. Repentance (Luke 23:39-43). Luke is the only Gospel account that mentions the penitent thief. The thief realized that he was getting the just deserts for his crimes but that Jesus was innocent of wrongdoing. Depending on what the thief knew about Jesus, this may have been more than an admission that Jesus was not a criminal. The thief may have been confessing the sinlessness of Christ. The thief acknowledged Him as Lord and requested to be remembered in Christ's kingdom. Whatever his understanding of Christ's kingdom, he seems to have understood it as an otherworldly kingdom (cf. John 18:36).

Granting him cleansing, Christ assured him they would meet that day in paradise (cf. II Cor. 12:4).

3. Release (Luke 23:44-49). From noon until 3:00 P.M., darkness covered the land. It was during this time that Jesus bore the wrath of His Father for the sins of humanity (cf. Matt. 27:46).

In the temple, the veil separated the holy place (where priests ministered) from the Holy of Holies (where the high priest entered only on the Day of Atonement). That the veil was torn indicates that Jesus opened heaven to all those who come to the Father through Him (Heb. 6:19-20). Because of this unhindered access, all Christians are priests (Rev. 1:6).

With His atoning work finished, Jesus voluntarily released His spirit from His body (cf. John 10:18).

The Roman centurion was deeply impressed by these events and confessed his faith in Christ (cf. Matt. 27:54). Both the bystanders and Jesus' disciples were likewise deeply moved.

AGE-GROUP EMPHASES

Children: Emphasize that God loved us so much that He allowed Jesus to suffer terribly for us.

Youths: Even though many teens have been desensitized to violence, try to impress upon them the tragedy of the cross.

Adults: Stress that Christ died for sinners. Urge them to reach the lost before it is too late (cf. Rev. 6:12-17).

—*John A. Owston.*

SCRIPTURE LESSON TEXT

LUKE 24:1 Now upon the first *day* of the week, very early in the morning, they came unto the sepulchre, bringing the spices which they had prepared, and certain *others* with them.

2 And they found the stone rolled away from the sepulchre.

3 And they entered in, and found not the body of the Lord Jesus.

4 And it came to pass, as they were much perplexed thereabout, behold, two men stood by them in shining garments:

5 And as they were afraid, and bowed down *their* faces to the earth, they said unto them, Why seek ye the living among the dead?

6 He is not here, but is risen: remember how he spake unto you when he was yet in Galilee,

7 Saying, The Son of man must be delivered into the hands of sinful men, and be crucified, and the third day rise again.

8 And they remembered his words,

9 And returned from the sepulchre, and told all these things unto the eleven, and to all the rest.

10 It was Mary Magdalene, and Joanna, and Mary *the mother* of James, and other *women that were* with them, which told these things unto the apostles.

11 And their words seemed to them as idle tales, and they believed them not.

12 Then arose Peter, and ran unto the sepulchre; and stooping down, he beheld the linen clothes laid by themselves, and departed, wondering in himself at that which was come to pass.

30 And it came to pass, as he sat at meat with them, he took bread, and blessed *it,* and brake, and gave to them.

31 And their eyes were opened, and they knew him; and he vanished out of their sight.

32 And they said one to another, Did not our heart burn within us, while he talked with us by the way, and while he opened to us the scriptures?

33 And they rose up the same hour, and returned to Jerusalem, and found the eleven gathered together, and them that were with them,

34 Saying, The Lord is risen indeed, and hath appeared to Simon.

35 And they told what things *were done* in the way, and how he was known of them in breaking of bread.

NOTES

The Resurrection of Jesus

(Easter)

Lesson Text: Luke 24:1-12, 30-35

Related Scriptures: Luke 23:50-56; Matthew 28:11-15; John 20:1-18

TIME: A.D. 30   PLACES: Jerusalem; Emmaus; Jerusalem

GOLDEN TEXT—"The Lord is risen indeed, and hath appeared to Simon" (Luke 24:34).

Introduction

In an article published over thirty years ago in *Christianity Today* ("Let the Pagans Have the Holiday," December 13, 1993), Rodney Clapp outlined and lamented the commercialization of Christmas, which has only accelerated since that time.

His purpose, however, was not simply to lament the commercialization of Christmas. Rather, he aimed to show that Easter is really our most important holiday (or better, celebration). We rejoice in the incarnation of our Saviour, which we celebrate at Christmas. But without the resurrection, which we celebrate at Easter, we have no Saviour; we are yet in our sins.

In this lesson we will focus on the resurrection of Christ and the glory and honor He deserves because of it. While we still want to maintain a proper spiritual focus at Christmas, we need to give even greater attention to Easter. We cannot concede this holiday to commercialization.

LESSON OUTLINE

I. THE WOMEN: VISITING THE TOMB—Luke 24:1-11

II. PETER: INVESTIGATING THE TOMB—Luke 24:12

III. THE DISCIPLES: MEETING THE RISEN SAVIOUR—Luke 24:30-35

Exposition: Verse by Verse

THE WOMEN: VISITING THE TOMB

LUKE 24:1 Now upon the first day of the week, very early in the morning, they came unto the sepulchre, bringing the spices which they had prepared, and certain others with them.

2 And they found the stone rolled away from the sepulchre.

3 And they entered in, and found not the body of the Lord Jesus.

4 And it came to pass, as they were much perplexed thereabout, behold, two men stood by them in shining garments:

5 And as they were afraid, and

bowed down their faces to the earth, they said unto them, Why seek ye the living among the dead?

6 He is not here, but is risen: remember how he spake unto you when he was yet in Galilee,

7 Saying, The Son of man must be delivered into the hands of sinful men, and be crucified, and the third day rise again.

8 And they remembered his words,

9 And returned from the sepulchre, and told all these things unto the eleven, and to all the rest.

10 It was Mary Magdalene, and Joanna, and Mary the mother of James, and other women that were with them, which told these things unto the apostles.

11 And their words seemed to them as idle tales, and they believed them not.

Coming to the tomb (Luke 24:1-2). Jesus had died, and Joseph of Arimathea, along with Nicodemus, had lovingly wrapped His body and put it in a tomb that Joseph owned (John 19:38-42). Some women who had come with Jesus from Galilee followed the two, taking note of the sepulchre and observing how Jesus' body was laid in it (Luke 23:55). These women were some of the more devoted followers of Christ and had come to His crucifixion (vs. 49).

The women then engaged in what they probably thought was their final act of devotion. They returned home to prepare spices and ointments to finish preparing the lifeless body of Jesus for burial. In keeping with their devotion to the Lord and His commandments, they rested on the Sabbath Day.

{After the Sabbath, having prepared the spices and ointments beforehand, the women and others with them came to the tomb early the next morning (the first day of the week) with the intent of anointing Jesus' body.}^Q1 (Luke's reference to the "first day of the week" [24:1] begins to show that the worship day for New Testament believers changed from Saturday to Sunday [cf. John 20:19; I Cor. 16:2].)

Mark 16:3 adds that on the way to the tomb, the women wondered who would roll the stone away from the entrance so they could anoint the body of Jesus. They asked that question because of two things they knew: the stone was large, and they would not be able to move it. When the women reached the tomb, they found to their surprise that the stone had already been moved away from the tomb entrance.

Entering the tomb (Luke 24:3-4). Still intending to anoint Jesus' body, the women entered the tomb. To their greater surprise, they did not see the body of the Lord Jesus! Earlier the women had seen the tomb and observed the place where Joseph had laid the body. So they knew they were looking in the right place. {However, because they did not see the body of Jesus, they were "much perplexed" about what had happened.}^Q2

They did not find the body of Jesus, their Saviour, but they saw two other men who are described as being clothed in dazzling robes. Matthew and Mark mention only one angel, but this is not a contradiction. Perhaps Matthew and Mark chose to write only of the one who spoke to the women. Mark 16:5 says the man had on a white robe and was at the right side of the tomb.

Meeting the angels (Luke 24:5). The women quickly recognized that these two men were angels. The sight of them moved the women from perplexity and surprise to fear and prostration. {The angels spoke to the women with the first reference to Christ's resurrection: "Why seek ye the living among the dead?"}^Q3 The women may not at that point have known exactly what happened, but they now knew that Jesus was alive. They had no use, then, for the spices and ointments they had brought to anoint His body.

Hearing the message (Luke 24:6-7). The angels spoke to the women with words that are etched into our memory: "He is not here, but is risen." {Then the angels gently chided them with the reminder that Jesus had told them He "must be delivered into the hands of sinful men, and be crucified, and the third day rise again."}Q4 The women should have remembered what Jesus had said and not have been surprised or afraid of what they found at the empty tomb.

Remembering Christ's words (Luke 24:8). Once the angels reminded them of Jesus' words, the women remembered what He had said. They had heard Him foretell His death and resurrection, but apparently in their grief and fear, they had forgotten His words until the angels spoke to them.

Jesus had also told the same thing to the disciples on more than one occasion, but "they understood none of these things: and this saying was hid from them, neither knew they the things which were spoken" (Luke 18:34). In fact, on one occasion Peter took Jesus aside "and began to rebuke him, saying, Be it far from thee, Lord: this shall not be unto thee" (Matt. 16:22). So the women were not alone in their forgetfulness.

After hearing the message from the angels and being reminded of Christ's words, the women went to the eleven disciples and other followers with the good news.

Reporting to the disciples (Luke 24:9-11). When the women found the disciples, they described what they had experienced. Verse 10 specifically names Mary Magdalene, Joanna, and Mary the mother of James. Mark 16:1 names Salome as another woman who was present. The several women, who were more than enough in number for a valid testimony (cf. Deut. 17:6), brought a firsthand account, but the apostles still refused to believe Jesus was alive. {Luke 24:11 records that the women's words were like "idle tales," or nonsense, to the men.}Q5

PETER: INVESTIGATING THE TOMB

12 Then arose Peter, and ran unto the sepulchre; and stooping down, he beheld the linen clothes laid by themselves, and departed, wondering in himself at that which was come to pass.

While the apostles generally did not believe the report of the women, Peter had enough interest that he decided to investigate the matter further. He ran to the tomb, stooped down, and looked inside. John 20:3-6 adds that John also ran to the tomb, with John arriving first but not entering. Peter arrived second and went inside. What he saw there eventually helped to convince him that Jesus was indeed alive.

Peter "beheld the linen clothes laid by themselves" (Luke 24:12). John 20:7 adds that he saw "the napkin, that was about his head, not lying with the linen clothes, but wrapped together in a place by itself." The picture that this description gives us is that even though the body of Jesus was gone, the linen clothes retained the shape of the body while the napkin over His face was laid aside. {If someone had stolen the body of the Lord, the clothes would have either been missing entirely or hurriedly piled in a heap. Tomb robbers would not have taken the time to lay the clothes neatly in place.}Q6

Did Peter realize that Jesus had come back to life and had literally passed through the graveclothes? Whatever he thought right then, the experience led to unshakable faith.

THE DISCIPLES: MEETING THE RISEN SAVIOUR

30 And it came to pass, as he sat at meat with them, he took bread, and blessed it, and brake, and gave to them.

31 And their eyes were opened, and they knew him; and he vanished out of their sight.

32 And they said one to another, Did not our heart burn within us, while he talked with us by the way, and while he opened to us the scriptures?

33 And they rose up the same hour, and returned to Jerusalem, and found the eleven gathered together, and them that were with them,

34 Saying, The Lord is risen indeed, and hath appeared to Simon.

35 And they told what things were done in the way, and how he was known of them in breaking of bread.

Eating with Jesus (Luke 24:30-31). In Luke 24:13-29, we find the record of two of Jesus' disciples (one named Cleopas and the other unnamed) walking from Jerusalem to Emmaus, a trip of about seven miles. As they walked along, the risen Christ met them, but the two disciples did not recognize Him. As they came near Emmaus, they invited Him to stay with them for a meal. At the meal Jesus "took bread, and blessed it, and brake, and gave to them" (vs. 30).

This action was similar to what Jesus had done in feeding the five thousand (Luke 9:10-17) and the four thousand (Mark 8:1-9) and in His institution of the Lord's Supper (Luke 22:14-23). {We see in Luke 24:35 that this action played a role in both disciples' recognition of Jesus, for as soon as He gave them the bread, they understood who He was.}[Q7] Bringing about this recognition apparently completed Jesus' purpose with those disciples, so He vanished from their sight.

{We should note that in His glorified body, Jesus could pass through graveclothes, appear and disappear (as He did in this text), and even pass through solid objects (cf. John 20:19, 26).}[Q8] We are not told that Jesus ate food with the disciples in Emmaus, but He later did so in the presence of the Eleven (Luke 24:42-43), showing that He had a real body and was not a phantom or ghost.

Returning to Jerusalem (Luke 24:32-33). After the Lord Jesus disappeared from their sight, the Emmaus disciples recounted their experience on the road with Him. "Did not our heart burn within us, while he talked with us by the way, and while he opened to us the scriptures?" they asked. Looking back, they now understood why Jesus' message made such a powerful impact on them. They knew that Jesus had risen from the dead.

Announcing the risen Saviour (Luke 24:34-35). The Emmaus disciples immediately left for Jerusalem to meet with the eleven apostles and the other believers assembled there. {When they arrived, they were greeted with the exclamation "The Lord is risen indeed."}[Q9] The two then related their experience in Emmaus and joyfully added their testimony to the resurrection of Jesus.

The Emmaus disciples were informed that Jesus had already appeared to Simon Peter (cf. I Cor. 15:5). This sequence of events seems to show that in His glorified body Jesus could travel immediately from place to place, for in this situation Jesus went back to Jerusalem ahead of the Emmaus disciples and met with Peter even before the disciples arrived from Emmaus. By the time they reached Jerusalem, the apostles were already aware of the resurrection and invited the two to share in the wonder of it all.

Luke 24:35 confirms the statement that Jesus' breaking of bread with the two disciples in Emmaus played a role in their recognition of Him.

We have found several indications in our study of Luke 24 that Jesus rose bodily from the dead. The two angels told the women He was living (vss. 5-6), the linen graveclothes were still intact (vs. 12), Jesus appeared to two disciples (vss. 30-32), and Jesus appeared to Simon Peter (vs. 34). These eyewitness accounts provide clear evidence of Christ's resurrection.

Luke 24 validates the truth of the bodily resurrection of Christ. It is also important in this Easter lesson to see the resurrection in its theological context.

• The resurrection of Christ was prophesied and foreshadowed in the Old Testament (Ps. 16:10; Isa. 53:10; Jonah 1:17—2:10; Matt. 12:40).

• Christ foretold His resurrection (Mark 8:31; Luke 9:22; John 2:18-22).

• New Testament writers attested to Christ's resurrection (Rom. 1:4; 6:9; Phil. 3:10-11; I Pet. 1:3; 3:21).

{• The resurrection of Christ is an indispensable part of God's salvation plan (Rom. 4:25; I Cor. 15:1-4).

• Belief in Christ's resurrection is essential for salvation (Rom. 10:9-10).

• Without Christ's resurrection, we have no salvation and no hope (I Cor. 15:17-18).}[Q10]

• Jesus' resurrection is the basis of our future hope (I Thess. 4:13-14).

• The resurrection is the motive for steadfast service to Christ (I Cor. 15:58).

• The resurrection of Christ is the reason for Christian morality (I Cor. 15:32-34).

• The resurrection of Christ is the basis for our Christian experience (Phil. 3:10).

• The resurrection of Christ is the measure of His power at work in our lives (Eph. 1:19-20).

During this Easter season, we need to take time to reflect on the importance of Christ's resurrection. It is the distinguishing mark of the Christian faith. No other religion has a founder who died and came back to life.

Let us meditate on the significance of Christ's resurrection by remembering these words from the chorus of Robert Lowry's well-known Easter hymn "Christ Arose":

Up from the grave He arose;
With a mighty triumph o'er his foes;
He arose a Victor from the dark domain,
And He lives forever with His saints to reign.
He arose! He arose! Hallelujah! Christ arose!
—Don Anderson.

QUESTIONS

1. Why did the women come to the tomb?

2. Why were the women perplexed when they came to the tomb?

3. How did the angels initially make known the resurrection of Christ?

4. What did the angels remind the women about?

5. How did the apostles at first react to the report of the women?

6. What was significant about the arrangement of the graveclothes in the tomb?

7. What did Jesus do that caused the disciples in Emmaus to recognize Him?

8. What do we learn about the resurrected body of Christ from this passage?

9. How did the apostles react to the arrival of the disciples from Emmaus?

10. What part does the resurrection play in our salvation?
—Don Anderson.

Preparing to Teach the Lesson

Today we conclude our unit on Jesus' power over death with the ultimate defeat of this last enemy—Christ's own resurrection from the dead. By His resurrection Jesus confirmed His identity as the Son of God (Rom. 1:4) and gave us assurance that we too will be raised with Him on the last day (I Thess. 4:14). What He did in His earthly ministry assures us that He is God come in the flesh. He will just as surely return to earth and complete the plan of God.

The best preparation for this lesson is to read the lesson text several times. Be sure you understand the story completely. You might also read it aloud to someone else. Memorizing portions of it would be splendid. The Word of God memorized is a great tool to be used by the Holy Spirit in your own Christian walk as well as in your teaching.

TODAY'S AIM

Facts: to understand the reality of the post-resurrection events recorded in Scripture.

Principle: to understand that the resurrection of Christ is crucial to the transformation of people.

Application: to give assurance that Jesus Christ physically rose from the dead and to make this truth central in our message to unbelievers.

INTRODUCING THE LESSON

Most people, even non-Christians, have heard the story of the resurrection of the Lord Jesus. Many of them are exposed to the story every year at this season. However, many of them also think the story is not true, that it is only a myth told to make a spiritual point or a fanciful story added to the Bible later to try to support the authority of the message of Christianity. The best way to combat these erroneous ideas is simply to present the truth of Scripture and let the Holy Spirit bring conviction and faith to people's hearts.

DEVELOPING THE LESSON

1. The women report the resurrection (Luke 24:1-10). The women went to the tomb of the Lord Jesus prepared to anoint His dead body with spices. They had no idea that He had risen from the dead, even though He had predicted it openly. Some detractors of the resurrection accounts claim that the witnesses merely saw what they wanted or expected to see. From this text, however, it is clear that the opposite is the case. Our text does not say how they expected to roll away the stone in order to get to Jesus' body, but when they arrived they found the stone already moved away from the entrance to the tomb.

The women entered the tomb. They did not find Jesus' body but did see two men in shining garments. Luke does not tell us here that these men were angels, but later in the passage they are so identified (vs. 23). Matthew 28:2-7 also makes it clear they were angels. The women were naturally frightened by their appearance.

As proof of their claim that Jesus had risen, the two angels reminded the women of what Jesus Himself had told them beforehand. When the women soon after told the apostles about their experience, the apostles did not believe them. The apostles, like everyone else, knew the Lord Jesus had been crucified. They knew the facts of the Lord Jesus' burial by Joseph of Arimathea.

It is true that the majority of the world's population does not believe that the Lord Jesus rose from the dead. However, there is no other plausible explanation for the sudden shift from the disciples' fearful unbelief in this passage to their boldness of faith that followed.

2. Peter verifies their report (Luke 24:11-12). Peter may not have really believed the women, either. Scripture says he was "wondering in himself at that which was come to pass." Even after Peter saw the empty tomb and the cloth in which the Lord Jesus' body had been wrapped, he still could not quite take it all in. We know that later Peter wholeheartedly believed in the resurrection and preached it openly and boldly.

Even the most devoted disciples of Jesus initially had trouble believing in His resurrection. This is important for us to remember when we tell unbelievers about Christ. We can expect people to push back against the truth of the resurrection at first. But this is the message people need to hear for their salvation, and in His perfect timing God will open the hearts of many unbelievers just as He did Peter's.

3. The Lord Jesus appears (Luke 24:30-35). Paul wrote, "After that, he was seen of above five hundred brethren at once; of whom the greater part remain unto this present, but some are fallen asleep" (I Cor. 15:6). There were enough post-resurrection appearances of the Lord Jesus to make it very plain to an unbiased person that Jesus did in fact rise from the dead. The two disciples who saw Him on the road to Emmaus recognized the Lord Jesus as He broke the bread at their table.

We can often recognize people, even at a distance, by their body movements, their habits of action, or their speech patterns. What a wonderful thing it is to be so familiar with the Lord Jesus as to thus recognize Him! The challenge of our lives is to be so familiar with the Lord and His Word that we recognize Him at work in our lives. We can then also recognize that which is false, should it appear.

ILLUSTRATING THE LESSON

The empty tomb is a powerful proof of the resurrection.

PRAISE GOD

CHRIST IS RISEN THE TOMB IS EMPTY

CONCLUDING THE LESSON

We will never have the same experience all these people had at the time of the resurrection. We did not see the Lord Jesus in His earthly ministry, His death, or His resurrection. We can only see these through the eyes of faith by believing the record of those who did see Him physically.

Over the years since that wonderful event, millions of people have trusted in Him. It would take many books to tell of all the transformed lives of those who came to faith in the resurrected Lord. God personally knows each one of them and treasures them as His own children. The power of the resurrection is seen in changed lives, healing of broken hearts, and the restoration of love in families and individuals worldwide.

ANTICIPATING THE NEXT LESSON

In our next lesson we will study the first of Jesus' mighty miracles (John 2:1-12) by which He displayed His divine power.

—*Brian D. Doud.*

PRACTICAL POINTS

1. When things do not go as planned, trust God's plan (Luke 24:1-3).
2. As we seek Him, the Lord does not leave us without clear guidance (vss. 4-6).
3. We can be confident that Jesus will do what He promised (vss. 7-8).
4. We must have the confidence to share the good news about Jesus, even when others do not believe (vss. 9-12).
5. Time spent with Jesus is a blessing (vss. 30-35).

—Valante M. Grant.

RESEARCH AND DISCUSSION

1. How does remembering Jesus' words prepare you for unexpected situations in life?
2. In what areas of your life do you find it difficult to believe the truth of Jesus' teaching?
3. What is an appropriate response in the presence of the resurrected Jesus (cf. Phil. 2:9-11)?
4. What seemingly impossible situations have you been in or are you currently in, and how does Jesus' resurrection help you face those?
5. Why is it important to continue to trust in Jesus, even when you do not understand what is going on?
6. What is the significance of Christ's resurrection for Christian living?
7. What is the responsibility of the believer when it comes to spreading the gospel of Christ?

—Valante M. Grant.

ILLUSTRATED HIGH POINTS

He is not here (Luke 24:6)

The following words appear on a tombstone in Nantucket, Massachusetts:

> Under the sod and under the trees
> Lies the body of Jonathan Pease:
> He is not here, there's only the pod
> Pease shelled out and went to God.

We are amused, but we should note two things regarding Pease's theology of the resurrection. First, it does not apply to Jesus since His resurrection from the tomb involved His body. Second, because of Christ's resurrection, Pease and all others who have trusted Christ as Saviour will be raised in the future, and even the "pods" will ultimately spend eternity in glory.

They remembered his words (vs. 8)

Flavius Josephus was a first-century Jewish priest. He wrote *The Wars of the Jews,* which includes a history of the Jewish revolt of A.D. 66, and a history titled *The Antiquities of the Jews.* In the latter, he mentioned Jesus, called Him the Messiah, and referred to His crucifixion and resurrection (18.3.3).

This reference to Jesus is extremely controversial and has been studied and debated by many scholars. Some accept it as authentic; others call it a fraud.

In the end it matters not. We accept the resurrection of Christ, not because of Josephus, but simply because the Bible says it happened.

And their eyes were opened (vs. 31)

As soon as the two disciples recognized Jesus during the breaking of the bread, He vanished. Forty days later He would disappear for a much longer time into the heavens. He has given us His Spirit to enable us to walk by faith and not by sight while He is not physically present.

—David A. Hamburg.

Golden Text Illuminated

"The Lord is risen indeed, and hath appeared to Simon" (Luke 24:34).

Our golden text this week is a ringing summary statement, part of which has become a common Easter response among Christians worldwide. Although almost no one speaks the "hath appeared to Simon" portion these days, the words "the Lord is risen indeed" are heard from many lips. The challenge is retaining our sense of wonder and excitement.

The lead-up to this joyful proclamation started earlier in the day when two downcast disciples, only one of whom is named, unknowingly met the resurrected Jesus, who joined them on their walk to the village of Emmaus (Luke 24:13-18). They unburdened themselves of their disappointment and sorrow and then were amazed at the inspired exposition of Scripture they heard on their way. But it was not until the enigmatic stranger broke bread at their destination and then abruptly vanished that they recognized who had stirred their hearts so profoundly (vss. 30-32).

Not wanting to keep this revelation to themselves for even one day, the two disciples rushed back to Jerusalem to inform the Eleven, who were gathered along with other followers of Jesus. As fast as they might have traveled, however, they did not come with breaking news, for it was those in the room who responded without hesitation, "The Lord is risen indeed." For the Emmaus disciples, it was confirmation, not the heralding of unheard tidings.

Those gathered in the room added in the same breath the detail "and hath appeared to Simon." This was important to them, for as yet the risen Lord had not been seen by any of the other apostles. They had heard the reports of the women and had been inclined to discount these (as had the two from Emmaus). But they could not so easily dismiss Simon Peter's testimony; the Lord's early appearance to Peter was foundational in overcoming their doubts and in proclaiming the risen Christ to the world (cf. I Cor. 15:5).

It is interesting that aside from the statement in our golden text, this initial appearance to Peter is not described in any of the Gospels. Many things that Jesus said and did are not recorded for us (cf. John 21:25), but what we are told is sufficient and reliable to build our faith on. The fact that Jesus would appear first to the disciple who had denied Him demonstrates His forgiving and loving approach to His own.

The Emmaus disciples were not denied the opportunity to relate their own experience with the risen Lord, and they did so with what must have been the greatest eagerness and joy (Luke 24:35). It was as they were finishing their report that the Lord Himself suddenly appeared among them all, greeting them with a word of peace (vs. 36).

We may wonder why He did not show Himself to all the disciples immediately after leaving the tomb, thus putting away all doubt at the outset. But the experience of hearing and relaying testimony must have been important. And even the personal appearance among them did not erase all doubts at first.

The appearance of the risen Christ is foundational to our faith, but He wants us to rely on the sure word of testimony that He has given us.

—Kenneth A. Sponsler.

Heart of the Lesson

Moments after I learned that my boyfriend had died unexpectedly, I called my mom. When I told her the news, she said, "Oh, Ann, not Tony!" and began to cry. That started my tears. Romances were not supposed to end this way. Whatever happened to "happily ever after" and our plans?

Jesus' followers felt deep grief at His death, but the story did not end there.

1. The women find the empty tomb (Luke 24:1-8). The women who followed Jesus knew where to find His body. They had followed Joseph of Arimathea when he took Jesus' body to the tomb (23:55). Now the Sabbath was over, and they returned to the tomb early Sunday morning, bringing spices to mask the odor of the body's decay. Likely their main concern, other than their grief, was how they were going to roll away the huge stone that sealed the tomb (cf. Mark 16:3).

But the stone was already gone. So they peeked inside the tomb. There was no body. It was missing. What? While they were puzzling over the situation, two men in shining white garments (angels; cf. Luke 24:23) appeared. Terrified, the women bowed low. The men asked them a strange question: Why were they looking for the living among the dead? The living? They had just seen Jesus die and His body buried.

The men clarified their question. Jesus, the one the women were seeking, was not here. He was risen. Did they not remember Jesus saying He would be crucified and then rise again on the third day? Slowly, His words came back to them.

2. The women report the empty tomb (Luke 24:9-12). The women abandoned their project and rushed back to the place where Jesus' followers were gathered in Jerusalem. The women excitedly poured out their story, but no one believed them.

Jesus' disciple Peter, however, slipped out to go see for himself. He found the stone rolled away as the women had said, looked inside the tomb, and saw the linen graveclothes lying in place. But there was no body. Peter returned home, wondering what had taken place.

3. Two disciples encounter the risen Jesus (Luke 24:30-32). Later that day, as two followers of Jesus were walking the seven miles from Jerusalem to Emmaus, a stranger joined them. They discussed what was on everyone's mind in Jerusalem: Jesus' death. Evening was drawing near, so the two invited the stranger to stay for the night.

As they dined together, the stranger picked up a loaf of bread and asked a blessing over it. Then He broke the bread and gave pieces to those with Him. The act was reminiscent of Jesus breaking bread at the Last Supper with His disciples. Suddenly, their eyes were opened. They knew who this stranger was—Jesus! Immediately, Jesus vanished.

The two reflected on how their hearts had burned within them as they listened to the stranger talk during their walk. They had felt something supernatural. Now they knew why. Jesus had been their Teacher.

4. The disciples trade resurrection stories (Luke 24:33-35). The two could not wait to tell the other disciples whom they had seen. They walked back to Jerusalem that night. But before they could tell their story, the other disciples were already sharing *their* good news. Jesus had appeared to the disciple Peter.

—Ann Staatz.

World Missions

One common principle in marketing is that a potential customer needs to see or hear about a product seven times before he will buy.

Interestingly, some have said that is also the average number of times a Muslim convert to Christianity encounters the gospel message before believing in Christ. This principle of seven can help our mindset when evangelizing the lost.

Let us consider the principle in light of the message of the resurrection. Jesus had told His disciples before His death that He would rise again. For the women, the angels' reminder of what Jesus had said, plus an empty tomb, was all they needed to believe. These are the success stories in missions— those who receive the message with joy and cannot wait to go tell others.

Jesus' other followers, however, were skeptical, and some were even resistant. How many times did it take for them to fully believe?

1. Jesus prophesied His resurrection before death (Luke 18:31-34).

2. The angels told the women, and they believed (24:4-6).

3. The women told the disciples, who thought it sounded like "idle tales" (vs. 11).

4. Peter left the empty tomb and wondered (vs. 12).

5. Jesus met two of His followers on the road to Emmaus and explained the Scriptures (vss. 13-27). Their eyes were opened, and they believed.

6. The Emmaus disciples told the others (vs. 35).

7. Jesus Himself appeared. They still had trouble believing until He ate with them and explained the Scriptures concerning Himself (vss. 36-49).

8. Thomas, not there at the time, did not believe until Jesus appeared personally to him (John 20:19-29).

As much as we would like to see people believe the very first time they encounter the gospel message, we should expect most to need to hear it more than once, and some will need seven times or more.

That should not discourage us— quite the opposite! If we share and our message is rejected, we can consider that we may be the second or fourth out of their seven. They may be one step closer to receiving salvation! Proclaiming the gospel is never wasted. God promises that His Word does not return void (Isa. 55:11). No matter the initial response, the Holy Spirit can nurture the truth in a person's heart over time.

Consider also how we can imitate the disciples' message, "We have seen the Lord" (John 20:25). We have not physically seen the resurrected Jesus, but God reveals Himself through creation (Rom. 1:20) and individually in people's lives. When we see God work, let us broadcast it to those around us. When we see Him in nature around us, let us show others.

Consider the Fibonacci spiral. I had never heard of it until recently, but now that I have studied it, I see it everywhere—in plants, human anatomy, weather patterns, flowers, music, thumbprints. I am in awe of the God who displays such creativity within such precise order. When I see something that fits the Fibonacci spiral, I can point it out and use it to lead to a discussion of its Creator.

We can all mention when we "see" the Lord, and perhaps that small reference will be one of the several encounters with the gospel God uses to lead a person to Himself.

He is risen. We have seen Him. Now let us go and tell the others!

— Kimberly Rae.

The Jewish Aspect

Passover remains one of the most important Jewish holidays. Immediately following Passover, the "counting of the omer" begins with the firstfruits offering, marking fifty days until Pentecost (Lev. 23:15-22). The first day of the counting of the omer is also known as the Festival of Firstfruits.

When the temple was in existence, Israel was primarily an agricultural society. During that period, the first crop of the land's barley harvest was brought to the temple as an offering for the Festival of Firstfruits.

The people would bring the firstfruits of the land to the temple and give them to the high priest. At the temple, the barley would be roasted over an open flame and winnowed to remove the unwanted chaff. Next, the priests would pass it through a sieve thirteen times, converting the barley into fine flour (Oakley, *Messiah and the Feasts of the Lord,* class notes, Colorado Theological Seminary).

According to the Law, the Festival of Firstfruits was to be celebrated the day after the first Sabbath following Passover (Lev. 23:11). Today Jews celebrate it on the second day of Passover. They do so on this date because the rabbis believe that the first festival day of Passover is a Sabbath regardless of the day of the week on which it falls. This means the second day of the Passover would always be the day after a Sabbath.

However, various Jewish sects have disagreed with the rabbis about the interpretation of "the day after the Sabbath." Some sects, including the first-century Sadducees, interpreted this to mean the first regular Sabbath after the beginning of Passover. In this interpretation, the omer celebration would have always taken place on a Sunday (Strassfeld, *The Jewish Holidays,* William Morrow).

This week's lesson tells the story of Jesus' resurrection. Because He was crucified during Passover, many believe that His resurrection took place on the day that the firstfruits offering was brought to the temple.

The counting of the omer connects two important holidays: Passover and Pentecost. Jews "count the omer" in anticipation and preparation for the holiday of *Shavuot,* or Pentecost.

Pentecost is a very important holiday for the Jewish people. It is a second firstfruits celebration. While the omer offering marked the barley harvest, Pentecost marked the wheat harvest. Two loaves of the new meal from the wheat crop were baked. The two loaves were then waved by the priests at the temple during a special ceremony. This celebration commemorated the second harvest.

Tradition holds that after the children of Israel arrived at Mount Sinai and met God, the Law was given on Pentecost. Thus, Pentecost celebrates the giving of the Law, as well as the sealing of the covenant and the experience of meeting the Lord as His voice was heard (Strassfeld).

Jesus became the "firstfruits" of eternal life when He conquered death, hell, and the grave with His death and resurrection (I Cor. 15:20). His victory ushered in the beginning of a harvest of believers. Seven weeks after Jesus' resurrection, on Pentecost, the second firstfruits occurred as the Holy Spirit fell on believers (Acts 2).

As we celebrate Jesus' resurrection this Easter, let us remember that He is also the firstfruits of our resurrection, graciously promised to us in Him.

—*Robin Fitzgerald.*

Guiding the Superintendent

Biblical Christianity is based squarely on history. The apostle Paul taught that the resurrection of Jesus was so important that if it did not happen, Christian faith is little more than a cruel joke (I Cor. 15:12-19).

The Easter lesson for this year explores several key facts that indicate that Jesus Christ has risen indeed.

DEVOTIONAL OUTLINE

1. Empty tomb—missing body (Luke 24:1-3). Early on Sunday morning, following the crucifixion and burial of Jesus, several women from the group came to Jesus' tomb with the purpose of anointing His body. To their complete surprise, they found that the stone was rolled away and the tomb was empty.

Over the centuries, skeptics have labored to explain why no body was found in the tomb. However, there can only be one explanation—Jesus Christ rose bodily from the grave.

2. Perplexity of the women (Luke 24:4). The women could not entertain the thought that Jesus had risen from the grave. Their first reaction was shock. They obviously were not expecting a resurrection.

3. Proclamation of the angels (Luke 24:5-8). Instead of finding a lifeless body, the women were greeted by two angels who said, "He is not here, but is risen." They reminded the women of Jesus' prophecy about His resurrection.

4. Disbelief of the disciples (Luke 24:9-12). The skeptical disciples were slow to believe. Even after hearing the testimony of the women, the disciples did not believe. The women's words seemed like nonsense to them. Peter ran to the tomb but left wondering at what he saw. Truly, the disciples were not expecting to see Jesus alive again.

5. Appearance of Jesus Christ (Luke 24:30-35). It was not until Christ physically appeared to the disciples that they were finally convinced of the fact of His resurrection. Only after Jesus took the role of table host with two disciples who had traveled with Him to Emmaus did these followers realize that He had risen from the grave.

These new witnesses hurried to tell the Eleven, who reported that "the Lord [had] risen indeed" (vs. 34).The final proof seems to be that Jesus Christ appeared to the one person who had denied Him so strongly—Peter.

The facts are irrefutable. Christian faith is based on real history. Jesus Christ actually rose from the grave and is alive today. The empty tomb proves it. Those who were present on the day of His resurrection were very reluctant to accept that He had risen, perhaps because it seemed too good to be true. The facts gradually convinced them. Jesus was risen indeed!

AGE-GROUP EMPHASES

Children: During Easter services around the world, many worship leaders will shout, "Christ is risen!" To which the people are to respond, "He is risen indeed!" This lesson would be a good time to introduce the children to this great proclamation of their faith.

Youths: By their nature, teens tend to be skeptical. Focus on how the facts from Luke 24 point to the truth that Jesus did physically rise from the grave.

Adults: Use this lesson to help reassure your adults about the historical basis for their faith.

—*Martin R. Dahlquist.*

SCRIPTURE LESSON TEXT

JOHN 2:1 And the third day there was a marriage in Cana of Galilee; and the mother of Jesus was there:

2 And both Jesus was called, and his disciples, to the marriage.

3 And when they wanted wine, the mother of Jesus saith unto him, They have no wine.

4 Jesus saith unto her, Woman, what have I to do with thee? mine hour is not yet come.

5 His mother saith unto the servants, Whatsoever he saith unto you, do *it*.

6 And there were set there six waterpots of stone, after the manner of the purifying of the Jews, containing two or three firkins apiece.

7 Jesus saith unto them, Fill the waterpots with water. And they filled them up to the brim.

8 And he saith unto them, Draw out now, and bear unto the governor of the feast. And they bare *it*.

9 When the ruler of the feast had tasted the water that was made wine, and knew not whence it was: (but the servants which drew the water knew;) the governor of the feast called the bridegroom,

10 And saith unto him, Every man at the beginning doth set forth good wine; and when men have well drunk, then that which is worse: *but* thou hast kept the good wine until now.

11 This beginning of miracles did Jesus in Cana of Galilee, and manifested forth his glory; and his disciples believed on him.

12 After this he went down to Capernaum, he, and his mother, and his brethren, and his disciples: and they continued there not many days.

NOTES

Jesus' First Miracle

Lesson Text: John 2:1-12

Related Scriptures: John 1:35-51; 20:26-31

TIME: A.D. 26   PLACE: Cana

GOLDEN TEXT—"This beginning of miracles did Jesus in Cana of Galilee, and manifested forth his glory; and his disciples believed on him" (John 2:11).

Introduction

The miracle recorded in this text is the first of seven that John included in his book to give evidence of Jesus' deity. They are usually referred to as "signs," because the purpose behind them was greater than merely the accomplishment of the miracle. The Greek word that has been translated "miracles" in John 2:11 is *semeion*, which refers to an indication or sign of something. The same word is used in John 4:54 after the healing of the nobleman's son in Capernaum. It too was a miracle pointing to Christ's deity.

A common activity, which takes place regularly all over the world—a wedding—turned into an event unlike any other wedding ever held. There was a significant purpose behind what happened, though, and it turned out to be the first of many revelations of Christ's glory.

LESSON OUTLINE

I. A COMMON ACTIVITY—
   John 2:1-5

II. AN UNCOMMON EVENT—
   John 2:6-10

III. A SPECIAL MANIFESTATION—
   John 2:11-12

Exposition: Verse by Verse

A COMMON ACTIVITY

JOHN 2:1 And the third day there was a marriage in Cana of Galilee; and the mother of Jesus was there:

2 And both Jesus was called, and his disciples, to the marriage.

3 And when they wanted wine, the mother of Jesus saith unto him, They have no wine.

4 Jesus saith unto her, Woman, what have I to do with thee? mine hour is not yet come.

5 His mother saith unto the servants, Whatsoever he saith unto you, do it.

The wedding (John 2:1-2). It is not certain what is meant by "the third day." The previous day mentioned by John was the day Jesus called Philip to follow Him (1:43). Thus, John 2 begins on the "third day" (vs. 1) after that. According to some sources, the expression may be equivalent to our expression "the day after tomorrow."

The majority of Jesus' early ministry was in Galilee. {Here He was in Cana, which, according to John 21:2, was the hometown of Nathanael. A wedding was being held there, and Jesus' mother, Mary, was present for the occasion.}Q1 The fact that she is mentioned before Jesus and His disciples indicates that she might have been a relative of the bride or groom, which would explain why Jesus and the disciples were among the invited guests. This was not far from Nazareth, Jesus' hometown, so He might have known the couple.

Cana is not mentioned by any of the other authors of the New Testament. John, however, referred to it as the location of Jesus' first miracle. It is not known today where this particular town was located, but it is fairly certain that it was just north of Nazareth, toward Capernaum. When a wedding was held in a town this size, everybody was probably invited, and it would have been an insult not to attend. At the time, Jesus had only called five disciples, so these five were probably the only ones in attendance.

{"Jesus' attendance and his actions at this wedding indicate His approval of the celebration.}Q2 . . . Images of Jesus as a dour-faced Messiah, passing judgment on all in his path simply fail to account for the biblical evidence that He was completely at home in festive occasions. . . . Jesus' life is the most profound statement ever made against joyless spirituality." (Barton et al., *Life Application Bible Commentary, John*, Tyndale).

The wine (John 2:3). Wedding celebrations in Jesus' day often lasted for a week, so it took careful planning to prepare for them. On this occasion a social disaster was about to occur. {Running out of wine would not merely be a source of embarrassment; it would be the height of disgrace and humiliation, as well as an insult to the invited guests.}Q3 The unwritten laws of hospitality would be violated and the hosts made to look ill-prepared and unthoughtful. It was much more of a disaster than it would be in our culture.

But that is exactly what happened on this occasion! {They ran out of wine, and it was Mary who came and informed Jesus about it. She simply told Him that they had no wine. We can only imagine the look of concern on her face, even though the statement sounds so perfunctory. One wonders whether Mary was the hostess for this wedding reception. If so, this would naturally be a great concern for her.}Q4 The fact that she was mentioned before Jesus in verses 1-2 suggests this could have been the situation.

"Hospitality in the east was a sacred duty. A wedding feast often lasted for a week. To run out of wine at such an important event would have been humiliating for the bride and groom. The family of Jesus was not wealthy, and it is likely their relatives and acquaintances were not either. This may have been a 'low-budget' wedding feast" (Radmacher, ed., *NKJV Study Bible,* Thomas Nelson). It is obvious that a critical situation had arisen, and Mary knew who could provide the solution to it.

The way forward (John 2:4-5). In our culture, to respond to a woman, and especially one's mother, the way Jesus did would be considered extremely rude and disrespectful. In Jesus' culture that was not the case. To address a woman as "woman" was a normal, polite way to speak, as can be seen by the several times Jesus Himself did so (cf. Matt. 15:28; Luke 13:12; John 4:21; 8:10). In fact, in John 19:26 Jesus again addressed His own mother as "woman" when He committed her future care to John. He was not being disrespectful in saying this.

The rest of Jesus' response to Mary has been viewed many different ways by Bible students. It is difficult to know exactly what He meant. The main idea, however, seems to be that His thoughts and hers were not converging at the moment. Jesus seemed to be indicating that the time for Him to fully reveal Himself as Messiah had not yet come. But did she want Him to do something that would reveal Him as Messiah, or was she simply trying to get Him to meet a critical need?

Homer Kent observed, "It can hardly be that Mary was asking simply that a miracle be performed, for in some sense Jesus seems to be rejecting what Mary asked, and yet He proceeded with the miracle. It is better to understand that Mary was hoping for Jesus to give the supreme manifestation of himself, perhaps to remove the suspicion of impurity that must have hovered over her those many years" (*Light in the Darkness,* Baker).

{Despite Jesus' response, Mary was not in the least deterred. She immediately turned to the servants and said, "Whatsoever he saith unto you, do it" (John 2:5).}[Q5] She knew that her son could not be aware of such a critical need and just ignore it. We can imagine her walking away with a contented smile on her face, eager to see what would happen next.

AN UNCOMMON EVENT

6 And there were set there six waterpots of stone, after the manner of the purifying of the Jews, containing two or three firkins apiece.

7 Jesus saith unto them, Fill the waterpots with water. And they filled them up to the brim.

8 And he saith unto them, Draw out now, and bear unto the governor of the feast. And they bare it.

9 When the ruler of the feast had tasted the water that was made wine, and knew not whence it was: (but the servants which drew the water knew;) the governor of the feast called the bridegroom,

10 And saith unto him, Every man at the beginning doth set forth good wine; and when men have well drunk, then that which is worse: but thou hast kept the good wine until now.

Putting water into pots (John 2:6-7). There were six stone water jars in the home where the wedding celebration was being held. Mark 7:3-4 explains how they were normally used in the homes: "For the Pharisees, and all the Jews, except they wash their hands oft, eat not, holding the tradition of the elders. And when they come from the market, except they wash, they eat not. And many other things there be, which they have received to hold, as the washing of cups, and pots, brasen vessels, and of tables."

These were various ritualistic washings that were important to the Jewish people and were ceremonially followed in obedience to their customs. The ceremonial law of the Jews stated that they were rendered unclean by touching things in their everyday activities, so they needed to be cleansed before meals and other events. Water from a jar would be poured over their hands in a symbolic gesture of washing away any impurities they had picked up in their daily contacts.

The capacity of the jars mentioned in John 2:6 was two or three "firkins," which amounts to 20 or 30 gallons per jar since a firkin was about 10 gallons in our measurements. If all the water was turned into wine and not just that which was drawn out, there would be 120 to 180 gallons of new wine available for the guests.

When Jesus told the servants to fill the jars with water, they filled them completely to the brim. There was no way even small amounts of wine could be added to the water. At the time of the miracle, the jars contained nothing but water.

Serving the master (John 2:8). "Our Lord's first miracle was not a spectacular event that everybody witnessed. Mary, the disciples, and the servants knew what had happened, but nobody else at the feast had any idea that a miracle had taken place. His first miracle was a quiet event at a wedding in contrast to His last miracle recorded by John (John 11), a public event after a funeral" (Wiersbe, *The Bible Exposition Commentary,* Victor). Jesus had not attended the wedding for the purpose of doing a miracle.

After the jars had been filled to the brim, Jesus told the servants to draw some of the water out and take it to the person in charge of the banquet (whom we might call the master of ceremonies). We are not told the exact moment when the water became wine. Did the servants obey with some amount of trepidation, fearing the wrath of the master of ceremonies upon being insulted with water? By the time they drew it out, did they realize what had occurred? If so, instead of trepidation they would have been filled with excitement.

What we see for certain is that the servants did exactly as Mary had told them and obeyed what Jesus told them to do. The master of ceremonies would have been the person in charge of the seating and serving, so if a shortage of wine occurred, it would have been his responsibility to inform the wedding couple, their parents, and the people in attendance. {If the servants suddenly served him water in front of all the guests, he would be terribly embarrassed, and they would be humiliated. Their action thus required some faith.}[Q6]

The text does not describe the moment of truth, when the master took the offered beverage and drank. We can imagine, though, the look on his face as he tasted what was now fresh wine.

Asking for an explanation (John 2:9-10). Some people are troubled by the fact that Jesus provided "wine" for the wedding guests. Many scholars argue that the wine of that day was fermented but heavily diluted with water and thus not the kind of drink that could easily produce drunkenness. Other scholars understand the "wine" that Jesus miraculously produced to have been pure grape juice, free from any alcoholic content.

What we ought to focus on, however, is the fact that a miracle took place on this occasion that revealed Jesus' deity to those who witnessed it. The master of ceremonies did not know where this wine had come from, even though the servants who handed it to him did. The water jars were evidently not in the room where the celebration was taking place, so no one in that room had witnessed the scenes leading up to this moment. The master immediately summoned the groom.

The logic he presented to the groom makes good sense. {As he explained, most hosts served the best wine at the beginning of a feast or celebration. Only after people had enjoyed the good wine and consumed all of it was the cheaper wine served. He could not understand why this groom had reversed that practice by serving the best wine last.}[Q7] The groom, of course, would have been totally surprised, for he had no idea where that last wine had come from.

A SPECIAL MANIFESTATION

11 This beginning of miracles did Jesus in Cana of Galilee, and manifested forth his glory; and his disciples believed on him.

12 After this he went down to Capernaum, he, and his mother, and his brethren, and his disciples: and they continued there not many days.

{We noted earlier that John chose to include seven specific miracles in his book in order to present Jesus as the Son of God and reveal His deity.}[Q8] The word *semeion*, which means an "indication" or "sign" of something, is used in John 2:11 and is translated "miracles." When Jesus turned this water into wine, it was the first of many times when He did something miraculous that proved He was more than a mere human being. For those who witnessed it, this was a sign.

John's recording of this miracle also makes it a sign for all of us. The way everything was accomplished reveals something extraordinary, something not possible by human means. Filling the six jars with water ensured that this was a miracle and not a trick or an accident. Taking the wine from the jars to the master of ceremonies guaranteed that the miracle was made known and the social disaster avoided. But more than that, the miracle revealed something about Jesus. As we read this and contemplate what happened, we should recognize that Jesus did something that only God could do. He was not just a man; He was the Son of God.

{In accomplishing this miracle, Jesus revealed His glory.}[Q9] This was the work of the Word who took on flesh, the One who is described in John 1 as the Creator of all that exists. {The first result of this miracle was belief in Him in the hearts of His disciples.}[Q10] This belief would be tested in days to come, and there would be much more spiritual growth, but at this point they needed to understand that they were indeed following the Son of God.

From Cana, Jesus went to Capernaum, which became the home base from which He reached out in His ministry. Instead of staying in town most of the time, He left often and traveled to other places.

—*Keith E. Eggert.*

QUESTIONS

1. In which town do we find Jesus and His disciples on this occasion, and who was already there (John 2:1)?

2. What does Jesus' attendance of the wedding tell us about Him?

3. Why was the shortage of wine of such momentous concern?

4. Who was the person who reported the problem to Jesus, and why might it have been of special concern to her?

5. How did Mary respond to what Jesus said to her?

6. Why did the servants' obedience to Jesus' instructions require faith?

7. What was the response of the master of ceremonies when He tasted the wine?

8. What does John indicate was the purpose of Jesus' miracles (cf. 20:30-31)?

9. How does the miracle at Cana fit into that purpose?

10. What response came from the disciples of Jesus? What response should come from us?

—*Keith E. Eggert.*

Preparing to Teach the Lesson

This week we learn how God's creative Word met the needs of a group of people who were celebrating a wedding in the village of Cana in Galilee. When Jesus meets our needs today, it should be motivation enough for us to fully trust Him.

TODAY'S AIM

Facts: to describe the details of the miracle of water turned into wine at Cana in Galilee.

Principle: to show that God's creative Word can meet all our needs.

Application: to encourage complete trust in Jesus, who is the creative Word who can meet all our needs.

INTRODUCING THE LESSON

Every now and then we all face a situation that is so desperate it seems we need a miracle from God to resolve it. God's ways of operating are very different from ours, though. Sometimes He works very slowly or through unexpected means. But in the end we have no doubt that He is the one who has done it for us, and our faith is strengthened. Our lesson this week presents a very powerful picture of our Lord Jesus as the creative Word who is always present to deliver us in times of trouble. He calls us to trust and follow Him.

DEVELOPING THE LESSON

1. A difficult situation (John 2:1-3). In our lesson this week, we find Jesus, His mother, Mary, and His disciples as guests at a wedding in the village of Cana in Galilee. A problem arose when the wine being served the guests ran out. Wine was the common drink of the day, and it was a social obligation to provide it at weddings. We see Mary, Jesus' mother, telling Jesus about the problem.

It is interesting that Mary would come to Jesus, who was also only a guest, to resolve the problem at hand. It does say something about the hierarchical situation of their society. Jesus was her oldest son, and it is possible that she came to Him because of that. It could also be because she knew Jesus was the Son of God (Luke 1:32) and that if anyone could help, He was the one. To her, Jesus was the only credible answer. Get the class to think through how they would have responded to that situation if they were in Mary's shoes.

Help the class think about where they go first when facing a difficult situation. Do they try all the earthly resources first before going to our Lord Jesus in prayer? As the creative Word of God, He can turn any situation around—and He can do it instantly, just as He created all things instantly by simply speaking them into existence. Emphasize to the class that God is on our side. He waits for us to call on Him so that He can act on our behalf. He is our creative Word, and He is here to help us.

2. A creative resolution (John 2:4-10). Jesus' response is somewhat hard to interpret. When Mary, His mother, came to Him with the problem, He seemed to indicate that it was not yet time for Him to get involved. Help the class see that God's delays are not God's denials of us. There is a specific time and place for everything that God does for us. And when He does it, it will be wonderful.

Jesus indicated that His "hour [had] not yet come" (vs. 4). Urge the students to assess their own responses to God's seemingly delayed help when they have needed it most. Emphasize that God's timing is always the best, even if it is delayed in our estimation.

Mary, however, knew her son well. She told the servants to do whatever He asked them. John noted that there were six large waterpots nearby that were used for the Jewish ceremonial washing rituals. Jesus commanded the servants to fill those pots with water and then serve some of that water to the master of ceremonies at the wedding. When the person in charge drank it, he found that it was wine, and he was impressed with how good it was. He asked the bridegroom why he had kept this drink till the very end, when everyone was already full.

We must note here that it was customary to serve the best wine first and the lesser quality of wine later, when the people were already full. Jesus shows us that no situation is too hard to remedy if we are willing to trust the creative Word in action in our worst situations. Get the class members to look at their own domestic life or other predicaments and visualize for themselves what God can do if they open the door to the working of His creative Word in those situations.

3. An increase in faith (John 2:11-12). Here we see that when God's creative Word steps into our broken world, there is restoration. The disciples who followed Him were now able to put things in perspective. This was no ordinary man. This was Jesus, the incarnate Son of God, the One who works miracles. These disciples, who were still growing in their understanding of who Jesus was, now saw a display of His glory and His wonder-working power.

Help the class realize what it really means to experience the glory of God in our broken lives. God invites us to call on Him in our broken situations, and then He responds with His custom-made answer for us. But like Mary, His own mother, we have to quietly trust in Him when we do not understand what He is doing.

This was the first miracle Jesus performed. It was the dawn of a new age for those around Him. The promised Messiah was now here. The disciples believed in Him. Our response must be like that of the disciples. We must fully trust our Lord Jesus, recognizing Him as God the Son and the creative Word. John tells us that after that miracle, Jesus retreated to Capernaum with His mother, His brothers, and His disciples. He stayed close to those who loved Him.

ILLUSTRATING THE LESSON

Our response in any difficult situation must be to call on the creative Word and believe in Him.

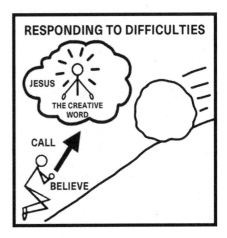

RESPONDING TO DIFFICULTIES

JESUS

THE CREATIVE WORD

CALL

BELIEVE

CONCLUDING THE LESSON

We are not alone in our deep and troubling situations. God's creative Word is always at work to help us. Leave the class with the challenge that we can trust our Lord to bring life into the impossible situations that face us. Our response must be simply to believe Him.

ANTICIPATING THE NEXT LESSON

In our lesson next week, we will see the deity of Jesus in His authority over demons.

—A. Koshy Muthalaly.

PRACTICAL POINTS

1. Jesus' disciples may freely celebrate God's goodness in this life and in heaven (John 2:1-2).
2. Though a prayer may seem trivial or impertinent, the Lord welcomes us to bring it to Him (vss. 3-5).
3. Those who are swift to follow Christ without question will accomplish His will (vss. 6-8).
4. Many who depend on the Lord's bounty are ignorant of where it comes from (vs. 9).
5. The Lord's provision is of supreme quality (vs. 10).
6. God's miracles promote His glory and our faith (vss. 11-12).

—*John Lody.*

RESEARCH AND DISCUSSION

1. What role should celebration play in the life of Jesus' disciples?
2. Are some needs too small for God to bother with? So trivial as to be beneath His dignity? Why or why not?
3. Does Jesus seem reluctant to address His mother's request? What reasons might He have had for this?
4. The master of ceremonies acknowledged the high quality of Jesus' wine. What does this tell us about people's knowledge of God through creation (cf. Rom. 1:19-22)?
5. What aspects of God's creation especially reveal His character to you?
6. What role do miracles play in God's purposes and plans? Do miracles happen today? Explain your answer, and discuss this issue.

—*John Lody.*

ILLUSTRATED HIGH POINTS

There was a marriage (John 2:1)

The story is told about a doctor addressing a large audience about troublesome food. He talked about the dangers of red meat and high-fat diets. He claimed that soft drinks corroded the lining of the stomach. He also mentioned foods that were loaded with MSG.

Then he said, "There is one thing that is the most dangerous of all. Could anyone here tell me what food it is that causes the most grief and suffering for years after eating it?"

After a few moments of silence, an elderly man in the front row raised his hand and wryly said, "Wedding cake."

Thankfully, this man's experience of marriage is not what God intended. He ordained marriage in the very beginning (Gen. 2:18, 21-24), and His plan of redemption will culminate in a wedding feast in heaven (Rev. 19:7-9).

Water that was made wine (vs. 9)

While Jesus' first miracle reminds us that celebration has a place in the Christian life, we must be careful not to use it as a license for sinful overindulgence.

God's invitation to enjoy His good gifts (cf. Ps. 104:14-15) is no excuse for abusing those gifts. As Warren W. Wiersbe has said, "If you use Jesus as your example for drinking, why don't you follow His example in everything else?" (*Be Alive,* Victor).

In another story, Wiersbe mentions a drunkard who was converted to Christ. A friend tried to confuse him by asking, "Do you believe that Jesus turned water into wine?"

"I certainly do!" replied the believer. "In my home He has [also] turned wine into furniture, decent clothes, and food for my children!"

—*David A. Hamburg.*

Golden Text Illuminated

"This beginning of miracles did Jesus in Cana of Galilee, and manifested forth his glory; and his disciples believed on him" (John 2:11).

Scripture tells us that the reason the Son of God became man was to ransom us from the penalty of sin by His death (Mark 10:45) and to defeat sin, death, and Satan by His resurrection (I Cor. 15:25-26; I John 3:8). So why did He perform so many miracles for three years leading up to that climactic victory at Calvary? Our text reveals to us two of the purposes of Jesus' miracles.

First, Jesus performed miracles in order to "manifest forth His glory." Throughout the Gospels, the disciples of Jesus consistently react to His miracles with amazement and, often, with fear. They are astounded as Jesus routinely does wonders that only the Creator of the universe is capable of doing (cf. Mark 4:41; John 3:2; 6:14).

In the Old Testament, the Israelites frequently reacted to the glory of God in a similar way. When the glory of God descended on the people of Israel in the wilderness, they trembled before Him and were afraid (Ex. 20:18). Not even Moses could enter the tabernacle when the awesome presence of God filled it (40:34-35). When the Lord appeared to Isaiah in the temple, Isaiah thought he was going to die because he had looked upon the glory of God (Isa. 6:1-5). Everyone who encountered the glory of God in the Old Testament was in awe of that glory; no one could come near it.

In Jesus, that same glory is now manifested. Like Old Testament Israel, Jesus' disciples react in amazement when He reveals this glory through miraculous works, recognizing Him as the Son of God. The only difference is, the disciples are now able to draw near to the glory of God, because He has become flesh (John 1:14).

Not only did Jesus manifest His glory through miracles, but He also intended His disciples to *respond* to His manifestation of glory. This brings us to the second purpose of Jesus' miracles. Our text tells us that Jesus performed miracles as signs to strengthen faith: When He did them, they "believed on him."

If Christ had lived His perfect life in complete obscurity before dying as an innocent victim and rising from the dead, He would still be the sinless Saviour, but no one would have known to put their faith in Him. His death and resurrection would have benefited no one but Himself. Therefore, His miracles served as one of the markers identifying Him as the Saviour of all who would believe in Him.

Every person Jesus encountered during His earthly ministry saw the glory of God in human flesh. Yet not everyone responded in the same way. Many who saw His signs believed in Him (2:11, 23; 7:31), but many others saw the same signs and refused to believe (12:37).

We are faced with the same choice today. We may not see the miracles of Jesus in person, but John tells us that he wrote down his Gospel account so that we might encounter the same signs and believe (20:30-31).

In other words, every time we read the Gospel accounts of Jesus (and, by extension, any part of Scripture), we are actually encountering the glory of God. So how do we respond? Are we so accustomed to the story that we have become numb to its power? Or will we be fearfully amazed and rejoice that the glory of God has drawn so near to us in Christ?

—*Matthew Robinson.*

Heart of the Lesson

John's Gospel is packed with theologically rich doctrines and miraculous events. From the very beginning, John prepares us and sets our minds in motion concerning the God-Man, Jesus Christ. John wrote, "In the beginning was the Word, and the Word was with God, and the Word was God" (John 1:1). Soon thereafter, John said, "And the Word was made flesh, and dwelt among us" (vs. 14). Since Jesus is truly God and truly man, we can anticipate great things from Him. In John 2:1-12 we see one of those great things. He performed His first miracle at a wedding at Cana.

1. The problem (John 2:1-5). If you have ever been to a wedding or at least heard about one, you know they never go according to plan. Someone is running late, the food is not prepared, somehow the appropriate music is forgotten, or any number of things. At the wedding in Cana, they had no wine. In Jesus' day, having enough wine at a wedding was a big deal. Running out was similar to a wedding in our day having no food (cf. vs. 10).

To us this problem seems easily fixed. Simply go to the store and purchase more wine. However, during the first century, getting more wine was not that simple.

Mary, having overheard that there was no wine, told Jesus. His response was quite striking: "Woman, what have I to do with thee? mine hour is not yet come" (vs. 4). Just a quick glance at Jesus' reply seems to heighten the problem. Was He going to help, and what was this "hour" to which He referred?

2. The solution (John 2:6-12). Jesus graciously provided the wine for the remainder of the wedding. In fact, He provided better wine than what had already been provided. The beauty of this story is that Jesus manifested His glory by performing a miracle and that His disciples believed in Him.

The solution and beauty of this story, however, provides a more glorious picture than simply turning large canisters of water into wine. In John 2:4, Jesus said, "Mine hour is not yet come." This theme of Jesus' "hour" runs throughout John's Gospel (4:21, 23; 5:25; 7:30). It points us to a time when Jesus' hour finally came.

John 17:1 says, "These words spake Jesus, and lifted up his eyes to heaven, and said, Father, the hour is come; glorify thy Son, that thy Son also may glorify thee." The hour to which Jesus frequently referred was that time when He would go to the cross to save His people from their sins (Matt. 1:21). Thus, when Jesus replied to Mary, "Mine hour is not yet come" (John 2:4), He was referring to His crucifixion and subsequent resurrection and ascension back to His heavenly Father.

There is more. John wrote, "And he saith unto me, Write, Blessed are they which are called unto the marriage supper of the Lamb" (Rev. 19:9). Jesus' miracle at Cana pointed forward to a greater wedding, when all the saints of God will feast together in heaven.

Thus, while the solution in John 2:1-12 provided a temporary fix for those at the wedding, our guarantee is that the greater problem—namely, our sin—has been dealt with in Christ. The solution He provided gives us access to the ultimate wedding in heaven.

—Leon Brown.

World Missions

At the marriage in Cana, Jesus won over His disciples, who "believed on him" (John 2:11). Although we may never do the miracles Jesus did, God has granted us the amazing opportunity to participate in His plan as He wins many more souls to belief in Jesus.

There was a man, now with the Lord, who took that opportunity very seriously. He awakened every day ready to be anywhere and do anything for the glory of Jesus Christ. That man was Walter L. Wilson, M.D., a Kansas City physician, business manager, pastor, and college president. The most important thing about Dr. Wilson was that he was a born-again believer who sought every opportunity to win someone to the Lord.

Many of Dr. Wilson's soul-winning adventures were captured for our enjoyment in a series of books he wrote over a long career of making Christ known. His books were gathered into one volume titled *Just What the Doctor Ordered* (BJU Press).

On the way to see a New York client, he passed a store that had a small, leather notebook in the window. Just what he needed! The merchant, a German man, stated the price as $1.10. He then asked Wilson what he would use the book for. Wilson explained that he entered prayer requests and the dates and then when the Lord answered, he filled in that information.

The German merchant came around from behind the counter with tears in his eyes and asked, "Can you get to Gott (God)?" The doctor replied that it was his main business. The poor merchant explained that he had gone to meetings in three New York boroughs without finding the way. Dr. Wilson led the merchant to Christ.

Wilson told of another time when he arrived by train in a certain city. There was no time for Bible reading or prayer. At 4:00 P.M. he felt that he might be able to catch up with the missing devotional time. "I asked the Lord whether in his infinite grace He would not find some troubled heart in that strange city." Wilson felt confident God would honor that request.

Over dinner he remembered that an old friend had a son living in the city. His name was Charlie Johnson, and he was unsaved. Dr. Wilson went through the Johnsons in the phone book and found his man. He took a taxi out to the Johnson home.

He found three people at home: Mrs. Johnson, her sister, and her sister's husband. Mrs. Johnson explained that Charlie was working nights. "Well, Charlie's business must be growing if he is working nights, too," Dr. Wilson said.

"Oh, Charlie's not in business; he is an engineer," Mrs. Johnson explained.

Clearly, Dr. Wilson was in the wrong home! He apologized and was starting to leave when he saw a dog-eared, well-thumbed Bible on the table.

"We love the Book," Mrs. Johnson said.

Dr. Wilson countered, "Have you found out from its pages how you may be saved and know it?"

All three broke into tears. Mrs. Johnson explained, "Dr. Wilson, when you rang the doorbell, we were on our knees praying that God would send someone to tell us how to be saved."

They knelt together around the table, and one by one, the three asked the Lord to save them.

May we learn from Dr. Wilson's example and never pass up an opportunity to glorify Christ by urging others to believe in Him.

—Lyle P. Murphy.

The Jewish Aspect

The account of Jesus' attendance at a wedding in Cana is very Jewish. A wedding in Israel is not only a joyous occasion but also an event related to the future promises of God, who is the Bridegroom of Israel. The purpose for recording this episode in John 2 is revealed in verse 11. It is about the Jewish theme of Messiah's coming and the signs He would give as He ushered in a new age of God's restoration and blessing.

In more than one place we read of ancient weddings continuing with daily celebrations for seven days. Samson's wedding feast with the woman of Timnath went on for seven days (Judg. 14:12). In a non-canonical book included in the Apocrypha, we find the same period for a wedding (Tobit 11:19).

With a wedding as a setting, Jesus' appearance at Cana already had messianic overtones. Isaiah 62:5 says God will rejoice over His people Israel as a bridegroom over a bride. In Jeremiah, the time of judgment is marked by the absence of the voices of bridegrooms and brides in the city (7:34; 16:9; 25:10), but the age of Messiah will see a return of the voices of the betrothed (33:10-11). When Israel is restored in the last days, God will be her Husband and Betrothed (Isa. 54:4-8; Hos. 2:16, 19).

Similarly, an abundance of wine is symbolic of the future blessing of God in the days of Messiah. The mountains will drip "sweet wine," and God's people Israel will drink in rejoicing (Amos 9:13-14). Wheat, wine, olive oil, flocks, and herds will abound (Jer. 31:12). God will give a feast of fattened meat and well-refined wine (Isa. 25:6).

The water jars Jesus used for His miraculous sign contained two to three firkins, or measures, apiece, each measure being just under nine gallons (Mounce, *The Analytical Lexicon to the Greek New Testament,* Zondervan). Jesus turned anywhere from 100 to 160 gallons of water into wine.

At an event that lent itself to messianic signs, Jesus performed His first sign, revealing to His disciples something of His identity. John called this the beginning of Jesus' miracles and explained this miracle's purpose as revealing Jesus' glory so that His disciples would believe in Him (John 2:11).

How did such a sign begin to reveal that Jesus has an exalted identity, status, and authority? It called to mind earlier miracles by Elijah and Elisha. Elijah once called upon God's power to provide a miraculous supply of grain and oil (I Kgs. 17:16), and Elisha healed a spring of water so that all could drink from it (II Kgs. 2:21-22). Elisha also caused oil to flow miraculously, filling as many jars as a widow could gather (4:3-6), and he caused a bitter stew to become edible (vss. 40-41).

In each of these miracles performed through Elijah and Elisha, the object was the staple food or drink of the people. These prophets were filled with God's power and spoke with authority to address the needs around them. Jesus frequently was thought of as an Elijah figure (Mark 8:28; Luke 9:8). On the cross, people thought He was calling for Elijah, as though Jesus might have been a disciple of that prophet (Mark 15:35).

Jesus' glory was first revealed to His disciples by providing the ordinary needs of the people in an ordinary setting. Though the miracle concerned the ordinary, it also was in a setting that had many messianic overtones. Jesus filled a wedding with joy, even as He will fill Israel and the world with joy in the age to come.

—Derek Leman.

Guiding the Superintendent

Of the several topics one could concentrate on in this portion of God's Word, we shall select three, with the prayer that they will enlighten, cheer, and challenge you in your life and ministry.

DEVOTIONAL OUTLINE

1. The shift of relationship (John 2:1-5). The wedding in Cana may have involved a relative or close friend of Jesus and His family, since they were specifically invited and Mary felt free to involve herself in matters regarding refreshments. When she approached Jesus about the need, Jesus addressed her as "woman." To our ears this seems disrespectful, but in that time and culture it was not.

It should be noted that in John's Gospel, Mary appears on only two occasions—here and when Jesus was on the cross. In both instances, Jesus addressed her as "woman" (cf. 19:26). At Golgotha, He provided for Mary's future by putting her in the care of John. Here, in Cana, a different matter was addressed.

The matter here was one of relationship. Jesus was stepping away from the family order that had been in place to that point so that He could begin His public ministry. Though Jesus would still honor His mother, as seen at the cross, He had to step away from her in order to follow the guidance of the Father and obey Him.

The focus today also should be upon Jesus, not Mary. Mary was God's chosen vessel to bear and raise the Messiah, but she had reached the point that she needed to step back and assume a different relationship with Him. We too should honor our parents as long as they are living, but Christ always wants first place in our lives.

2. The supply of the need (John 2:6-10). Though Jesus expressed His independence when Mary spoke to Him, He was sympathetic to the need of the wedding host and guests and responded accordingly.

Here is a great truth that the apostle Paul would later learn and teach—that the Lord can and will supply the needs of those who look to Him (cf. Phil. 4:19). Do we have a need (not a want)? Are we looking to Jesus to meet that need?

We should note also that when Jesus met the need at the wedding, He did not do just enough to get by. He did His best. The Creator created again, and that act in Cana was not simply a miracle but a sign that pointed to His creative ability and hence His divinity.

3. The sign that brought faith (John 2:11-12). One of the purposes of John's Gospel is to present Jesus as the Son of God and point readers to Him, where they can find life and light. The miracles/signs he recorded were designed to do just that. The Jews looked for such signs (cf. I Cor. 1:22).

John wrote this last Gospel at the end of the first century to direct all his readers, and especially the Jews, to Jesus as the Son of God. John's evangelistic heart desired that as many as possible believe in Christ. He added that the disciples of Jesus believed at that point.

AGE-GROUP EMPHASES

Children: Lead children to see that Jesus can meet needs.

Youths: Young people need to honor and obey their parents but also practice following Jesus as they grow toward independence.

Adults: Parents need to recognize that their ultimate goal is to equip their children to follow Christ on their own.
—Darrell W. McKay.

SCRIPTURE LESSON TEXT

MARK 9:14 And when he came to *his* disciples, he saw a great multitude about them, and the scribes questioning with them.

15 And straightway all the people, when they beheld him, were greatly amazed, and running to *him* saluted him.

16 And he asked the scribes, What question ye with them?

17 And one of the multitude answered and said, Master, I have brought unto thee my son, which hath a dumb spirit;

18 And wheresoever he taketh him, he teareth him: and he foameth, and gnasheth with his teeth, and pineth away: and I spake to thy disciples that they should cast him out; and they could not.

19 He answereth him, and saith, O faithless generation, how long shall I be with you? how long shall I suffer you? bring him unto me.

20 And they brought him unto him: and when he saw him, straightway the spirit tare him; and he fell on the ground, and wallowed foaming.

21 And he asked his father, How long is it ago since this came unto him? And he said, Of a child.

22 And ofttimes it hath cast him into the fire, and into the waters, to destroy him: but if thou canst do any thing, have compassion on us, and help us.

23 Jesus said unto him, If thou canst believe, all things *are* possible to him that believeth.

24 And straightway the father of the child cried out, and said with tears, Lord, I believe; help thou mine unbelief.

25 When Jesus saw that the people came running together, he rebuked the foul spirit, saying unto him, *Thou* dumb and deaf spirit, I charge thee, come out of him, and enter no more into him.

26 And *the spirit* cried, and rent him sore, and came out of him: and he was as one dead; insomuch that many said, He is dead.

27 But Jesus took him by the hand, and lifted him up; and he arose.

28 And when he was come into the house, his disciples asked him privately, Why could not we cast him out?

29 And he said unto them, This kind can come forth by nothing, but by prayer and fasting.

NOTES

Jesus' Authority over Demons

Lesson Text: Mark 9:14-29

Related Scriptures: Matthew 17:14-21; Luke 9:37-42;
Mark 5:1-13; Acts 8:3-8

TIME: A.D. 26   PLACE: possibly near Mount Hermon

GOLDEN TEXT—"Jesus said unto him, If thou canst believe, all things are possible to him that believeth" (Mark 9:23).

Introduction

What would it have been like to be a student learning from the Son of God? It took Jesus' disciples a while to fully understand who He was, but throughout the process of learning, they were being mentored by the One who had been anticipated for centuries in Israel. One of the greatest privileges was given to Peter, James, and John while they were with Jesus at the transfiguration (Mark 9:1-13). It was the most glorious mountaintop experience they could possibly have had.

God graciously gives us high points in our Christian walk. He knows we need the training that comes from painful situations, but He also knows the encouragement that comes from spiritually exhilarating times. We must realize that these are special blessings.

LESSON OUTLINE

I. A NEEDY SON—Mark 9:14-20

II. A BELIEVING FATHER—
   Mark 9:21-24

III. A POWERFUL SAVIOUR—
   Mark 9:25-29

Exposition: Verse by Verse

A NEEDY SON

MARK 9:14 And when he came to his disciples, he saw a great multitude about them, and the scribes questioning with them.

15 And straightway all the people, when they beheld him, were greatly amazed, and running to him saluted him.

16 And he asked the scribes, What question ye with them?

17 And one of the multitude answered and said, Master, I have brought unto thee my son, which

hath a dumb spirit;

18 And wheresoever he taketh him, he teareth him: and he foameth, and gnasheth with his teeth, and pineth away: and I spake to thy disciples that they should cast him out; and they could not.

19 He answereth him, and saith, O faithless generation, how long shall I be with you? how long shall I suffer you? bring him unto me.

20 And they brought him unto him: and when he saw him, straightway the spirit tare him; and he fell on the ground, and wallowed foaming.

A question for the scribes (Mark 9:14-16). Jesus, Peter, James, and John immediately faced the reality the other disciples had been trying to handle in their absence. It involved a problem that had arisen among the people who were around them, and it involved the power and workings of a demon in a young boy. "This is the last exorcism that Mark recorded. . . . The disciples' lack of glory in this story contrasts with Jesus' glory in the Transfiguration" (Constable, *Thomas Constable's Notes on the Bible,* Tyndale).

{A large crowd of people surrounded the nine disciples who were waiting for Jesus' return. Jesus and the three with Him saw that there were arguments going on.}^{Q1} The word translated "questioning" in verse 14 is the Greek word *suzēteō,* and it indicates investigative discussion— that is, a dispute or controversy. Mark did not mention the subject of their discussion, nor did he explain why the people were amazed when they saw Jesus. The Greek term signifies that they were absolutely astonished!

There is no reason to believe that Jesus had some type of visible glow left over from the transfiguration experience, for He had specifically told His three companions not to tell anyone about the event (vs. 9). The people's

amazement may have simply come from suddenly seeing Jesus drawing near, for they immediately ran to meet Him.

Jesus began by addressing the scribes with a question. Apparently they had been the ones leading the arguments (not an unusual situation in which to find them!). It is very likely that they had been watching the disciples and taunting them about their attempts to do something at which they were miserably failing. Jesus' question was direct: "What question ye with them?" (vs. 16). It must have been extremely comforting to the disciples to have Jesus appear and immediately take up their cause in the conflict.

A request from a father (Mark 9:17-18). {Upon hearing Jesus' question, a man stepped up and explained his dilemma, which apparently was the focus of the dispute taking place.}^{Q2} He said he had brought his son to Jesus to have Him exorcise a demon that had robbed the boy of speech and hearing (vss. 17, 25). The demon was causing him to be self-destructive. This initial description given by the father sounds like epileptic convulsions, but it would soon become clear that the demon was causing more than this.

{The father described the boy as being seized by the demon and thrown to the ground, where he would foam at the mouth, gnash his teeth, and turn rigid (with plants, "pine away" meant to lose all moisture and thus become dried up and rigid).}^{Q3} The father then explained that he had spoken to Jesus' disciples about helping him, since Jesus Himself was absent, but they had failed in their attempts.

Jesus had previously given His disciples the power to cast out demons (cf. Mark 3:15; 6:7, 13), so it was not out of line that this father approached them when Jesus was not personally present. What caused them to be ineffective this time? Perhaps they were relying on their own power, thinking that since Jesus had given them this ability before, they could now do it again on their own.

We need to understand that a sickness such as epilepsy or a condition like deafness does not automatically indicate demon possession. There have been people with epilepsy who have had well-meaning acquaintances traumatize them by trying to cast demons out of them. This father was accurate in his diagnosis, but we must be careful not to draw premature conclusions about such symptoms when we see them in others.

A rebuke for that generation (Mark 9:19-20). "Jesus had given His disciples authority to cast out demons (Mark 6:7, 13), and yet their ministry to the boy was ineffective. No wonder the Lord was grieved with them! How often He must be grieved with us when we fail to use the spiritual resources He has graciously given to His people!" (Wiersbe, *The Bible Exposition Commentary,* Cook).

Jesus' words were biting and direct and were probably meant for everyone present, including the father and the disciples. He had encountered so much unbelief that we can understand why He took such a direct tone. Later He indicated that His disciples' faith was not strong in this incident. {He expressed frustration over the fact that He was still encountering so much unbelief in everyone.}Q4 How much more did He need to do and say to convince them about Himself and His abilities?

Nevertheless, Jesus would not let a needy boy go without help, so He asked that he be brought to Him. {When the boy saw Him, the demon in him convulsed him and threw him to the ground immediately.}Q5

"When the evil spirit saw Jesus, it knew that its rule over the boy would soon end. The demon responded with one last attack, throwing the boy to the ground, showing its contempt for and rebellion against Jesus. . . . Watch this demon demonstrate. It's as if the demon wants one more round of child's play before the end—an exercise in futility, one final shudder of pitiful posturing" (Osborne, ed., *Life Application Bible Commentary,* Tyndale).

A BELIEVING FATHER

21 And he asked his father, How long is it ago since this came unto him? And he said, Of a child.

22 And ofttimes it hath cast him into the fire, and into the waters, to destroy him: but if thou canst do any thing, have compassion on us, and help us.

23 Jesus said unto him, If thou canst believe, all things are possible to him that believeth.

24 And straightway the father of the child cried out, and said with tears, Lord, I believe; help thou mine unbelief.

An explanation about the son (Mark 9:21-22). Why did Jesus ask how long the boy had been afflicted? No doubt He did so for the sake of the father, who needed to acknowledge his desperate need for help from Jesus. {Perhaps his faith had been shaken when Jesus' disciples were unable to do anything for his son when he thought they could.}Q6 He had seen his son like this ever since early childhood, so it was indeed a seemingly impossible situation. Perhaps Jesus also asked the question for the benefit of the crowd, so they would know that only the power of God could help the boy.

The description the father gave of what repeatedly happened to his son reveals that his condition was more than epilepsy. These were the destructive activities of a demon. From other Gospel accounts we know that such activity was a typical sign of demon possession. A demon's goal was the destruction of the person it inhabited (cf. Mark 5:5). What was now stated by the father amplified what he had said earlier (9:18). This boy was clearly at the mercy of the indwelling demon.

The father recognized that his son's problems were the work of the demon. His description of the demon's actions sounds like something working on the boy from outside his own body. It was the demon that often threw him into fire and water, and the father understood that it was trying to destroy him. He had probably been forced to rescue him many times. {Although his faith had been shaken by the disciples' inability to help, he made an appeal to Jesus even in his doubt. The word "if" in verse 22 indicates his uncertainty.}[Q7]

The man asked for compassion for his son. One of the encouraging truths we encounter in reading the Gospels is the regularity with which we read of Jesus' compassion upon needy people. We must never give up hope!

A challenge to have faith (Mark 9:23-24). Jesus also used the word "if" in His response. {"Jesus took up the father's words of doubt, ['if thou canst'], to show that the point was not His ability to heal the boy but the father's ability to trust in God who can do what is humanly impossible"}[Q8] (Walvoord and Zuck, eds., *The Bible Knowledge Commentary,* Cook). It was not a question about Jesus' ability but rather a question about the father's belief in Him and what He could do.

Modern-day "faith healers" often emphasize the necessity of having a certain amount of faith instead of drawing attention to the Person who should be the object of their faith. Jesus did not say the father did not have enough faith; He merely pointed out that he needed to believe in Him. In any given situation, we do not need to summon up a certain amount of faith in order for God to respond to our needs. We need to strive to know our Father well enough to understand His ability to respond to those needs.

The father's response was immediate and strong. He declared his faith, but he also acknowledged that it was frail and needed to be built up. Instead of again calling Jesus "Master" (vs. 17), he now called Him "Lord" (vs. 24). Most of us can identify with this man's assessment of himself. We have put our trust in God and believe He will provide and protect, but then we experience pangs of doubt when facing a difficult situation. We too then cry out, "Lord, I believe; help thou mine unbelief."

A POWERFUL SAVIOUR

25 When Jesus saw that the people came running together, he rebuked the foul spirit, saying unto him, Thou dumb and deaf spirit, I charge thee, come out of him, and enter no more into him.

26 And the spirit cried, and rent him sore, and came out of him: and he was as one dead; insomuch that many said, He is dead.

27 But Jesus took him by the hand, and lifted him up; and he arose.

28 And when he was come into the house, his disciples asked him privately, Why could not we cast him out?

29 And he said unto them, This kind can come forth by nothing, but by prayer and fasting.

A demon's lack of power (Mark 9:25-27). Jesus never wanted to draw attention to Himself just for the sake of attention. At this moment, many people were running to see what was going on, and He apparently sought to spare the father any unneeded spectacle. So without further delay, He commanded the demon to come out of the boy and never enter him again. His words were an authoritative charge. No demon could ever defy this.

{Once again the demon reacted violently, convulsing the boy and letting out a shriek of rage.}[Q9] The wording of the text indicates an extreme spasmodic convulsion. We get the impression that the boy was violently thrashing around and screaming at the same time. This was happening as the demon was departing his body, and afterward he lay there looking as if he were dead. As the people gathered around, they concluded that he was, indeed, dead, for there was no longer any sign of life coming from him.

But at that moment, Jesus calmly reached down and took his hand and helped him stand up. It appears that the demon had done his best to kill the boy, but it now became obvious that the power of Jesus was more than sufficient to overcome all such attempts. The boy's healing was complete. Not only was he free of the demon, but he also had full physical strength to stand and go on as normal.

"We can imagine the demon saying, 'Ha, I left this kid like a corpse. Your move, Jesus!' And as the crowd watched and the father winced at his son's stillness, Jesus took the boy's hand and brought him to his feet" (Osborne).

An answer concerning the disciples' lack of power (Mark 9:28-29). Jesus and His disciples left the crowds of people and entered into the privacy of a house, where the perplexed disciples immediately asked why they had failed so miserably. What they had been unable to accomplish, Jesus had done with relative ease. Where were they lacking?

"The thing that must have bothered the disciples most was the fact that they had been given authority over unclean spirits (6:7) and had been able to cast them out before (6:13). Now for some reason, they do not experience that same miracle power, but at least they go to the right person to find out why" (Douglas, ed., *New Commentary on the Whole Bible,* Tyndale). {Jesus' answer indicated indirectly that they had relied on themselves instead of on the power of God.}[Q10] This was also one of the more powerful demons.

Matthew adds a fuller explanation by Jesus: "Because of your unbelief: for verily I say unto you, If ye have faith as a grain of mustard seed, ye shall say unto this mountain, Remove hence to yonder place; and it shall remove; and nothing shall be impossible unto you" (17:20).

If those who lived in Jesus' presence so constantly faltered in their belief, how much easier is it for us to falter? We must daily renew our trust in Him.

—Keith E. Eggert.

QUESTIONS

1. What did Jesus and the three disciples encounter when they came down the mountain?
2. What happened when Jesus asked the scribes what they were discussing with His disciples?
3. How did the father describe his son's actions, and to what did he attribute it?
4. What exasperated Jesus about the whole situation?
5. What happened when the boy first saw Jesus?
6. What seemed to have happened to the father's faith? Why?
7. How do we hear this in his request to Jesus (Mark 9:22)?
8. Why did Jesus say "If thou canst believe" to the father (vs. 23)?
9. What happened when Jesus commanded the demon to leave?
10. How did Jesus explain the disciples' inability to succeed?

—Keith E. Eggert.

Preparing to Teach the Lesson

"Faith" is one of the key words in our Christian life. We are saved by faith (Eph. 2:8-9), and we live by faith (II Cor. 5:7). While we have to exercise faith, we do not generate it within ourselves. It is a wonderful gift from God through His Spirit.

Often our walk of faith is tested by trials that God allows to come our way. God designs these tests to grow and deepen our faith (Jas. 1:2-5). In this lesson, we look at a great test of faith.

TODAY'S AIM

Facts: to get a clearer picture of the role of faith in our daily Christian lives.

Principle: to understand the power of faith in God to change situations.

Application: to pray with greater confidence in the power of the Lord for a current struggle.

INTRODUCING THE LESSON

Americans are enamored with power. (Ask your learners for examples of powerful people or things that attract us.) We like to hear or follow powerful people. We are captivated by powerful race cars. We are fascinated by powerful athletes. We seem to be obsessed with power.

When it comes to our Christian lives, however, we are usually not as concerned about power. Our testimony for Christ is weak, not powerful. Our prayer life is weak, not powerful. Our faith is weak, not powerful. Today we will examine Mark 9 to help us get a clearer picture of what it means to have a powerful faith.

DEVELOPING THE LESSON

1. The disciples' disputing (Mark 9:14-18). As Jesus, along with Peter, James, and John, descended from the Mount of Transfiguration (vss. 2-13),

He found the rest of the disciples and the Jewish scribes disputing among themselves. As the exchanges continued, a large crowd of people gathered to observe the event (vs. 14). When Jesus approached the crowd, they immediately turned toward Him and greeted Him. Jesus then asked the people the reason for their arguing and disputing.

One of the men in the crowd addressed the Saviour and told Him that the issue concerned the pitiful situation his son faced. A demon had afflicted his son so that he could not speak or hear (cf. vs. 25). Furthermore, "wheresoever he [the demon] taketh him, he teareth him: and he foameth, and gnasheth with his teeth, and pineth away" (vs. 18). The man continued by saying, "I spake to thy disciples that they should cast him out; and they could not." Apparently, the disciples attempted to drive out the demon but were unable to do so.

2. The Lord's questioning (Mark 9:19-23). Jesus was moved by the boy's condition and the disciples' inability to heal the child. Addressing the crowd as a whole, He said, "O faithless generation, how long shall I be with you? how long shall I suffer you? bring him unto me" (vs. 19). When the evil spirit saw Jesus, it caused the boy to go into seizures that threw him to the ground in helplessness.

In response to Jesus' question, the father explained that his son had been afflicted from his childhood, probably indicating a period of several years. The father further stated that the demon had often tried to destroy his son by burning and drowning him.

At this point the distraught father

cried out to the Lord Jesus, "If thou canst do any thing, have compassion on us, and help us" (vs. 22). Jesus responded in tenderness with the assurance that "all things are possible to him that believeth" (vs. 23).

Jesus had identified the heart of the issue—belief or faith. He encouraged the man to exercise confidence in Him and have faith in His power to deliver the boy from demon possession.

3. The father's believing (Mark 9:24-27). The father was ready to exercise faith in the Lord, but he also recognized the weakness of his faith. "Lord, I believe; help thou mine unbelief" (vs. 24).

The father had given enough evidence of faith that the Lord responded by healing the son. "He rebuked the foul spirit, saying unto him, Thou dumb and deaf spirit, I charge thee, come out of him, and enter no more into him" (vs. 25). The evil spirit had to obey the Lord, but in doing so the spirit afflicted the boy one last time so severely that many thought he was dead. The Lord tenderly lifted the boy and returned him to his grateful father.

4. The Lord's teaching (Mark 9:28-29). Later Jesus' disciples asked Him why they could not cast out the demon from the boy. The Lord responded that "this kind can come forth by nothing, but by prayer and fasting." This kind of miracle could only occur with prolonged and focused prayer and fasting and dependence on the Lord, which they apparently had not done. Those who rely on the Lord can have a powerful faith.

ILLUSTRATING THE LESSON

We should pray with great confidence, knowing that all things are possible with God.

PRAY WITH GREAT CONFIDENCE IN THE LORD

HE IS ABLE

CONCLUDING THE LESSON

We who have placed our faith in the Lord and believe in the power of prayer sometimes find ourselves in the same situation as the father in today's study. "Lord, I believe; help thou mine unbelief" (Mark 9:24). We believe that the Lord has the power to change matters, but we occasionally still struggle with our confidence in Him.

What challenges to your faith are you facing right now? (Allow time for personal reflection.)

What steps can we take today to grow in our faith and confidence in the Lord? We can identify and claim certain promises from Scripture. We can review God's working on our behalf in the past. We can ask a friend to pray that we will increase in our faith.

Having greater confidence in the power of the Lord does not mean He will grant all our requests. It does mean, however, that we can have complete confidence that the Lord is able to act on our behalf as He sees fit.

ANTICIPATING THE NEXT LESSON

In the next lesson, we will examine Jesus' healing of a man on the Sabbath.

—*Don Anderson.*

PRACTICAL POINTS

1. Before we get into an argument, we should remember that we will answer to Jesus about it (Mark 9:14-16).
2. God does not want excuses; He wants our faith (vss. 17-19).
3. We must never doubt God's ability to act, no matter what the odds are (vss. 20-23).
4. We do not need rock-solid faith; we just need faith in Jesus (vs. 24).
5. The work of God in our lives can be frightening, but it leads to lasting peace (vss. 25-27).
6. Where human strength fails, prayer avails (vss. 28-29).

—*Kenneth A. Sponsler.*

RESEARCH AND DISCUSSION

1. Why were the people overwhelmed with wonder when they saw Jesus approach (Mark 9:15)?
2. Jesus' words in verse 19 imply that He thought His disciples should have been able to cast out the demon. Was this realistic (cf. Luke 9:1)?
3. Why did Jesus ask for specifics about the boy's demon possession (Mark 9:21)? If the disciples had asked this, would they have been successful? Why or why not?
4. How is Jesus' assertion in verse 23 to be understood? For example, is it possible for a person to play professional sports at age sixty if he only believes?
5. How do we discern when a situation or need calls for prayer and fasting (vs. 29)? Why do we neglect this?

—*Kenneth A. Sponsler.*

ILLUSTRATED HIGH POINTS

Bring him unto me (Mark 9:19)

On August 2, 1922, a *New York Times* headline read, "40 Lourdes Pilgrims Killed, 52 Hurt." Hoping to receive miracles, parents had attempted to take their crippled children to a famous "healing" shrine in Lourdes, France. Two trains, each transporting about 500 travelers, met with disaster. On a steep hill, one of the overloaded locomotives lost traction and rolled back onto the other, resulting in the many deaths.

A father seeking a miracle for his possessed child (Mark 9:17) initially took him to Christ's disciples. He had come to the right source. Yet the power to heal does not lie in any site, object, or human being. It is foolish to attribute God's power to things, people, places, or methodologies. When someone is in need, Jesus simply says, "Bring him unto me" (vs. 19).

Cried out, and said with tears (vs. 24)

The Chugach Electric Association of Anchorage, Alaska, had a problem: ravens were continuously hitting the power lines. The solution came in the form of an earsplitting, forty-second screech, broadcast every five minutes. This disturbing sound, designed to mimic the distress call of ravens, successfully deflected the bothersome birds.

Several passages in Scripture depict young ravens calling out for food from their Maker (cf. Job 38:41; Ps. 147:9). Perhaps that is an appropriate parallel to what we find in Mark 9:24: a desperate father crying out to the Lord for help. Can such undignified, demonstrative behavior have a place in faith and prayer? Indeed, faith, though often understood as a quiet waiting upon the Lord, may also express itself with spontaneous cries. Such was the cry of the father in our text.

—*Therese Greenberg.*

Golden Text Illuminated

"Jesus said unto him, If thou canst believe, all things are possible to him that believeth" (Mark 9:23).

Some believers say that miracles were only for biblical times, while others insist that they are still happening. Still others fall in between, and there are those who are not sure what to believe. Perhaps the greatest challenge for each of us, though, is the hopelessness we sometimes feel when our present need seems beyond the scope of the possible.

That is what the father in this lesson was facing. His situation seemed impossible, beyond hope. He was almost ready to give up.

Try to place yourself in his shoes. His only child was suffering, caught in a demon's grip for years. He was forced to watch as his child was destroyed more each day, and he was absolutely helpless to find a remedy.

From the passage, we know that this father loved his son. He had likely sought out rabbi after rabbi and tried remedy after remedy to find a cure. Still, his son grew worse.

When he approached Jesus, he was desperate. He did not know where else to turn, and he had heard stories about the healings this Prophet had performed.

Initially, he asked the disciples for help, but they were unsuccessful (vs. 18). By then, discouragement and despair were foremost.

That was when Christ stepped in. He had just come down from the mountain after the transfiguration. He found His disciples being mocked because of their failure.

Curiously, Christ did not heal the child immediately. Instead, He asked the father how long his son had been that way. The father did not hesitate to say. However, he did show doubt in Christ: "if thou canst do any thing" (vs. 22).

Christ told him that anything was possible if he would just believe. I think this was a challenge. He was checking just what this man was willing to risk when it came to faith.

The man's response is one we all have cried: "Lord, I believe; help thou mine unbelief" (vs. 24). If we think, all of us can remember a circumstance that seemed hopeless. It was not that we did not believe but rather that the situation seemed impossible. We find ourselves setting limits on our Saviour. Belief and unbelief often reside within the same person, since faith is not always perfect.

Watch what happened. After this man's exclamation, Jesus did not expound on some message concerning the necessity of faith in daily life. Instead, He cast out the demon, and the boy was healed.

For those of us familiar with Scripture, this healing does not come as a surprise. It seems obvious to us. To this father, it was not. Like Abraham, he was being asked to place his only child completely in God's hands (Gen. 22:1-19).

In both instances, that faith was rewarded. God asks us to trust in Him and His work even when we cannot see Him working (Heb. 11:1). He asks us to walk by faith and not by sight (II Cor. 5:7).

Faith that is powerful has conviction and confidence in God's authority over all. Someone with powerful faith believes that he has been given that faith through Christ. If we believe this, then we have faith to go out and do even the most formidable task for His glory. Let us cultivate and practice such a powerful faith.

—*Jennifer Lautermilch.*

Heart of the Lesson

One often hears the statements "keep the faith" or "I believe." Popular culture has made the words "faith" and "believe" prominent in Christian and non-Christian homes alike. This cultural trend makes it all the more important that we look to Scripture to see what faith really is. Not everything we refer to as "faith" is pleasing to God (cf. Heb. 11:6). What matters is not merely that we have faith but in *whom* we have it

In today's lesson we see three types of faith and Christ's response to each.

1. The presumptuous faith of the disciples (Mark 9:14-19). Having descended from the Mount of Transfiguration, Jesus, along with Peter, James, and John, encountered a heated discussion taking place between His other disciples and the Jewish scribes. Upon His inquiry, Jesus found that the discussion centered on the disciples' inability to heal a demon-possessed boy, something they, and apparently those around them, expected they should have been able to do (cf. 6:7).

Jesus strongly rebuked His disciples, calling them part of a faithless generation—not because they did not have faith but because they were presumptuous. When questioned privately later about their inability to cast out the demon, Jesus said that powerful faith is dependent on the will of God, which can be known only through biblically grounded prayer and fasting (9:28-29).

As God's people, we must never presume to use God's gracious gifts to accomplish our own wills or bring ourselves glory. We must not forget that, like Jesus, we need to first seek the Father's will and then faithfully act (cf. John 5:30; 8:28).

2. The weak faith of the boy's father (Mark 9:20-23). At the command of Jesus, the boy was brought to Him. Immediately, the demon convulsed him. In His compassion, Jesus inquired about the boy's history and gave the father an opportunity to share his grief and heartache. In his anguish, the father cried out, "If thou canst do any thing, have compassion on us, and help us" (vs. 22).

Jesus immediately identified the father's weak faith by focusing on his words "if thou canst." Jesus wanted him and us to understand that faith is believing that He can do all things and then trusting Him to do what is good. Faith allows us to trust the ability of Jesus to do anything. We can expect Him to do what He knows is best.

3. The growing faith of the boy's father (Mark 9:24-29). In response to Jesus' challenge, the man tearfully cried out, "Lord, I believe; help thou mine unbelief" (vs. 24). In response to the father's growing faith and the son's predicament, Jesus simply commanded the evil spirit to leave. After a final convulsing, it left and was forbidden to enter the son again.

The boy was restored to his father, and both learned a vital lesson that we too must understand. Powerful faith is not dependent on who we are or the gifts we have. Powerful faith is centered on Jesus as the Author and Perfecter of our faith (Heb. 12:2). Our prayer and fasting is directed toward Him (Mark 9:28-29). Powerful faith believes Jesus can and will do whatever accomplishes the Father's will and is best for us. Powerful faith is powerful because Jesus is all-powerful and we simply rely on Him.

—*Don Kakavecos.*

World Missions

"If God gave her a forty-thousand-dollar jet, He must want me to have one too."

This was said by a pastor in Uganda, a land with much poverty, nearly two million orphans, and the largest refugee population in Africa. A famous female "evangelist" had just visited his country. Her message of health and wealth received a great response, but she left behind people like this pastor, who used her message as an avenue for personal greed. Many others, when God did not heal or grant their requests, became disillusioned about Christianity or felt like spiritual failures.

Verses like this week's golden text give us hope. Faith can move mountains. Faith is the victory. However, some who call themselves Christians will use such verses to spread their claim that God wants everyone to be happy, healthy, and rich in this life and that anyone who is not must not have enough faith. Those in ministry around the world will encounter people who either have been disillusioned by such claims or who want to believe it because they want comfortable lives.

Ironically, though today's main verse could be used as ammunition by those who preach health and wealth, when read in context, the full passage is an argument against the idea that your level of faith determines the result of your request. In the passage, the disciples were unable to heal the boy due to their own lack, not because the person in need of healing lacked anything. Also, Jesus healed at the request of the father, not the boy. The level of faith of the actual sick person was never mentioned. And the healing was not based on the father having a great level of faith, either. He himself said, "Lord, I believe; help thou mine unbelief" (Mark 9:24).

Anyone in outreach today needs to know how to respond to the health and wealth message. Following are some biblical refutations.

1. The reason for faith should not be to get what we want. James 4:3 says we do not receive what we ask for when we "ask amiss, that ye may consume it upon your lusts." Our prayers should be for the will of God more than our personal desires.

2. The Bible clearly states that we will have suffering in this life (cf. Ps. 34:19; John 16:33; II Cor. 4:8-11). In heaven, all will be wonderful. Here it is not.

3. Getting what we want is not always representative of our level of faith. The first half of Hebrews 11 is about people doing wondrous things by faith (vss. 2-12), but the last half talks of ones who suffered horrible things—also by faith (vss. 17-38).

4. Our comfort does not always fulfill God's purposes. When Lazarus sickened and died (John 11), Jesus did not say it was because of a lack of faith. He said it was for the glory of God. (See also the man born blind in John 9.)

In the final analysis, using our prayers to demand health and wealth is selfish, a way to sound spiritual while seeking only our own desires. We in ministry need to help seekers and believers alike understand the Christian life as the Bible presents it so they will not be swayed by false teachers. As Jesus said, what good is it if a person gains the whole world but loses his soul (Matt. 16:26)?

—*Kimberly Rae.*

The Jewish Aspect

When Jesus came down from the Mount of Transfiguration, He found His disciples arguing with the Jewish scribes (Mark 9:14). Who were the scribes, and what made them important?

The word "scribe(s)" occurs fifty-four times in the Old Testament and sixty-six in the New. Prior to the Babylonian Exile, the term referred to those capable of writing who served in various capacities, such as keeping financial and military records (II Kgs. 12:10; II Chr. 26:11). Many Levites were also scribes (I Chr. 24:6), and there were "families of the scribes" (2:55). Because of their literary skills, they were accepted as men of wisdom.

After the temple's destruction in 586 B.C., scribes became more central to Jewish life. They became the teachers of the Mosaic Law. The most well-known biblical scribe of that time was Ezra (Ezra 7:11-12). He made the reading, study, and interpretation of the Law a central focus of Jewish culture (Neh. 8:1-18). Jewish tradition holds that he was instrumental in founding the Great Synagogue, the precursor of all later synagogues. The apocryphal book of Ecclesiasticus describes the office of scribe in detail (38:24; 39:1-11). He was "schooled in the law and religious wisdom, understanding the implications of both the written law and oral traditions. As a result of his learning, he enjoyed prominence in public assemblies, and both understood and exercised justice among the people" (Tenney, ed., *The Zondervan Pictorial Encyclopedia of the Bible,* Zondervan).

During Jesus' time, the scribes were most closely associated with the Pharisees. Twenty-two times in the New Testament they are directly linked. In His rebukes of Jewish hypocrisy, Jesus specifically said, "Woe unto you, scribes and Pharisees, hypocrites!" (Matt. 23:13). While some Pharisees were scribes, not all were.

The scribes diligently passed their knowledge from scholar to student. They were the theologians of New Testament times. "Only fully qualified scholars . . . were legitimate members of the guild of scribes" (Bromiley, ed., *Theological Dictionary of the New Testament,* Eerdmans).

Jesus frequently confronted the scribes during His ministry. He said that their "righteousness" (Matt. 5:20) was insufficient to enter the kingdom of heaven. He indicted them for their vanity (Mark 12:38-39) and their hypocrisy (vs. 40). Jesus further rebuked the scribes, asserting that their traditions contradicted the commands of God (Matt. 15:3-9) and that they were "blind guides" (23:16).

As a group, the scribes felt so threatened by Jesus and what He taught that they ultimately called for His crucifixion (Luke 22:2; 22:66—23:1). Not all religious leaders opposed Jesus, however. The Pharisee Nicodemus opened his life to Christ and did not participate in His crucifixion.

The New Testament testifies that at least two other scribes were open to Christ's teaching. One scribe said, "I will follow thee whithersoever thou goest" (Matt. 8:19). Whether he actually did, Scripture does not record. Another scribe asked Jesus which commandment was the greatest (Mark 12:28-33). After their interaction, Jesus told the scribe that he was "not far from the kingdom of God" (vs. 34). We can only hope that more scribes turned from their self-sufficiency and trusted in the revealed Messiah.

— *R. Larry Overstreet.*

Guiding the Superintendent

"Now faith is the substance of things hoped for, the evidence of things not seen" (Heb. 11:1). Biblical faith has substance—a solid, meaningful quality that impacts believers' lives in expressive ways.

This week, we will discover the quality of powerful faith. "Of course, power does not inhere in faith itself; faith is not a magical way to manipulate reality. Instead, faith is effective because it is the means by which we access the help of God Himself, with whom all things are possible (Matt. 19:26). Faith is the conviction, John Calvin comments, that 'God will never forsake us, if we keep the door open for receiving his grace.' And He cannot help but move in the lives of those who cry out to Him day and night (Ex. 2:23—3:8; Luke 18:1-8)" (Ligonier Ministries, "Small but Powerful Faith," ligonier.org).

DEVOTIONAL OUTLINE

1. Prelude: Jesus and the multitude (Mark 9:14-19). Jesus saw a multitude engrossed in conversation. When the multitude saw Jesus, they rushed to Him in amazement. A question-and-answer period ensued, and a frustrated and disappointed parent shared with Jesus his emotional story of his son's demon possession and the disciples' failure to cure him. Jesus' unanticipated response reminds us how He constantly endured the unbelief of the masses and weakness of faith in even His own followers.

2. Main event: Jesus and the healing (Mark 9:20-26). When the demon-possessed boy came into Jesus' presence, he was overcome with convulsions. The boy's father shared his son's disturbing history with Jesus and implored Him to intervene with His compassionate assistance.

Jesus responded to the father's desperate plea with an emphasis upon genuine personal faith. The father replied with vulnerability, confessing both the reality and weakness of his faith. Jesus then exerted His spiritual authority over the demon. The healing experience was so traumatic that the boy looked as if he were lacking life.

3. Postlude: Jesus and His disciples (Mark 9:27-29). Jesus lovingly helped the boy to his feet. His disciples asked Him about their failed effort to heal the boy. Jesus then taught His disciples that spiritual victory over the powers of hell demands a commitment to God through prayer and self-denial.

AGE-GROUP EMPHASES

Children: Use Jesus' healing of the young boy to illustrate to your children how much the Lord loves them. He is willing to battle the powers of darkness to rescue them from anything that would do them harm.

Youths: Young people often believe that they are invincible, that they can "rush in where angels fear to tread" with impunity. Help your young people develop a healthy respect for the powers of darkness along with a maturing dependence upon the Lord's power for their safety and protection.

Adults: Many parents have been in situations they were unable to control that required them to entrust their children to the Lord. This act of faith can be challenging and frightening. In fact, some adults have not experienced a good outcome after doing so. Remind your adults that the power of faith in Jesus Christ will overcome any disappointment they may have experienced in life.

—*Thomas R. Chmura.*

SCRIPTURE LESSON TEXT

LUKE 6:1 And it came to pass on the second sabbath after the first, that he went through the corn fields; and his disciples plucked the ears of corn, and did eat, rubbing *them* in *their* hands.

2 And certain of the Pharisees said unto them, Why do ye that which is not lawful to do on the sabbath days?

3 And Jesus answering them said, Have ye not read so much as this, what David did, when himself was an hungred, and they which were with him;

4 How he went into the house of God, and did take and eat the shewbread, and gave also to them that were with him; which it is not lawful to eat but for the priests alone?

5 And he said unto them, That the Son of man is Lord also of the sabbath.

6 And it came to pass also on another sabbath, that he entered into the synagogue and taught: and there was a man whose right hand was withered.

7 And the scribes and Pharisees watched him, whether he would heal on the sabbath day; that they might find an accusation against him.

8 But he knew their thoughts, and said to the man which had the withered hand, Rise up, and stand forth in the midst. And he arose and stood forth.

9 Then said Jesus unto them, I will ask you one thing; Is it lawful on the sabbath days to do good, or to do evil? to save life, or to destroy *it?*

10 And looking round about upon them all, he said unto the man, Stretch forth thy hand. And he did so: and his hand was restored whole as the other.

11 And they were filled with madness; and communed one with another what they might do to Jesus.

NOTES

Law was good
- Jesus shows you inspite of the Law
- Scribes go by the Law.

- Do you save on the Sabbath day?

- Law impaires us from doing the right thing in certain situations

- Sabbath is made for man

Healing on the Sabbath

Lesson Text: Luke 6:1-11

Related Scriptures: Deuteronomy 5:12-15; I Samuel 21:1-6; Luke 13:10-17

TIME: A.D. 28   PLACE: Galilee

GOLDEN TEXT—"And he said unto them, That the Son of man is Lord also of the sabbath"
(Luke 6:5).

Introduction

Jesus was thoroughly Jewish, and He kept God's commandments for the Jewish people, including the Sabbath. He attended synagogue on the Sabbath in keeping with the way it was observed in His time. Yet He became involved in disputes with other Jewish groups about what was and was not permitted on the Sabbath. The fourth commandment stipulated that no work should be done on the Sabbath (Ex. 20:8-11; Deut. 5:12-15), but the Bible does not specify exactly what that "work" includes.

Jesus used the Sabbath as an occasion for teaching not only with His words but also with His actions. Those who came to observe and criticize Him found that they were not able to defeat Him with arguments.

The themes of healing and the Sabbath come together in Luke 6:1-11. There is more to the Sabbath than Jesus' opponents understood. There is more to Jesus than they understood. Only Jesus truly understood what the Sabbath was all about, and He left us an enduring lesson.

LESSON OUTLINE

I. **LORD OF THE SABBATH—Luke 6:1-5**

II. **DOING GOOD ON THE SABBATH—Luke 6:6-11**

Exposition: Verse by Verse

LORD OF THE SABBATH

LUKE 6:1 And it came to pass on the second sabbath after the first, that he went through the corn fields; and his disciples plucked the ears of corn, and did eat, rubbing them in their hands.

2 And certain of the Pharisees said unto them, Why do ye that which is not lawful to do on the sabbath days?

3 And Jesus answering them said, Have ye not read so much as this, what David did, when himself was an hungred, and they which were with him;

4 How he went into the house of God, and did take and eat the shewbread, and gave also to them that were with him; which it is not lawful to eat but for the priests alone?

5 And he said unto them, That the Son of man is Lord also of the sabbath.

Rubbing grain on the Sabbath (Luke 6:1). Two Sabbath events involving Jesus are found in this Gospel prior to chapter 6. Luke 4:16 records Jesus teaching in the Nazareth synagogue, attending the synagogue on Saturday, "as his custom was." In verses 31-37, we find Him teaching in the Capernaum synagogue on the Sabbath, amazing the people with His power and casting out an unclean spirit.

On this third Sabbath, Jesus was passing through a grain field with His disciples. Presumably, He and the disciples had already attended the synagogue service and were walking in the afternoon or evening. {This was probably a short walk, since Jesus appears to have observed the traditional understanding about limited travel on the Sabbath (cf. Matt. 24:20).}[Q1]

The "corn fields" in Luke 6:1 (and elsewhere in the Bible) were either barley or wheat fields ("corn" in British English is a general word for grain). The husk around each seed of wheat or barley can be removed by rubbing it between two hands. The uncooked seeds are edible and nutritious. It was not considered theft to pick for one's immediate needs: "When thou comest into the standing corn of thy neighbour, then thou mayest pluck the ears with thine hand; but thou shalt not move a sickle unto thy neighbour's standing corn" (Deut. 23:25).

Not lawful on the Sabbath (Luke 6:2). The Pharisees were a fraternity of middle-class men whose common goals included an increased observance of the commandments of Scripture. The Pharisees were respected by the common people but were not the governing religious authority. The party with real political power was the Sadducees, which included the chief priests. They ran the temple and dominated Judea. The Pharisees were based in Jerusalem, not Galilee, and must have been following Jesus to evaluate whether He was a threat, a genuine teacher, or something else.

{What the Pharisees objected to was the disciples picking grain on the Sabbath. By A.D. 200, the rabbis had clarified that thirty-nine types of work were not permitted on the Sabbath, including "reaping" (Mishnah Shabbat 7:2).}[Q2] As for the beliefs of the Pharisees in the first century, the New Testament is our primary source. There are no rabbinic writings earlier than the Mishnah in A.D. 200. So we can make a historical guess that the thirty-nine prohibited types of work were already largely in place for the Pharisees who observed Jesus.

{It is important to realize that neither Jesus nor His disciples violated basic laws like the Sabbath. The disputes between Jesus and the Pharisees over the Sabbath concerned additional rules about what was forbidden on the Sabbath.}[Q3] The rabbis themselves called the Sabbath rules they devised "mountains hanging by a hair" of evidence (Mishnah Hagigah 1:8). In other words, they believed their interpretation of Sabbath rules was strictly a guess and not a biblical requirement.

Thus, the disputes Jesus had with the Pharisees on this matter do not concern overturning the Sabbath law of the Bible as a requirement for Jews. The Sabbath was and remains today a sign between God and the Jewish people (Ex. 31:13). There is no evidence in the Bible that the same Sabbath observance was ever required of Gentiles. Although Christians differ on whether Sunday has replaced Saturday as the "Christian Sabbath," the New Testament implies that observance of the Jewish Sabbath is not required of non-Jewish Christians (Acts 15:19-20; Rom. 14:4-10).

A Sabbath riddle (Luke 6:3-4). The Pharisees observed Jesus, watching for Him to make a mistake that they could publicly criticize. They accused Him of allowing His disciples to break the Sabbath (by their interpretation). Jesus typically answered criticism with riddles and by suggesting interpretations that were beyond the skill of His critics.

Jesus gave His critics a true riddle to ponder with the story from I Samuel 21:6 about David receiving the sacred bread from the tabernacle at Nob (cf. Ex. 25:30). The consecrated bread in the tabernacle was replaced every Sabbath, and it was to be eaten by the priests alone (Lev. 24:5-9). Yet David and his men ate the bread, and the high priest Ahimelech allowed it.

What exactly was Jesus saying? Many think He was teaching that hungry people are permitted to eat even food reserved for priests by ceremonial law. Others think He was pointing to David's authority, as a godly ruler, to make new rulings about what is permitted in relation to the law. Yet there is another way to understand Jesus' riddle.

The event in David's life resembles what was happening with Jesus and the disciples. Jesus may be compared to David, the disciples to David's men, and the Pharisees to Doeg the Edomite and Saul's men who were pursuing David (cf. I Sam. 21:7). {So it does seem that Jesus was claiming to have a moral and royal authority like David's.}Q4 He and His disciples were doing God's work, as David had been, and He had the authority to authorize His disciples to pick grain in a field on the Sabbath. Jesus was using the David story as a sort of parable and illustration of His authority. The Pharisees in this parable are the villains, like Saul's men who persecuted David.

A Sabbath principle (Luke 6:5). There are two prevailing interpretations of what Jesus meant that "the Son of man is Lord also of the sabbath." It is possible that both interpretations are correct, since a teacher of Jesus' caliber can make profound statements that contain more than one truth at the same time. The first interpretation is that "Son of man" here refers to all people. In this interpretation, Jesus would be saying that people are more important than the Sabbath (cf. Mark 2:27). Filling human needs like hunger should not be interfered with by any interpretation of Sabbath laws. According to this way of thinking, doing what is necessary to bring food to the hungry is not to be considered work or a violation of the Sabbath.

{The second interpretation, which fits with the understanding of Jesus' use of the David story above, is that the Son of Man here is Jesus. He was claiming that He had a special authority to make rulings about what was permitted on the Sabbath.}Q5 No doubt this offended the Pharisees, who viewed themselves as experts in the law and authoritative teachers.

It was a startling claim for Jesus to make to people who did not believe in Him. He expected full faith from these Pharisees. By observing Him, they should have been able to see that He truly was worthy of faith as the Lord of the Sabbath and even of the entire law of God.

DOING GOOD ON THE SABBATH

6 And it came to pass also on another sabbath, that he entered into the synagogue and taught: and there was a man whose right hand was withered.

7 And the scribes and Pharisees watched him, whether he would heal on the sabbath day; that they might find an accusation against him.

8 But he knew their thoughts, and said to the man which had the

withered hand, Rise up, and stand forth in the midst. And he arose and stood forth.

9 Then said Jesus unto them, I will ask you one thing; Is it lawful on the sabbath days to do good, or to do evil? to save life, or to destroy it?

10 And looking round about upon them all, he said unto the man, Stretch forth thy hand. And he did so: and his hand was restored whole as the other.

11 And they were filled with madness; and communed one with another what they might do to Jesus.

Two ways on the Sabbath (Luke 6:6-7). The man was full grown and had a hand that had probably been disabled from birth. There was nothing urgent about his condition. He apparently was not in pain. His life was not in danger. Some might argue that Jesus should have waited until after the Sabbath to heal him. Yet, as will be seen later in this passage, there is a principle to be taught here about what is and what is not permitted on the Sabbath. {Jesus deliberately used the occasion of meeting this person not only to do a deed of loving-kindness but also to teach the Pharisees and the people watching what the Sabbath is really about.}Q6

Two ways of observing the Sabbath are on display in verses 6-7. The way of Jesus is teaching and healing. In the synagogue He observed the Sabbath according to the customs of His people, focusing on the words of God in Scripture. He was also observing the Sabbath with the intention of doing good deeds, the work of God in the world.

The opposite way of observing the Sabbath is seen in the reactions of the Pharisees. {They were probably in Galilee to observe and evaluate Jesus (since they likely were from Judea). They were apparently there to criticize.}Q7 They would be caught by Jesus' words (vs. 9) and exposed as lacking true devotion to what the Sab-

bath is supposed to be about.

They wanted to find an accusation against Jesus. Perhaps they expected Him to teach something in the synagogue that they deemed wrong or even blasphemous. Perhaps they expected to see Him heal someone, which in their minds was a violation of the Sabbath.

A Sabbath question (Luke 6:8-9). Did Jesus know their thoughts because He is divine and therefore omniscient? Or did He know them because He understood human hearts? The Gospels often show Jesus knowing things supernaturally (cf. John 16:30; 21:17). Yet they do not require us to see Him as independently exercising omniscience during His earthly ministry.

This is the mystery of the incarnation. When the Son of God became a man, He did not for a moment relinquish His omniscience or any other divine attribute. Yet He also took on all the weaknesses and limitations of fallen humanity, except for sin (Heb. 2:17; 4:15). Scripture indicates that as a man, Jesus did not rely on His own divine omniscience for His knowledge but on the guidance of the Holy Spirit and the revelation of His Father, so that He would be "like unto His brethren" (2:17).

Whether from His knowledge of the human heart or because His Father revealed it to Him, Jesus knew the intent and thoughts of the scribes and Pharisees. So He asked the man with the disabled hand to rise. While the man was standing, Jesus asked a question. As He did when He healed a paralyzed man (cf. Luke 5:23-24), Jesus used this occasion to teach something His disciples would never forget. It was a lesson about the meaning of the kingdom, the people of God, and the mission God has given Messiah and His disciples.

Jesus' question is not just about what is or is not permitted on the Sabbath. It is a question that penetrates to the very heart of God's will. It tells us that a Jewish Sabbath or a Christian Sunday worship service is not automatically godly simply by virtue of being held on the "correct" day. Jesus took these scribes and Pharisees beyond the external form of religion by placing two options before them: to do good on the Sabbath or to do evil.

{The scribes and Pharisees planned evil—to accuse Jesus and get Him into trouble. Jesus planned good—to teach and to heal a man with a disability.}[Q8] Jesus' lesson was pointed and simple: merely keeping the form of a command does not make one righteous. These scribes and Pharisees were in the synagogue on the Sabbath Day, but they were doing evil. {A godly person keeps the intent and the form of God's commands.}[Q9] It is good to obey a commandment like honoring the Sabbath or gathering with the church. Yet the wrong intent or the lack of desire to do what is right ruins even an act of outward obedience.

Life and death on the Sabbath (Luke 6:10-11). Many things in this world need to be restored. The Bible tells us what is broken in people and in creation. The world was subjected to God's curse because of human sin, and it groans for wholeness (Rom. 8:20-22). Jesus came to do the work of God, to teach disciples what God is doing, and to save a people (within Israel and beyond the Jewish people) who would have faith in Him as Messiah. {Jesus is the Restorer of the broken world, and all things will be gathered together in Him (Eph. 1:10).}[Q10]

The question He asked (Is the Sabbath intended for good or evil?) was answered in the miraculous healing of the man with the withered hand. This healing confronted the scribes and Pharisees with two questions. First, how could Jesus have divine power to heal unless He was doing God's will? Second, how could people have any doubt

about the authority of His teaching when such a miracle demonstrated it?

However, the scribes and Pharisees were untouched by the miracle. They were angry at being rightly condemned by His words. The miracle only added to their anger because they were so thoroughly proved wrong.

Jesus' teaching is not just about the Sabbath; it is about all of the commandments that are God's will. Jesus did the Father's work on the Father's day, and Jesus' disciples are to imitate Him.
—*Derek Leman.*

QUESTIONS

1. What might lead us to believe that the walk through the grain field was a short one?

2. Why did the Pharisees think Jesus' disciples were breaking the Sabbath law?

3. Did Jesus and His disciples actually violate God' s Sabbath law? Explain.

4. What was Jesus' point in citing the example of David and the tabernacle bread?

5. Who is the Lord of the Sabbath, and what does that mean?

6. Why did Jesus not wait until after the Sabbath to heal the man with the withered hand?

7. Why were the Pharisees in Galilee?

8. How was Jesus keeping the Sabbath for good while the scribes and Pharisees were keeping it for evil?

9. What principle about obedience did Jesus teach through His question to the scribes and Pharisees?

10. How is Jesus' Sabbath restoration of what was broken a picture of what is to come?
—*Derek Leman.*

Preparing to Teach the Lesson

The lesson this week deals with honoring the Sabbath. It came to the fore in the life of Jesus because of the rules the Pharisees added to the original Sabbath law. These became—to them, at least—more important than the commandment God had given. Jesus did not share their perspective.

TODAY'S AIM

Facts: to reveal how traditions became more sacred than the Word of God to the scribes and Pharisees.

Principle: to show that God's Word can stand on its own and does not need man's rules added to it.

Application: to obey God from the heart, not just in outward form.

INTRODUCING THE LESSON

Within the Christian community, one finds a wide range of ideas about the Sabbath Day. Some follow the Old Testament and honor Saturday because God rested on the seventh day of Creation (Gen. 2:2-3). The Jews followed that pattern.

Early on, the church worshipped on the first day of the week (Sunday) because it was the day the Lord was raised from the dead. But Jewish believers continued to observe Saturday as the Sabbath Day as well. As time went by and the church became more Gentile in makeup, Sunday became the Christian day of rest and worship.

Today there are differing opinions and convictions as to what is allowable and what is not on the Lord's Day. It is often pointed out that the commandment concerning the Sabbath is the only one of the Ten Commandments that is not repeated in some form in the New Testament, thereby granting liberty in that regard. Ask the class where they stand on the matter. There will likely be differences of opinion.

DEVELOPING THE LESSON

We will examine two episodes in the life of Jesus to gain something of a grip on how He viewed the matter.

1. Caring for one's own needs (Luke 6:1-5). Each of the three Synoptic Gospels contains the accounts found in this week's lesson (cf. Matt. 12:1-14; Mark 2:23—3:6) and should be consulted. Each has something unique to report. That there are variations within the reports should not be cause for concern, for even today several writers might report different aspects of the same story without contradicting one another. Besides that, keep in mind that the Holy Spirit is behind all Scripture, superintending its formation. We have what He wanted us to have.

Jesus and His disciples traveled through a grain field on the Sabbath Day. They picked some heads of grain and removed the chaff in order to eat. This caught the eye of some Pharisees. In their minds, what the disciples had done was nothing less than harvesting and threshing—unlawful work for that day of the week.

In response to their query, Jesus challenged the Pharisees to remember the Scripture where David and those with him took and ate the shewbread from the tabernacle. This was usually reserved for priests only, and yet they were not guilty before God (cf. I Sam. 21:1-9). In fact, 22:10 implies that the priest asked God whether granting David his request for the bread was permissible and was obviously told it was.

The use of that example from Scripture was pertinent and seems to have been chosen to communicate that since it was fine for David and his men, it should also be fine for the Son of David and His men to meet their needs on the Sabbath. Though not explicit in the Samuel text, it is quite likely the incident occurred on a Sabbath Day since 21:6 indicates that the shewbread had just been replaced.

Then Jesus proclaimed Himself Lord of the Sabbath, a statement that claimed deity, for it certainly was God who established the day. Luke was silent on the Pharisees' reaction until after the following episode.

2. Caring for the needs of others (Luke 6:6-11). On another Sabbath Day, Jesus was teaching in a synagogue. Present in the congregation was a man with a withered hand. Also present were some eagle-eyed Pharisees and scribes who were watching Jesus to see whether He would heal on the Sabbath. They obviously hoped He would so they could bring a charge of breaking the Sabbath against Him.

However, knowing their intentions, Jesus took up the challenge and asked the man with the infirmity to stand where everyone could see him. Jesus then directed a question to everyone present about the lawfulness of doing good on the Sabbath. He gave them time to respond as He looked at each man. The account in Mark tells us that Jesus was "grieved for the hardness of their hearts" (3:5).

The afflicted man held out his hand at Jesus' request and was healed. The earlier episode involved Jesus referring to a text for His argument, but here He performed a miracle to make His case. There could be no doubt whatsoever that Jesus was a miracle worker, furthering His claim to deity, but that mattered little to His accusers. Filled with rage, they took counsel with one another about how to handle this lawbreaker.

Jewish tradition, built over a long time, had taken the place of Scripture. The tradition was based on a misunder-

standing of Scripture, and Jesus was attempting to show and teach them the correct way to view the Sabbath. Mark 2:27 records that Jesus said the whole point of a day of rest and worship was for man's benefit. The Creator knew that man needed such a day, but it did not mean he could not care for himself or for the needs of others on that day.

ILLUSTRATING THE LESSON

Man needs a day of rest and worship for physical, emotional, and spiritual reasons.

A DAY OF WORSHIP AND REST

A DAY OF RENEWAL

CONCLUDING THE LESSON

There is a reason why both Mark and Luke precede these episodes with the parable of new wine. As new wine needed new wineskins, so Jesus' teaching required a new mind set. Christians need to continually search the Scriptures and make God's Word the basis for their decisions.

ANTICIPATING THE NEXT LESSON

Jesus is Lord of the Sabbath because He is the Creator of the Sabbath. Next week we will see how His authority over the wind and sea shows us that He is the Creator of all things.

—*Darrell W. McKay.*

PRACTICAL POINTS

1. God's people were required to provide food for the hungry; we should likewise care for the poor (Luke 6:1; cf. Deut. 23:25).

2. Self-righteous people are always enforcing rules that enable them to condemn others (Luke 6:2).

3. The heart of the law leads us to praise God (Luke 6:3-4; cf. I Sam. 21:1-6).

4. Jesus is to be honored as Lord on the Sabbath—and on every other day (Luke 6:5).

5. We humans tend to look for opportunities to criticize other people (vss. 6-7).

6. Believers in Jesus have many opportunities to honor Him by doing good—sometimes at great personal cost (vss. 8-11).

—Paul R. Bawden.

RESEARCH AND DISCUSSION

1. Is it ever necessary to violate the letter of one law in order to obey the spirit of another (cf. I Sam. 21:1-6)?

2. What lesson did Jesus teach when He healed on the Sabbath?

3. What does Jesus' healing of the man's withered hand tell us about Him and His power?

4. What was Jesus telling the Pharisees about their traditions, and how does that apply to us?

5. Why did Jesus' words and actions stir up such anger in the scribes and Pharisees (Luke 6:11; cf. John 5:18)?

—Paul R. Bawden.

ILLUSTRATED HIGH POINTS

Have ye not read? (Luke 6:3)

It is simply amazing how much of what we read influences us and even changes the way we think and how we look at different things.

Martin Luther was a devout seeker of God who was not satisfied with the rituals of the church he was in. He searched the Scriptures for an answer. One day as he was reading the Bible, he came across the glorious truth that the just shall live by faith. A burden was lifted off his shoulders, and Luther was a free man. It transformed his life. The Bible is God's living Word, and it speaks to our hearts if we only read it. The Pharisees in our lesson this week missed that message.

Is it lawful on the sabbath days to do good, or to do evil? (vs. 9)

Legalism is a dangerous thing, especially when it comes to matters of faith, for it focuses on outward things rather than on matters of the heart.

It is common to experience something akin to this in a high school or college speech class. On one occasion my fellow classmates were to critique a speech I made. I was appalled to hear one student comment that a spot on my shirt had caught his attention and distracted him from listening to what I was saying. While the spot was certainly noticeable, it was inconsequential compared to my speech.

Legalism is often like that situation. It focuses on the things that are not really so important and ignores that which needs our attention. In religion, we can often be distracted from doing what God wants us to do and instead create our own rules. Jesus pointed out that the practice of our faith should transform the world.

—A. Koshy Muthalaly.

Golden Text Illuminated

"And he said unto them, That the Son of man is Lord also of the sabbath" (Luke 6:5).

The Pharisees had developed a complex, detailed set of rules regarding the Sabbath. With a catalog of thirty-nine types of work to avoid, (with subdivisions further classifying these), they had very clearly laid out what activities they considered appropriate and inappropriate on the Sabbath. When they saw Jesus' disciples plucking grain, the Pharisees immediately accused them of harvesting and reaping, which was forbidden. They confronted Jesus. Why wasn't He stopping His disciples?

The confrontation would get even more personal when it came to healing a man on the Sabbath. There it was not the disciples but Jesus Himself who was accused of wrongdoing.

Jesus' response to them was straightforward: "the Son of man is Lord also of the sabbath." The Pharisees claimed to have the authority to determine what was and was not appropriate on the day, but they were wrong; Jesus is the only one who has the authority to decide such things. The Pharisees had created long lists of human traditions, but only God's Word is binding on His people.

Jesus used an example to emphasize His point: in I Samuel 21, David goes to the priest Ahimelech and is given the shewbread, which was designated as ceremonially special and for the priests alone to eat (cf. Lev. 24:9). That was not a man-made tradition; it was a divinely appointed provision.

Under any normal circumstances, it was not lawful for David and his men to eat the shewbread. Jesus rightly reasons that if the priest had the authority to give David this divinely designated bread, how much greater authority did He—the Son of Man and the Lord of the Sabbath—possess to do away with the man-made traditions of the Pharisees! Just as David was not condemned for eating the shewbread when it was a necessity and given by the priest, so the disciples should not have been condemned for plucking grain to eat on the Sabbath.

When Jesus later healed the man with a withered hand, He declared that the Sabbath had been given to do good and to save life. The Pharisees were so caught up in their traditions that they had missed the entire point of the Sabbath. But as Jesus pointed out in Mark 2:27, the day had been given to be a blessing, not to burden people with rules.

God certainly prohibited work on the Sabbath, but His intent was to provide people with a day of rest, not to force them to literally count the number of steps taken outside the home, (as some Pharisees did) or to condemn people for doing necessary things like eating, or for doing good things like healing.

Of course, it was one thing for Jesus to *claim* to have the authority to brush aside all of their traditions. Anyone can *claim* to have authority, but actually *having* authority is a different matter. I could claim to be the president of the United States, but the guards are not likely to let me walk into the Oval Office! By miraculously healing the man's withered hand, Jesus not only did something good and merciful; He also demonstrated that He truly was the Son and the Lord of the Sabbath, and He has the authority to determine what is right.

—*Tom Greene.*

Heart of the Lesson

We live in a world full of rules and regulations. While some laws seem unnecessary and some laws are annoying, laws are given for a reason and are to be heeded. Whether we agree with a law or not, it is the law. In Luke 6 we read that the Pharisees interrogated Jesus regarding what they felt were illegal acts by His disciples.

1. Out of necessity (Luke 6:1-5). The law says to remember the Sabbath, to keep it holy, and to refrain from work. The disciples were not trying to break the law by plucking grain on the Sabbath; they were simply hungry. Had the religious leaders forgotten that the Sabbath existed to benefit people?

In our culture, we have posted speed limit signs; however, an ambulance in the midst of an emergency is allowed to go beyond the posted speed limit without penalty. Why? Because there is a life-and-death situation. In the midst of a possible fatal circumstance, seconds count.

Jesus reminded the Pharisees that even King David ate bread that was reserved only for the priests. Jesus informed the Pharisees that He has authority over the Sabbath and the laws regarding the Sabbath. Who knows the law and how to interpret it better than the One who made it?

2. Mercy (Luke 6:6-10). The Pharisees were tired of Jesus pushing their religious buttons. Jesus challenged their mindset and their traditions. They said it was unlawful to heal on the Sabbath; however, was it better to observe their self-imposed protocols or to save a life?

In some churches, men are not allowed to pray with women and vice versa. Often this is wise practice. However, one time a friend of mine was pressed by God to pray for a gentleman who had come to our church. She had not seen him before and could not shake the feeling that she needed to go over and pray for him. When she saw two male elders praying with the man, she figured he was all right; nevertheless, the urgency in her spirit never left. She never did pray for the man. Did she miss an opportunity to see God's work in someone's life simply because of protocol?

Jesus had mercy on the man with the withered hand and healed him despite what day of the week it was. God is not bound by our rules and regulations. He will confound the religious traditionalists if necessary to display His unfailing love, mercy, and grace.

3. Outrage (Luke 6:11). When God manifests His glory, it often puts those who hate Him to shame. The Pharisees were so angry with the way Jesus had outsmarted them again that they plotted against Him.

When we listen to the still, small voice inside of us that urges us to step outside of man-made traditions to bring about freedom for the captive, healing for the infirm, and peace for the oppressed, we may be labeled as rebels. We may endure scorn and shame; nevertheless, what is our reputation compared to the eternal destiny of a soul?

At the same time, we should not ignore protocols simply for the sake of ignoring them. We must acknowledge the *motives* of Jesus and His disciples. The disciples plucked grain out of necessity, and Jesus healed because He is merciful. Remember that the purpose of the Sabbath was to worship God and give man rest.

—*Kristin Reeg.*

World Missions

Eric Liddell's testimony was so stunning that his story was not only written about but also made into a movie. However, the most incredible parts of his story—his years in missionary service in China and his internment in a war camp until his death—are not the things most of the world knows about him.

The world knows about him through one choice he made regarding God's day of rest and worship. Eric Liddell was a runner, the best in all of Scotland. He was good enough to be in the Olympics. He was on his way to fame and victory until he found out that one of his Olympic races was scheduled for Sunday.

It was an important race. At the time it seemed his entire future hinged on it. And in a way, it did. People pushed and prodded Eric to go ahead and race on the Lord's Day. God would understand. It was, after all, the Olympics. He could not just back out.

However, that is exactly what Eric Liddell did. Making a very difficult personal decision, he did not run the race. He wanted to honor and obey God more than find his own glory.

And in the "upside-down" way God works, God used that very decision to give Eric Liddell worldwide fame.

Liddell was concerned that if he gave in and ran a race on Sunday, his testimony before the world would be damaged. Instead, he would show the world that his commitment to the Lord and His ways was stronger than whatever distraction might come up.

What about us? If we go to ball games, play sports, or do other activities on God's Day, what does that do to our witness?

Perhaps, if asked, you would say, "Well, sure, it's important for a pastor or a church leader not to do those things. People are watching them. But with us regular Christians, it's not that big of a deal."

That is what people kept saying to Eric Liddell: "It's not a big deal."

Had he raced, he would likely have won and gained a fleeting pleasure and some glory. The fact that he did not, though, shot him to a level of witness that is still affecting people today!

Is that not preferable to "It's not a big deal"? Now it is true that genuine believers differ on how the Sabbath applies today. Each of us needs to prayerfully search Scripture to determine what God requires of us on the Lord's Day (cf. Rom. 14:5). But however God convicts us, we should not stray from that. If we compromise what God has pressed on our hearts, what influence will that have on those around us? What influence will that have on our children?

Note that Jesus never encouraged making a bunch of rules just to say you were keeping rules. He never wanted the Sabbath to be all about pride in what you did or did not do, particularly when it comes to judging others. Jesus did good on the Sabbath. He brought people out of darkness into light, and He helped those in need. To Him, it was less about certain activities and more about honoring God and His day.

Setting aside a day for the Lord is not an easy thing to do in today's fast-paced, activity-filled society. Saying no to certain activities might be difficult. You might be mocked or criticized for it, and your children might complain. In the end, however, that very choice may be the thing God uses to bring people to Himself.

Eric's last words, those that summed up his life, were "It's complete surrender."

—Kimberly Rae.

The Jewish Aspect

Jews have rigorously observed the Sabbath for over two thousand years. During the intertestamental times, numerous nonscriptural practices arose. By the time of Jesus, these had become set regulations.

Jewish belief concerning the Sabbath is seen in the conflict between Jesus and the Pharisees when "his disciples plucked the ears of corn [that is, wheat or barley], and did eat, rubbing them in their hands" on a Sabbath (Luke 6:1). The Pharisees challenged, "Why do ye that which is not lawful to do on the sabbath days?" (vs. 2).

The Pharisees viewed the disciples' actions as a violation of the Sabbath. According to their traditions, merely plucking the heads of grain was the same as reaping. Rubbing grain in one's hand was the same as threshing. Throwing away the husks of grain was the same as winnowing. By eating the grain, they showed that they had prepared food. All four of those actions were violations of their Sabbath traditions. The four acts were included in a list of thirty-nine actions that Jewish rabbis taught were forbidden on the Sabbath. Because God repeated the Sabbath commandment in the context of instructions for building the tabernacle (Ex. 31:13-17), the rabbis concluded that all types of work that were required in building the tabernacle must cease on the Sabbath. Reaping, threshing, winnowing, and preparing were among these forbidden actions.

Contemporary, observant Jews still assert that "all of these tasks are prohibited, as well as any task that operates by the same principle or has the same purpose. In addition, the rabbis have prohibited handling any implement that is intended to perform one of the above purposes (for example, a hammer, a pencil or a match)" (Judaism 101, "Shabbat," www.jewfaq.org).

Because of the Sabbath prohibitions, observant Jews carefully prepare for it. All food preparation is done in advance so that nothing is made on the Sabbath. Washing of clothes should be done on Thursday, with bathing on Friday afternoon, along with cleaning the house and setting the table. "It is customary in Jewish communities to signal or announce the arrival of the Sabbath half an hour or an hour in advance, so that people can stop working and complete their preparations" ("Preparations for the Sabbath," torah.org).

Observant Jews are also careful about Sabbath activities. Playing a board game, for example, is permitted only if no one writes down the score. A game would not be appropriate if it is a business-oriented game. Playing chess is permitted, since it is considered a pastime activity ("Scrabble, Monopoly and Chess on Shabbat," ohr.edu).

Jesus did not argue the fact that God set apart the Sabbath as a day to rest and honor the Lord. He did, however, strongly refute the Pharisaical additions to the law. David's example of eating the shewbread, which was restricted to the priests, showed that the support of human life took priority over obeying the letter of the law (Luke 6:3-4). More important, Jesus asserted that He was Lord of the Sabbath (vs. 5). Since the Sabbath originated with God, Jesus' claim to be Lord of the Sabbath declared that He was equal to the God who gave the Sabbath. Jews and Christians alike must be careful about adding personal restrictions to the laws God has given us, whether concerning the Sabbath, Sunday, or any other holy day.

—R. Larry Overstreet.

Guiding the Superintendent

"I say unto you, That except your righteousness shall exceed the righteousness of the scribes and Pharisees, ye shall in no case enter into the kingdom of heaven" (Matt. 5:20). In the process of ushering in God's new kingdom reign, Jesus challenged many aspects of what the religious leaders of His day taught and what the vast majority of people believed. This week we see Him challenging the Pharisees' teaching on how to keep the Sabbath.

On the surface, the fourth commandment is pretty clear: "The seventh day is the sabbath of the Lord thy God: in it thou shalt not do any work" (Ex. 20:10). As basic as this command might appear, it has a long history of being a very difficult passage of Scripture to apply. The people of Jesus' day were no exception. The Pharisees had pretty well figured out a system of what they could and could not do on the Sabbath. Jesus turned all this on its head. In the process, He conveyed to us a couple of great truths about the Sabbath.

DEVOTIONAL OUTLINE

1. A time for doing good for others (Luke 6:1-5). It seems that the disciples and Jesus were walking through a grain field one Sabbath. As was the custom, they were picking and eating some of the grain. This action greatly disturbed the Pharisees, who understood this type of action as a violation of the prohibition against working on the Sabbath. The problem was really *when* they were doing this—on the Sabbath.

The scribes and Pharisees complained to Jesus, who responded by quoting from Scripture. He reminded them how David had set aside certain ceremonial laws when he ate the special bread that was intended only for the priests.

Jesus followed this with an appeal to His own sovereignty. As the Lord of the Sabbath, He had the right to determine what could be done on the Sabbath. As the Lord of the Sabbath, Jesus taught that a person can obey the Sabbath law and still use the day to help others with their needs.

2. A time for works of mercy (Luke 6:6-11). In the Pharisees' view, healing of most kinds was considered work and was thus prohibited on the Sabbath. At the most, an injury could be kept from getting worse; it was not to be made better.

To make a point, Jesus healed a man with a deformed hand on the Sabbath. He could have waited one more day, but He did not. Before the healing, Jesus asked the crowd if it was right to do good on the Sabbath. The answer, of course, is yes!

For Jesus, the Sabbath was a time to help those in need. He drove home His point by asking whether it was right to do harm on the Sabbath, implying that the Pharisees were the ones breaking the Sabbath by plotting to kill Him. The key to Sabbath observance is doing good for those around you.

AGE-GROUP EMPHASES

Children: This is a great lesson to help children understand the true meaning of taking a day off to serve God. How can they serve? Have them suggest ways they can do good for others.

Youths: Have the teens suggest someone they know who could use some help from the group after church this week.

Adults: God has ordained that His people take one day off to serve Him. This lesson can help adults understand what that service is all about.

—*Martin R. Dahlquist*

SCRIPTURE LESSON TEXT

MATT. 14:22 And straightway Jesus constrained his disciples to get into a ship, and to go before him unto the other side, while he sent the multitudes away.

23 And when he had sent the multitudes away, he went up into a mountain apart to pray: and when the evening was come, he was there alone.

24 But the ship was now in the midst of the sea, tossed with waves: for the wind was contrary.

25 And in the fourth watch of the night Jesus went unto them, walking on the sea.

26 And when the disciples saw him walking on the sea, they were troubled, saying, It is a spirit; and they cried out for fear.

27 But straightway Jesus spake unto them, saying, Be of good cheer; it is I; be not afraid.

28 And Peter answered him and said, Lord, if it be thou, bid me come unto thee on the water.

29 And he said, Come. And when Peter was come down out of the ship, he walked on the water, to go to Jesus.

30 But when he saw the wind boisterous, he was afraid; and beginning to sink, he cried, saying, Lord, save me.

31 And immediately Jesus stretched forth *his* hand, and caught him, and said unto him, O thou of little faith, wherefore didst thou doubt?

32 And when they were come into the ship, the wind ceased.

33 Then they that were in the ship came and worshipped him, saying, Of a truth thou art the Son of God.

34 And when they were gone over, they came into the land of Gennesaret.

35 And when the men of that place had knowledge of him, they sent out into all that country round about, and brought unto him all that were diseased;

36 And besought him that they might only touch the hem of his garment: and as many as touched were made perfectly whole.

NOTES

Jesus' Mighty Power

Lesson Text: Matthew 14:22-36

Related Scriptures: Matthew 8:23-27; Luke 8:22-25; Matthew 9:27-31, 35

TIME: A.D. 29   PLACES: by the Sea of Galilee; Sea of Galilee; Gennesaret

---

GOLDEN TEXT—"When they were come into the ship, the wind ceased. Then they that were in the ship came and worshipped him, saying, Of a truth thou art the Son of God" (Matthew 14:32-33).

Introduction

We often think of Jesus' miracles as expressions of His compassion. The Gospels do, in fact, record several instances when Jesus' healings were motivated by His compassion for the suffering (cf. Matt. 14:14; 20:34; Mark 1:41). And it was compassion that moved Him to miraculously feed the multitude (Matt. 15:32-38).

However, Jesus' mighty works were not designed *merely* to relieve the suffering of people who would suffer again and eventually die. His miracles had another, greater purpose: they revealed who He was.

Through the working of miracles, Jesus was fulfilling messianic prophecy. Thus, the miracles confirmed that He was Israel's Messiah (11:2-6). As such, the miracles also validated Jesus' teaching (cf. John 3:2).

While the nation of Israel ultimately rejected Christ—even in the face of His miraculous works—certain individuals, especially His disciples, grasped what the miracles truly revealed about the Lord. When they did so, they responded in humble worship.

LESSON OUTLINE

I. PRAYER ON THE MOUNTAIN—
   Matt. 14:22-23

II. TROUBLE ON THE SEA—
   Matt. 14:24-33

III. MINISTRY ON THE SHORE—
   Matt. 14:34-36

Exposition: Verse by Verse

PRAYER ON THE MOUNTAIN

MATT. 14:22 And straightway Jesus constrained his disciples to get into a ship, and to go before him unto the other side, while he sent the multitudes away.

23 And when he had sent the multitudes away, he went up into a mountain apart to pray: and when the evening was come, he was there alone.

The events recorded in Matthew 14 took place in the third year of Jesus' public ministry. {At this point, Israel's religious leadership had made it clear they would never accept Him (cf. 12:22-45), and Jesus' ministry was now focused primarily on the training of His twelve disciples.}^Q1

The miraculous feeding of the multitude recorded in 14:13-21 was yet another confirmation of Jesus' messiahship, but it was also used to instruct the disciples, whom Jesus employed in carrying out the work.

When the crowd's hunger had been satisfied, Jesus had further instructions for His disciples. He "constrained" them to get into a boat and "go before him unto the other side" (vs. 22). "Constrained" has the idea of using force. It suggests a very forceful command to the disciples. Why this was necessary is not altogether clear, but they did not want to be separated from Jesus at this time.

The group was at the northeastern end of the Sea of Galilee. Jesus' plan was apparently to send the disciples ahead of Him and meet them later at Gennesaret (vs. 34), on the western shore of the sea. Presumably, He would walk the six or seven miles around the northern shore to join them there.

{The reason for sending the disciples away becomes clear in verse 23, for as soon as they departed, Jesus "went up into a mountain apart to pray."}^Q2 Though He is God the Son, in becoming man, Jesus was dependent on His Heavenly Father, just as we are. The crowd He had fed was so enthusiastic that they wanted to "take him by force, to make him a king" (John 6:15). The religious elite hated Him, and His own disciples often misunderstood Him. There was much He needed to pray about.

Knowing what lay ahead, Jesus took time alone with the Father to pray. Undoubtedly, His prayers concerned His disciples as well as Himself. Jesus' example reminds us of the priority prayer should have in our lives. As important as Jesus' work on earth was, He took time alone to pray. So should we.

TROUBLE ON THE SEA

24 But the ship was now in the midst of the sea, tossed with waves: for the wind was contrary.

25 And in the fourth watch of the night Jesus went unto them, walking on the sea.

26 And when the disciples saw him walking on the sea, they were troubled, saying, It is a spirit; and they cried out for fear.

27 But straightway Jesus spake unto them, saying, Be of good cheer; it is I; be not afraid.

28 And Peter answered him and said, Lord, if it be thou, bid me come unto thee on the water.

29 And he said, Come. And when Peter was come down out of the ship, he walked on the water, to go to Jesus.

30 But when he saw the wind boisterous, he was afraid; and beginning to sink, he cried, saying, Lord, save me.

31 And immediately Jesus stretched forth his hand, and caught him, and said unto him, O thou of little faith, wherefore didst thou doubt?

32 And when they were come into the ship, the wind ceased.

33 Then they that were in the ship came and worshipped him, saying, Of a truth thou art the Son of God.

The storm (Matt. 14:24). In contrast to the quiet mountain refuge where Jesus prayed, the disciples in the boat were being battered by waves that were pushed by the strong winds of a storm. While the trip would normally not have taken the boat far from shore, it was now "in the midst of the sea." They had been driven some three or four miles out from the land (cf. John 6:19) by a wind from the opposite direction.

The Saviour (Matt. 14:25-26). Jesus was very much aware of the disciples' situation. {He was the one who had sent them out on the sea, and He was praying for them, so they were protected despite the dangerous waters.}[Q3]

The Lord may send us into difficult places, but He never abandons us. He is the Master who sends, the Intercessor who prays, and the Saviour who delivers.

Deliverance for the disciples came when the Saviour arrived, walking on the sea (vs. 25). It was "in the fourth watch," or between 3:00 A.M. and 6:00 A.M., that Jesus appeared. This suggests they had probably been battling the waves for a number of hours.

The sight of someone walking on the water unnerved the disciples. They had witnessed many of Jesus' miracles, but they did not immediately associate the figure they saw with Jesus. {They were fearful and assumed this must be a ghost. After all, a man could not walk on water!}[Q4]

The assurance (Matt. 14:27). In the midst of their fear, the disciples heard the reassuring voice of their Master. "Be of good cheer" means "take courage" or "be comforted." Together with Jesus' words "be not afraid," this conveyed a sense of comfort to the disciples. There was no need to fear the waves or the figure walking on the sea, because the one approaching them was Jesus Himself.

The test (Matt. 14:28-29). {We might be tempted to fault Peter for his request that Jesus allow him to also walk on the water. However, Jesus did not fault him but rather granted his request.}[Q5] It seems Peter's request was not designed merely to prove to himself that this was really Jesus. On the contrary, it was an act of faith. Gone was the fear that had encompassed the disciples moments before. Now Peter simply wanted to be with the Lord.

"Anybody can sit in the boat and watch. But it takes a person of real faith to leave the boat and walk on the water" (Wiersbe, *Meet Your King,* Victor). At Jesus' command to come, Peter left the boat and walked on the water toward Jesus. "Peter's full attention had been centered in faith on Jesus, and the Lord had honored his faith by granting him supernatural power" (Pfeiffer and Harrison, eds., *The Wycliffe Bible Commentary,* Moody).

The failure (Matt. 14:30-31). Peter's faith did not endure for long. When he saw how strong the wind was, fear gripped him and he began to sink. The faith that had moved him to get out of the boat now failed him. As soon as his attention turned away from the Lord and onto his circumstances, his faith faltered.

There is an obvious lesson here for all of us. As long as our attention is focused on our circumstances rather than on the Lord who controls our circumstances, our faith will not grow and will not sustain us over the long term.

While Peter's faith faltered, he was not altogether without faith. As he began to sink, he called out to the One he knew could save him. Jesus immediately reached out and caught Peter.

Along with giving Peter His hand to pull him from the waves, Jesus also offered a rebuke. He described His disciple as having "little faith" (vs. 31). Peter had been with Jesus for more than two years. He had witnessed much and learned much from his Master, but his faith was still small. Nevertheless, Peter did have faith, and that faith, once mature, would make him a bulwark of the early church, a man of extraordinary commitment to Christ.

{What made Peter's faith small at that moment was doubt.}Q6 The Greek word in this context is a combination of two words and conveys the image of being "pulled two ways" (Robertson, *Word Pictures in the New Testament,* Broadman). Peter's faith in Christ pulled him toward the Lord, but his fear of the waves overwhelmed him and pulled him down.

Temptations constantly tug at us, attempting to pull us toward the world. Trying situations that come into our lives pull us toward worldly solutions. It takes a strong and growing faith to keep us walking in paths of righteousness, and faith comes from hearing the Word of God (Rom. 10:17). The best thing we can do to grow in our faith is to consistently read, learn, and obey Scripture.

The result (Matt. 14:32-33). {When Jesus and Peter reached the boat and entered it, the wind stopped.}Q7 The cessation of the wind at that very moment could conceivably be understood as natural, but the timing and the reaction of the disciples suggest it was miraculous. On another occasion, a raging storm on the sea ceased at Jesus' command (Mark 4:39).

{Those in the boat responded to Jesus' appearance, His walking on the water, and the calming of the sea not just with astonishment but with reverence. They came before Him and "worshipped him" (Matt. 14:33).}Q8 This indicates that they fell at His feet in an act of reverence. {It is clear this was not an act appropriate for any great person; it was an act of true worship, for the disciples acknowledged Jesus as the Son of God.}Q9

The term "Son of God" was probably "equivalent to the Divine Deliverer, the Messiah or Christ. Though such identification had been made earlier by the disciples ([John] 1:41, 49), there was an ever increasing realization by the Twelve of what these terms meant" (Pfeiffer and Harrison). While they may not have understood the full implications of Jesus' deity, they acknowledged Him as such in an appropriate way—through worship.

Apparently, only the disciples witnessed the miracle recorded in these verses. Furthermore, the miracle may not have been "necessary" in the sense of being needed to save the disciples. The experienced fishermen among them may well have been able to weather the storm and in time bring the boat safely to shore. And, of course, Jesus knew when He insisted that they go ahead of Him what they would face on the sea.

All this points to the fact that the miracle was designed to teach the disciples more about the Lord Jesus. As a result of it, they saw Him more clearly as the God-sent Messiah. They learned that He has authority even over nature and began to appreciate more deeply that He knows, cares for, and never abandons His own.

MINISTRY ON THE SHORE

34 And when they were gone over, they came into the land of Gennesaret.

35 And when the men of that place had knowledge of him, they sent out into all that country round about, and brought unto him all that were diseased;

36 And besought him that they might only touch the hem of his garment: and as many as touched were made perfectly whole.

Arrival in Gennesaret (Matt. 14:34). Matthew simply records the arrival of the boat with Jesus and the disciples at Gennesaret. John 6:21 says that when Jesus and Peter got into the boat, the vessel immediately was at Gennesaret, indicating another miraculous event.

Gennesaret is a fertile plain along the Sea of Galilee south of Capernaum. In fact, the Sea of Galilee was also called the Lake of Gennesaret (cf. Luke 5:1).

Response in Gennesaret (Matt. 14:35-36). {It appears that Jesus had not been to this place previously; however, there were men there who recognized Him, perhaps having seen Him or heard of Him in other parts of Galilee. These men quickly spread the word throughout the area that Jesus was present.}[Q10]

The news of Jesus' arrival attracted many people from around the region. They brought people who were suffering from disease that they might merely touch the edge of Jesus' garment. In doing so, these people experienced divine healing. Perhaps they had heard of the woman who had been healed in Capernaum when she touched the hem of Jesus' garment (9:20-22). Their faith was evident in their actions. They sought no special attention or favor but simply the slightest contact with Jesus, believing this was all that was needed.

Even if they did not fully understand who Jesus was or put their faith in Him personally, the people of Gennesaret believed He had the power to heal. Yet, "the *main* point of the story is not the faith of men—whether of the sick or of those who brought them—but the power and love of Christ" (Hendriksen, *The Gospel of Matthew,* Baker).

The miracles on the sea, as well as the healing miracles at Gennesaret, reveal to us again the mighty power of Christ. But they also reveal our all-powerful Saviour as the loving Shepherd who knows us and cares for us. He takes time to teach His children about Himself and to model the kind of love and compassion we are to exhibit to the world around us.

We should stand in awe of Christ's power and the way He used that power to minister to people. Just as the Lord sent His disciples out onto the sea, so He has sent us into the world (John 17:18). It is not an easy place to live and serve the Lord, but the One who sent us has also equipped us with the power of the Holy Spirit. In His power we are to minister to the hurting, the unloved, and the lost, sharing the gospel of Christ as His representatives on this earth.

—Jarl K. Waggoner.

QUESTIONS

1. What was the focus of Jesus' ministry at this time?
2. Why did Jesus send the disciples ahead of Him?
3. Why can we say that the disciples were not really in danger?
4. Why were the disciples frightened when they saw Jesus approaching the boat?
5. What request did Peter make of Jesus? How did Jesus respond?
6. In what sense was Peter's faith "little" (Matt. 14:31)?
7. What happened as soon as Jesus and Peter reached the boat?
8. How did the disciples respond to what they had witnessed on the sea?
9. Who did the disciples proclaim Jesus to be?
10. How did the people of Gennesaret respond to Jesus' arrival there?

—Jarl K. Waggoner.

Preparing to Teach the Lesson

Over the past few weeks we have considered how the power of Jesus over demons, sickness, and circumstances demonstrates His divine authority. Today we will see that Jesus also has authority over creation itself, because He is its Creator.

We will also see that when we follow Christ by faith, we experience the benefits of His divine authority. We can have confidence in Him even during our greatest challenges, because all power belongs to Him and He will always be with us (cf. Matt. 28:18, 20).

TODAY'S AIM

Facts: to get a fresh glimpse of the power of Christ.

Principle: to have greater confidence in the power of Christ to work on our behalf.

Application: to trust the all-powerful Christ for the challenges we face.

INTRODUCING THE LESSON

People generally are awestruck by demonstrations of power. Auto racing fans are captivated by the power of the cars as they speed around the track. Spectators at air shows are fascinated by the power in the jets that fly overhead. We are a people who love powerful things.

Far more than being captivated by the power of engines, we should be in awe of the power of the omnipotent Christ. Let us get a clearer picture of the power of Christ and trust Him for the challenges we face.

DEVELOPING THE LESSON

1. Jesus prays (Matt. 14:22-23). Jesus' miraculous feeding of the five thousand (vss. 13-21) was not only an act of great compassion toward thousands of hungry people but also a demonstration of His great power to His disciples. After that event, Jesus wanted to give the disciples another demonstration of His power, so He sent them away in a boat across the Sea of Galilee (vs. 22).

Jesus then left His disciples and went to a mountain alone to pray. Spending time in prayer at night was a habit of our Lord (cf. Mark 1:35; Luke 5:16; 6:12; 9:18). His model stands as a great example for us to imitate.

2. The disciples row (Matt. 14:24). As the Lord prayed alone, the disciples found themselves some distance from the shore (cf. John 6:19) in the middle of a storm. Matthew tells us that they were "tossed with waves: for the wind was contrary" (14:24). Mark adds that they were "toiling in rowing" (6:48). The disciples certainly faced a difficult situation!

3. Jesus walks (Matt. 14:25-27). As Jesus observed His struggling disciples, He left His mountain prayer site and walked toward them on the surface of the water! Jesus walked to them during the fourth watch of the night, which would have been between three o'clock and six o'clock in the morning. Here is another demonstration of the awesome power of Christ.

At first, all that the disciples could see was a ghostlike figure coming toward them in the midst of the raging waves. They were understandably frightened, and "they cried out for fear" (vs. 26).

Jesus, sensing their fear, immediately called to them, "Be of good cheer; it is I; be not afraid" (vs. 27). The phrase "it is I" was probably more than a simple greeting. With these words, Jesus identified Himself as the great and powerful "I Am," the self-existent One (cf. Ex. 3:14; John 8:58; 18:5-6).

4. Peter sinks (Matt. 14:28-31). In a moment of faith mixed with doubt, Peter said to the Lord, "Lord, if it be thou, bid me come unto thee on the water" (vs. 28). He apparently wanted to make sure it was Jesus.

Jesus honored Peter's faith by inviting him to come to Him on the water. And he did! Peter stepped out of the boat and walked on top of the water toward Jesus—another demonstration of the power of Christ.

After a few moments, however, Peter took his eyes off Jesus, was distracted by the storm, and began to sink. Jesus immediately rescued him and gently chided him for his lack of faith: "O thou of little faith, wherefore didst thou doubt?" (vs. 31).

5. The disciples worship (Matt. 14:32-33). When Jesus and Peter climbed into the boat, the storm immediately ceased (cf. 8:26). The sudden end to the storm was yet another evidence of the power of Christ. On seeing the miraculous events of the past few minutes, the disciples "worshipped him, saying, Of a truth thou art the Son of God" (14:33).

6. Jesus heals (Matt. 14:34-36). When Jesus and His disciples reached the other side of the lake, He again showed His power by healing people. The sick people were so confident of the power of Christ that they thought that if they could just touch the hem of His robe, they would be healed (cf. 9:21).

In Matthew 14 we can see many demonstrations of the power of Christ.

- He fed five thousand men, as well as women and children, with only a small amount of food.
- He walked on the surface of the Sea of Galilee.
- He identified Himself as God, the great "I Am."
- He enabled Peter to walk on the water.
- He calmed the storm.
- He healed many people. We should certainly stand in awe of the power of Christ.

ILLUSTRATING THE LESSON

We can have full confidence in the power of Christ at any and all times.

RELY ON CHRIST'S POWER

CALENDAR

THROUGHOUT THE YEAR

CONCLUDING THE LESSON

We can expect to face many challenges as we walk with Christ, because Christ Himself told us we will have trouble in this world (John 16:33). We may already know of some challenges, but others may suddenly come upon us. We may face life-threatening illnesses or job loss.

The Scripture we have studied should cause us to stand in awe of the power of Christ. He can help us meet any challenge we face.

We do not know how Christ will use His power on our behalf. He may choose to reverse a life-threatening illness, or He may help us endure it. No matter what happens, we can have confidence in His power on our behalf. As we face each challenge, let us affirm what Jesus taught: "With God all things are possible" (Mark 10:27).

ANTICIPATING THE NEXT LESSON

Next week we will focus on Jesus' healing of a paralytic and His authority to forgive sins.

—Don Anderson.

PRACTICAL POINTS

1. Like Jesus, we should set aside time to pray (Matt. 14:22-23).
2. Jesus has authority over creation, because He is the Creator (vss. 24-26).
3. We can trust Jesus' power because He controls all creation (vs. 27).
4. Jesus cares for His people when they are fearful.
5. We should always keep our eyes fixed on Jesus (vss. 28-30).
6. Jesus' mercy and power make it clear that we can trust Him as the Son of God (vss. 31-33).
7. One day Jesus will fully reverse the effects of sin in the world, and all creation will be restored (Matt. 14:34-36; cf. Rev. 21:1-5).

—*Stuart Olley.*

RESEARCH AND DISCUSSION

1. How does our society distract us from Jesus? How can we fight those distractions (Matt. 14:23)?
2. What purpose(s) might Jesus have had for walking on water in front of the disciples (vs. 25)?
3. In what areas of life do you need more confidence in God's power (Matt. 14:27; cf. II Pet. 1:3)?
4. How did Peter demonstrate faith in Jesus (Matt. 14:28-29)? What are some ways God calls us to demonstrate our own faith?
5. What stops us from having faith in Jesus' power (vs. 30)?
6. How could seeing Christ's restoring power cause a person to come to Him (vss. 34-36)?

—*Stuart Olley.*

ILLUSTRATED HIGH POINTS

To pray (Matt. 14:23)

A prominent evangelical Bible teacher told about a time when he was preaching away from home. Tired after a long day, he entered an elevator. The only other occupant was a woman. Her body language suggested that she was available for the night. He said he was grateful for memorized Scripture that came to mind to help him overcome the temptation.

Jesus must have been tired after a long day of teaching and feeding the five thousand. He too was facing a severe temptation—the people's desire to make Him their political king. His recourse was to pray—and stay the course that led to the cross.

Lord, save me (vs. 30)

It is interesting when people with no spiritual concern comment on a situation in which people were injured or died. They usually say something like "Our thoughts and prayers go out to the family." May we never offer such disinterested "prayers," but instead pray with the desperation of a dying man.

Wherefore didst thou doubt? (vs. 31)

One Christian apologist has written, "To believe is to be 'in one mind' about accepting something as true. To disbelieve is to be 'in one mind' about rejecting it. To doubt is to waver between the two, to believe and disbelieve at once and so be in two minds" (Guinness, *In Two Minds*, InterVarsity).

This describes Peter's predicament. He thoroughly believed Jesus was standing on the surface of the lake and that he could join Him. His problem came when he looked around and saw the effects of the wind. With a divided mind, he began to sink. Happily, he cried out in faith, and Jesus rescued him.

—*David A. Hamburg.*

Golden Text Illuminated

"When they were come into the ship, the wind ceased. Then they that were in the ship came and worshipped him, saying, Of a truth thou art the Son of God" (Matthew 14:32-33).

When reading this week's lesson text, most people focus on Peter's adventure. Other than Jesus, he is the only known person to have walked on water—an impressive achievement to be sure if he had done it on his own.

In a way, he did. It was Jesus' power that held him up, of course, but Peter seems to have taken the initiative. While he kept his focus on Jesus, he was able to do amazing things. But when he looked at the danger around him, he sank.

There is a good lesson for us in this story. We should not esteem too highly the so-called heroes of the faith; rather, we should esteem the Saviour in whom they placed their faith. When someone spends his life in service to God, we should honor him as the Bible instructs (I Tim. 5:17) but not esteem him too highly (cf. Rom. 12:3-8). Merely human leaders sometimes fall. Peter fell that day, and his greatest fall was yet to come. Only Jesus deserves our worship. Only He never fails, never falls.

This is essential to our faith and even to our very existence, since God's Word is what upholds all things. Think about all that is being upheld at this exact moment by Jesus' power. In a handful of dirt, there are billions of organisms, all acting according to God-created natural laws. Creatures of the land and sea, weather patterns, our own minds and bodies—all are upheld by His power.

What we see all around us is beyond comprehension. We are microscopic if viewed from the moon, and the moon is miniscule when compared to our universe.

Amazingly, all it takes is a look around to remember what power Jesus has. Too often we are so absorbed in our own small realm of existence, our own particular handful of troubles, that we forget who Christ really is and how much absolutely everything—every heartbeat, every breath—is fully and completely dependent upon the power of His Word.

Jesus knew the storm was coming when He sent the disciples out in their small, inadequate fishing boat. In fact, He told them to go to the other side, something they would not be able to physically accomplish because of the storm. He asked them to do the impossible. Then, when they realized they could not—at their time of helplessness and fear—Jesus came through. Even after all the miracles He had performed, it was at this moment they recognized He was the Son of God—not when He had delivered others but when He delivered them.

At times we may feel we are in an inadequate boat in a deadly storm. We are tempted to panic, knowing we cannot get to the other side, knowing we are helpless.

We should not fear. If God has asked us to do the seemingly impossible, He knows about the storm and is ready to show His power. As He said, even in the midst of the storm, "Be of good cheer; it is I; be not afraid" (Matt. 14:27).

The storms we go through may be the very thing God wants to use to manifest Jesus' power. And when the storm is over and the wind has calmed, we will worship Him, saying, "Of a truth thou art the Son of God."

—*Kimberly Rae.*

Heart of the Lesson

It must have been hard for the disciples of Christ to understand that He was God. They walked the dusty roads of the land of Israel with Him, they ate with Him, and they listened to Him combat the arrogance and criticism of the opposition. While they certainly recognized from the outset that He was an exceptional person and teacher, they did not seem to be in awe of Him as God until several events had occurred. This week we look at two of them.

1. Awesome prayer life (Matt. 14:22-23). It would be hard to overemphasize the importance of prayer in the earthly life of the Lord Jesus. A thorough study of the Gospel accounts reveals that the Lord Jesus often prayed before a big day of teaching or working miracles.

Jesus sent His disciples away, and He was alone with His Heavenly Father. Public prayers and kneeling at an altar have their place, but sometimes real, deep, life-changing prayer can take place only alone with God. The Lord Jesus sent the disciples away so that He could be alone to pray. We would do well to follow His example.

2. Awe-inspiring deliverance (Matt. 14:24-33). The Lord Jesus could have chosen any number of ways—miraculous or not—to join the disciples. But He chose to appear to them walking on the water of a strongly troubled sea. No doubt He did so for the benefit of the disciples, so that they would know for certain that He was the Son of God.

Impetuous, brash Peter had to learn his total dependence on the Lord Jesus. What a lesson he learned! I must keep my eyes on the Lord Jesus, not the circumstances. If the Lord bids me to do something, He will enable me to do it in His strength and His way, not in my strength and my way.

The disciples got the point and worshipped Jesus as God. We observe that He never refused worship. To do so would have been to deny the truth about Himself (cf. John 8:55).

3. Sovereign healing power (Matt. 14:34-36). The Lord Jesus' reputation had preceded Him, so when He arrived in Gennesaret, people brought the diseased to Him for healing.

My wife had polio when she was nine and was quite severely handicapped. Her mother took her to a healing meeting. When the faith healer looked at her, he said, "I cannot help her." He did not even try. He knew the limitations of his gift, whatever it was.

The Lord Jesus has no limitations, either then or now. We were not there to see what happened when He healed people. The testimony of Scripture is that those who touched the hem of His garment were made perfectly whole. We may be sure that observing these miracles further established the fact of His deity in the minds of His disciples.

As we read of these physical healings, let us remember that the ultimate miracle is the regeneration of a person's spirit. We were dead in trespasses and sins (Eph. 2:1) until we were made alive in Christ Jesus. We are already seated in the heavens in Him. We have been made sons of God through faith in Him. Every day of our lives is in His hands. Our future is as bright as the promises and prophecies of God. We have been given everything that pertains to life and godliness. We can trust Him completely because He is God.

—*Brian D. Doud.*

World Missions

As one who teaches courses on the Bible and on world religions at a Christian university, I am often asked the question "Why should I believe in your Jesus?" Students often ask why Christianity is unique and special. They assume that all spiritual paths lead to the same God. It is not easy to answer these claims. However, we can point these people to the God of the Bible, who is very actively involved in the lives of His people. When mankind submits to God, He can accomplish the impossible. He also can be trusted to meet our daily needs.

In the Old Testament, we see God actively involved in guiding the Jews to their land and delivering them from their enemies. In the New Testament, we see Jesus impressing His hearers with His words of wisdom and His acts of power—healing the sick, making the lame walk, and even raising the dead. This is the God we worship. Should we not then fully trust Him for our daily needs? When we see the works of God in our lives, we must praise Him in recognition of His powerful acts.

The apostle Paul recognized this when Jesus told him, "My grace is sufficient for thee" (II Cor. 12:9). In other words, even though Paul's physical ailment would continue to afflict him, God's grace toward Paul would enable him to overcome it. There is power in God's presence. We no longer grope in the dark. In many religions, there is no assurance that people's sacrifices have ever been accepted by the god they worship. That is not true in Christianity, for our God is powerful and continually shows us that He is with us. After all, He reveals Himself as "Emmanuel" which means "God with us" (Matt. 1:23).

The world needs to know that people no longer have to grope in the darkness, not knowing where they are going or whether what they believe is the truth.

Tracy Johnson tells the story of how she stole a Bible from a hotel. While reading it, she was delivered from drugs and witchcraft. She was reading Deuteronomy 18:10-13, where such acts are referred to as abominations in the eyes of God. She repented, and her life completely changed. All this happened to her because of the power of our loving God.

We should stand in awe of our great and powerful God, who is actively involved in pursuing us with His love. Do we think that He does not care about the millions of people who are following false gods? This is where world missions comes in. Each of us who bears the name of Jesus has a calling and a task to fulfill. He calls us to proclaim the gospel of His grace. Salvation is not something to keep to ourselves! We are to let the whole world know this good news.

God's power is revealed when the lives of the most hardened sinners are changed by the love of God. God's power is seen when creation shows forth His work, as in the glory of a mighty waterfall. We see His power and His grace when we look at the colors in a rainbow. We see His handiwork in a newborn child as we gaze at the miracle of a new life. All the works of God are a glowing testimony to His power in the world. He is deeply engaged every day. This is worth proclaiming to the world!

Unlike the silent, inactive idols that are worshipped by false religions (cf. Isa. 44:9-20), our God is a God who not only speaks to us but also cares enough to listen to us. It is His powerful engagement in our lives that prompts us to respond in gratitude and humility. Jesus is truly the Son of God!

—A. Koshy Muthalaly.

The Jewish Aspect

As we read in our text, Jesus and His disciples were in a ship on the Sea of Galilee. The word "ship" occurs over forty times in the Gospels. What did a Jewish boat in Jesus' day look like? How large were the boats? Of what materials were they built? Until recently, Bible scholars could only conjecture what a Galilean boat looked like based on descriptions by Josephus and some mosaics on floors of excavated Galilean homes.

That changed in January 1986. Israel had been enduring several years of drought, during which time "the water level of the Sea of Galilee [had] dropped by several meters and the shoreline had receded considerably" (Geva, "The Roman Boat from the Sea of Galilee," www.biblical.world). Two Galilean brothers, Yuval and Moshe Lufan, were walking along the shore and saw a distinct oval-shaped object poking up out of the mud. The brothers reported that at the time of their discovery, "a double rainbow appeared in the sky" ("Galilee Boat," www.greatarchaeology.com).

Over the next eleven days, as people worked day and night, the boat was carefully removed from the mud. Workers had to avoid damaging it and yet get it out quickly so that coming rains would not bury it underwater again.

Once it had been fully removed, the boat "was submerged in a chemical bath for 7 years to preserve it before it could be displayed" ("The Jesus Boat," www.earlychurchhistory.org). During these years, the rotten wood in the boat was replaced with a special wax. When the repairs were completed, the temperature of the chemical bath was slowly raised over a span of several months until workers could remove the boat from its bath and put it on display. Scholars date the boat to the first century A.D. Evidence indicates it was likely in use for many decades.

Jesus may never have actually ridden in this particular boat, but it testifies concretely to a type of boat in use at that time. It was made primarily of oak and cedar, but various repairs were made with twelve kinds of wood.

The Gospels make it clear that the boats of Jesus' day were large enough to accommodate Jesus and His disciples. The Galilean boat demonstrates how large at least one type of boat was. This boat measured 27 feet long, 7.5 feet wide, and 4.5 feet deep. Scholars calculate that it would have accommodated five crew members and about ten passengers. Without passengers, it could have held between 600 and 2,000 pounds of fish ("The Jesus Boat"). That should help us appreciate the size of the catch of fish Jesus gave the disciples that caused two boats to start sinking (Luke 5:1-7)!

In addition to Matthew's account, both Mark (6:45-52) and John (6:15- 21) record the event of the disciples in a boat on the storm-tossed Sea of Galilee. Jesus walked on the water to them, got in the boat, stilled the storm, and brought them safely to land. Mark says they were "toiling in rowing" (6:48). Reading those words, many used to picture rows or oars on both sides of the boat and all twelve disciples hard at work seeking to bring the boat through the stormy waters.

The discovery of the Galilean boat, however, gives us a new picture. Four of the disciples would have been rowing, with a fifth at the helm. The other seven were merely passengers. Whoever rowed, we can better imagine the frightening scene. We now have a good idea of the kind of boat these men used.

—R. Larry Overstreet.

Guiding the Superintendent

It was dark. They were in a boat on the lake. They were fishermen. There was a storm, and they were horribly scared. And so we enter one of the greatest worship stories in the Bible. Everything was so different from the setting in which we normally worship. There was no worship band. There was no worship leader. There was no worship choir. Yet there was worship.

This true story is one of the most famous accounts of Jesus found in the Gospels. It is referred to as the account of Jesus walking on the water. The incident left a lasting impression on the disciples.

While three of the four Gospel writers tell us about Jesus walking on the water, only Matthew tells us that it ended with the disciples worshipping Him as the Son of God. A person can never truly worship Jesus Christ until he gets a clear picture of who He is.

DEVOTIONAL OUTLINE

1. The storm (Matt. 14:22-30). To really understand the Gospels, one must always look at the reactions of the people in the accounts. The story of Jesus walking on the water is no exception.

The disciples had just witnessed and been a part of Jesus' preaching and then the feeding of the five thousand (vss. 13-21). Surely they must have been wondering who He really was. Then Jesus sent them out onto the Sea of Galilee with directions to go to the other side. They obediently complied. Jesus then went up onto a nearby mountain to pray.

When the boat got out onto the lake, a storm came up. Given how the disciples reacted, it is apparent that this storm was unusually strong. They were troubled. They were "tossed with waves: for the wind was contrary" (vs. 24).

It was now the darkest part of the night (between three and six o'clock in the morning). Suddenly, they saw what they thought was a ghost walking on the water, and "they cried out for fear" (vs. 26).

Then they heard Jesus speaking: "Be of good cheer; it is I; be not afraid" (vs. 27). Peter then got out of the boat and headed toward Jesus, walking on the water for a time. But then he took his eyes off Jesus and started to sink into the water. Jesus rescued him and got him back into the boat.

2. The worship (Matt. 14:31-36). All of this had a profound impact on the disciples. Who was this person?

There in the boat, with the storm suddenly subsiding, these men demonstrated their devotion by worshipping Jesus as the Son of God. It is interesting to note that there is no record of Jesus rebuking them for this worship. Jesus truly was the Son of God.

The most important thing about worship is *whom* we worship, not where or how it takes place. In this account, the disciples were on a lake. It was possible to truly worship God even in those circumstances.

AGE-GROUP EMPHASES

Children: Jesus is more than just a good individual. He is God's Son. This lesson will help children understand exactly who Jesus is.

Youths: Worship for many Christian teens is all about music. This lesson will help them understand that worship is all about Jesus.

Adults: Adults need to learn that Jesus can be worshipped anywhere and in any situation.

—*Martin R. Dahlquist.*

SCRIPTURE LESSON TEXT

MARK 2:1 And again he entered into Capernaum after *some* days; and it was noised that he was in the house.

2 And straightway many were gathered together, insomuch that there was no room to receive *them,* **no, not so much as about the door: and he preached the word unto them.**

3 And they come unto him, bringing one sick of the palsy, which was borne of four.

4 And when they could not come nigh unto him for the press, they uncovered the roof where he was: and when they had broken *it* **up, they let down the bed wherein the sick of the palsy lay.**

5 When Jesus saw their faith, he said unto the sick of the palsy, Son, thy sins be forgiven thee.

6 But there were certain of the scribes sitting there, and reasoning in their hearts,

7 Why doth this *man* thus speak blasphemies? who can forgive sins but God only?

8 And immediately when Jesus perceived in his spirit that they so reasoned within themselves, he said unto them, Why reason ye these things in your hearts?

9 Whether is it easier to say to the sick of the palsy, *Thy* sins be forgiven thee; or to say, Arise, and take up thy bed, and walk?

10 But that ye may know that the Son of man hath power on earth to forgive sins, (he saith to the sick of the palsy,)

11 I say unto thee, Arise, and take up thy bed, and go thy way into thine house.

12 And immediately he arose, took up the bed, and went forth before them all; insomuch that they were all amazed, and glorified God, saying, We never saw it on this fashion.

NOTES

Healing and Forgiveness

Lesson Text: Mark 2:1-12

Related Scriptures: Matthew 9:2-8; Luke 5:18-26

TIME: A.D. 28   PLACE: Capernaum

GOLDEN TEXT—"But that ye may know that the Son of man hath power on earth to forgive sins, (he saith to the sick of the palsy,) I say unto thee, Arise, and take up thy bed, and go thy way into thine house" (Mark 2:10-11).

Introduction

Persistence in spiritual matters pays off. When Jerry B. Jenkins was working with Billy Graham on Billy's autobiography, he asked him, "How do you maintain your own spiritual disciplines?" Billy responded, "We are told to do two things: to pray without ceasing and search the Scriptures daily." After hearing him talk about his prayer life, Jenkins asked Billy, "How about searching the Scriptures? What form does that take?"

"Wherever I am in the world, I put my Bible where I can see it during the course of the day," Graham replied. "If I'm in a hotel room, I open it and put it on the bed. If I'm in my office, I open it and put it on the edge of my desk. If I'm at home I put it someplace where I'm going to see it frequently. . . . Anytime I notice that open Bible, I stop and read a verse or two, a chapter or two, or I read for an hour or two. This is not for sermon preparation. It's just for my own edification. It's my spiritual food" (Shaw and Clough, *Amazing Faith*, Moody).

LESSON OUTLINE

I. A PHYSICAL NEED—Mark 2:1-5

II. A COMPLETE HEALING—Mark 2:6-12

Exposition: Verse by Verse

A PHYSICAL NEED

MARK 2:1 And again he entered into Capernaum after some days; and it was noised that he was in the house.

2 And straightway many were gathered together, insomuch that there was no room to receive them, no, not so much as about the door: and he preached the word unto them.

3 And they come unto him, bringing one sick of the palsy, which was borne of four.

4 And when they could not come nigh unto him for the press, they uncovered the roof where he was: and when they had broken it up, they let

down the bed wherein the sick of the palsy lay.

5 When Jesus saw their faith, he said unto the sick of the palsy, Son, thy sins be forgiven thee.

Jesus' popularity (Mark 2:1-2). A good example of persistence is recorded for us in this biblical incident. It was the persistence of four friends who helped a man get to Jesus for healing. Jesus had recently returned from a Galilean tour (1:39) to Capernaum. {This time He was not in a synagogue but in a house, probably the house in which He Himself was staying.}[Q1] It did not take long for word to get around town that He was home, and the crowds began to gather immediately.

{Jewish custom allowed uninvited people to come into a home for special events, so the house was soon filled to capacity, and a large crowd stood outside.}[Q2] {Luke gives the added detail that there were Pharisees and teachers of the Law in the crowd and that they had come from every town in Galilee and Judea and from the capital city of Jerusalem (5:17).}[Q3] Jesus' reputation had spread far and wide, and after hearing so much about Him, the religious leaders felt it was their duty to investigate His teachings.

Instead of resenting the presence of so many people, Jesus was delighted to have them and to have the opportunity to preach God's message to them. He knew that He spoke to a mixed group. Some were there with longing hearts, hoping to be encouraged with spiritual truth. Others were there with critical attitudes. The religious leaders, for the most part, were not genuinely interested in His message. They were feeling threatened by His growing popularity and were incensed that He was exposing their true character.

This is Mark's first account of a growing antagonism and organized opposition to Jesus from the religious leaders of Israel. It did not take long for a clear distinction to arise: Jesus was filled with integrity and truth, while they were full of hypocrisy and pretended piety.

Friends' determination (Mark 2:3-4). Since the paralytic in this incident was carried by four men, it is possible he was a quadriplegic. It is obvious that they brought him specifically for the purpose of being healed. Upon arrival, they realized from the crowd standing around outside the door that there was no way they could reach Jesus in the normal fashion. They would not be able to get through such a crowd carrying a stretcher without being terribly rude and obnoxious. And yet they were determined.

Most of the homes in Israel had flat roofs on which the people sat in the cool of the evening or slept during hot weather. An external stairway led up to the roof, which was probably made of slabs of dried clay spread over supporting beams that reached from wall to wall. A layer of wet clay might then have been spread over the entire area to make it waterproof. It was apparently this type of roof to which the paralytic's friends took him and in which they created an opening by removing some of the clay slabs.

In order to understand the persistence of this man's friends, we need to imagine all the events that took place that day. As the people crowded into the home and stood many deep around the front door, no doubt there was much craning of necks as each person tried to get a glimpse of Jesus. Those nearby could hear His voice, while those on the perimeters may have strained to hear some of His preaching. All at once there was a disturbance from behind them as four men approached carrying another on a stretcher.

Those standing outside must have wondered as they watched the men ascend the stairway to the roof. Soon all eyes inside the house stared upward as noise came from above. Jesus no doubt paused in His preaching and looked upward with them. {A hole soon emerged in the roof and gradually became bigger. After it was enlarged, a stretcher descended (perhaps on ropes) into the room.}Q4 Comments and smirks may have passed quickly from person to person as they witnessed this audacious act of determination. They realized immediately that someone needed healing.

Paralytic's forgiveness (Mark 2:5). Imagine the silence that momentarily prevailed as everyone in the room watched to see how Jesus was going to respond to this intrusion. Would He resent it? Would He ignore the man and simply go on preaching? Would He scold the four men and tell them to remove the intruding person? Surely such an entrance was a rude interruption and should not be tolerated—at least, that is what some of those present would have thought, for they themselves would have resented such an intrusion into their lives.

Mark gives us a peek into the mind of Jesus at this moment, explaining that He observed the faith of these men, who apparently believed He was the Messiah. When they heard Jesus was in town, they probably became very excited at the prospect of a healing. Their initial inability to get close to Jesus was not going to stop them when they were so certain He could heal the one who was paralyzed. Jesus knew this was in their hearts, and it was to that faith that He responded, "Son, thy sins be forgiven thee."

It was a common belief in Israel that every disease or physical impairment was the result of sin in that person's life. While all sickness and suffering is the result of sin in the world, not every instance of suffering is the

result of one's personal sin (cf. John 9:2-3). Jesus did not suggest that this man's situation was caused by his sin, but He did recognize the man's need for forgiveness. He also recognized the man's faith. Jesus knew he had a repentant heart and wanted to be right with God as well as healed of his disease.

Jesus' words were a response to the man's trusting heart, and he became a forgiven man. Jesus also intended to reveal significant spiritual truth in the way He handled this situation.

A COMPLETE HEALING

6 But there were certain of the scribes sitting there, and reasoning in their hearts,

7 Why doth this man thus speak blasphemies? who can forgive sins but God only?

8 And immediately when Jesus perceived in his spirit that they so reasoned within themselves, he said unto them, Why reason ye these things in your hearts?

9 Whether is it easier to say to the sick of the palsy, Thy sins be forgiven thee; or to say, Arise, and take up thy bed, and walk?

10 But that ye may know that the Son of man hath power on earth to forgive sins, (he saith to the sick of the palsy,)

11 I say unto thee, Arise, and take up thy bed, and go thy way into thine house.

12 And immediately he arose, took up the bed, and went forth before them all; insomuch that they were all amazed, and glorified God, saying, We never saw it on this fashion.

Pious criticism (Mark 2:6-7). The religious leaders reacted in their minds immediately, accusing Jesus of blaspheming. Mark describes them as sitting there "reasoning in their hearts." No one spoke his thoughts, but it is certain that all the religious leaders were contemplating the same thing. {Since they knew that only God could forgive sins, they heard Jesus' words of forgiveness as a claim of equality with God.}Q5

"Rabbinical theology taught that all physical infirmity was a sign of divine displeasure and came as a punishment from God for specific sin. Since God was the One displeased with sin, and the One who, according to the Rabbis, had punished this paralytic because of sin, only God could forgive sin. Christ was, then, claiming the prerogatives that belong to God" (Pentecost, *The Words and Works of Jesus Christ,* Zondervan).

The Law forbade anyone from claiming the prerogatives of God, with death being the punishment for doing so (cf. Lev. 24:16). We noted earlier that this is Mark's first recorded incidence of organized opposition to Jesus. It marked the beginning of a controversy that would not end short of Christ's death. {The religious leaders refused to believe His words and completely rejected Him.}Q6 It is ironic that at the same time, multitudes of the common people were flocking to Jesus, hopeful that their Messiah had finally come.

Pointed question (Mark 2:8-9). It must have come as a shock to the religious leaders when Jesus revealed that He knew their thoughts. The phrase "perceived in his spirit" indicates a supernatural knowledge made known to Jesus by His Father. Although Jesus' human mind operated under natural human limitations (cf. Heb. 2:17; Mark 13:32), the Father made known to Him everything necessary for His earthly ministry (cf. John 5:19-20). When He questioned the religious leaders, they were unprepared to give a response. In fact, He did not give them an opportunity for a response but continued with a very pointed question. It left them no room for argument.

Jesus' question was whether it is easier to say "Thy sins be forgiven thee" or "Arise, and take up thy bed, and walk" (Mark 2:9). The answer is simple. There is no visible proof of the former. It is easy to speak forgiveness, because forgiveness takes place in a person's heart and cannot be physically verified. It is quite another thing to command someone who is paralyzed to get up and walk, because it will immediately be evident that he either can or cannot do so. If he cannot, the one giving the command will be exposed as a fraud.

{The religious leaders were critical of Jesus because of His statement to the man that his sins were forgiven.}Q7 Jesus responded by setting up a situation in which He could prove that He did indeed have the power to forgive sins. He was not simply saying something that could not be proved; He was doing something that truly God alone can do, namely, forgive people their sins. The religious leaders were not about to accept the fact that He had the authority to forgive sins, but what Jesus did next proved otherwise.

Powerful evidence (Mark 2:10-11). In His next statement Jesus put everything in the open: "But that ye may know that the Son of man hath power on earth to forgive sins." The scribes and Pharisees knew that only God can forgive sins, and they were not going to accept that Jesus was divine, so Jesus determined to demonstrate His authority to do what only God can do. What He was about to do would leave them without argument and discredit them before the people.

{Jesus often referred to Himself as the Son of Man. Mark used this title fourteen times in his book. In every instance, Jesus was referring to Himself. It is a messianic title that combines the ideas of heavenly glory and earthly suffering.}Q8

Daniel 7:13 is one Old Testament passage that clearly refers to the Son of Man as a divine figure: "I saw in the night visions, and, behold, one like the Son of man came with the clouds of heaven, and came to the Ancient of days, and they brought him near before him." Daniel saw the Son standing in front of the Father, referred to as "the Ancient of days." The next verse describes the power, authority, and dominion given to Him in an eternal kingdom never to be destroyed.

Jesus' command to the paralyzed man was "Arise, and take up thy bed, and go thy way into thine house" (Mark 2:11). This was to be a complete and permanent cure, not a sideshow for entertainment. {From that day on, people would be able to point to this man as proof that Jesus did indeed have the authority to forgive sins, for He proved it in the accompanying act of physical healing.}[Q9]

Praise-filled amazement (Mark 2:12). The scribes thought they had Jesus pinned down. "But their accusation of blaspheming had only served to emphasize the justification of Jesus of His right to forgive sins and His consequent declaration of His divinity. . . . His miracle made it unnecessary for Him to refute the Scribes further. He had now met His enemies and had gained over them a signal victory" (Shepard, *The Christ of the Gospels,* Eerdmans).

Jesus' claim was verified even as the words left His mouth. The man responded immediately. There was no hesitation, for the miracle was instantaneous. Does not the power of the word of Christ assure us of the power of the Word of God today? When Jesus merely spoke, the man did exactly what He said: he got up, picked up his bed, and left to go home, walking strongly all the way there. The relief was no doubt written all over his face as his countenance glowed with joy.

The effect on the people present was evident. They had never observed such a display of power before. It was obvious that this was not a staged demonstration of magic or false healing. The unexpected incident had occurred before their eyes and left them staring at one another in amazement. {It caused them to think as Jesus wanted them to think, for they glorified God because of what they had seen.}[Q10]

The paralyzed man was made completely whole. God does not always provide immediate healing, but He will always heal spiritually those who come to Him in faith and repentance. And even our physical ailments will all be healed when He raises us up in the new heavens and new earth (Rev. 21:4).

—Keith E. Eggert.

QUESTIONS

1. Where was Jesus at the time of this incident?
2. Why were there so many people in the house where Jesus was?
3. Which of Jesus' critics were present and listening to Him?
4. What happened that interrupted Jesus' teaching?
5. What was so shocking about Jesus' first words to the paralytic?
6. What was the reaction of the religious leaders to Jesus' words?
7. What was it about Jesus' statement that upset the leaders?
8. What did Jesus call Himself, and what did this title convey?
9. What did Jesus prove by healing the paralytic?
10. How did the people respond to the miracle?

—Keith E. Eggert.

Preparing to Teach the Lesson

Healing was an important part of Jesus' ministry on earth. When our Lord healed people, He always made them completely whole people. Healing and wholeness were therefore synonymous terms from Jesus' perspective.

TODAY'S AIM

Facts: to show how Jesus healed a paralyzed man.

Principle: to underscore that God is more concerned about spiritual wholeness than physical well-being.

Application: to help students make spiritual concerns a priority in their lives.

INTRODUCING THE LESSON

When God does something, He always does a perfect job. When He finished creating the universe, He looked at it and said that it was "very good" (Gen. 1:31). When Jesus touched people and made them well, it was always a task that was completed to perfection. His touch restored people to wholeness. Our lesson explores the concept of wholeness in relation to healing and shows us that while God is concerned about our physical well-being, His higher priority is that we know the truth and experience forgiveness and spiritual wholeness.

DEVELOPING THE LESSON

1. Jesus' response to the needs of a paralyzed man (Mark 2:1-5). After journeying through Galilee, Jesus returned to the town of Capernaum (literally, "village of Nahum"). The news of His arrival spread quickly, and the house where He stayed was soon packed with curious people. There was no room for any more people, even around the doorways. They wanted to see what Jesus would do next. Jesus used this opportunity to preach the good news of the kingdom of God to them.

It is in this context that four men desperately tried to get their paralyzed friend to Jesus so that he might be healed. Paralysis in a human being is the ultimate state of physical helplessness. If you have ever known a paralyzed person, you understand how frustrating it can be. The mind is often alert, but the muscles do not obey the dictates of the will. The muscles are immobile and uncooperative.

In our lesson this week we see how Jesus took on one of the most difficult human conditions. Since the house where Jesus was preaching was so crowded, the men went up the outside stairway that led to the roof of the house and then cut through the roof in order to let the man down in front of Jesus. They certainly showed great determination in their desire to see their friend healed.

The biblical record tells us that Jesus responded to their faith and spoke to the man, telling him that his sins were forgiven. Ask the class whether that was a response that they would have expected if they had been there, especially if they had been in the shoes of the paralyzed man. Discuss Jesus' purpose in that statement. Did the sick man get what he wanted?

2. Jesus' response questioned (Mark 2:6-7). From God's perspective, the forgiveness of sins was probably the only healing that was truly necessary. Physical healing, after all, is only temporary until the renewed creation at Jesus' second coming. It seems that God was primarily concerned with the spiritual healing of this man. Encourage the students to talk about this.

The scribes were teachers of the Law, and some were present in the house in Capernaum. They were not at all concerned about the paralyzed man. Their concern was the words Jesus had spoken.

In their thoughts the scribes accused Jesus of taking the place of God by claiming to forgive sins. Only God had that prerogative. According to them, Jesus had just committed blasphemy, which was punishable by stoning according to the Law (Lev. 24:16).

Blasphemy means to speak of God with a lack of reverence. It must be remembered that the Jewish leaders thought of themselves as having great reverence for God. In fact, they did not even pronounce God's name lest they violate its sacredness. In their eyes, Jesus had usurped a privilege that belongs only to God. With cold and stoic religiosity, they rejected Jesus' claim because they could not accept the fact that He is God.

3. Jesus' demonstration of power (Mark 2:8-11). Here Jesus taught the true meaning of wholeness. While it was easy for Jesus to speak the words of forgiveness, which the scribes considered blasphemy, His authority to forgive sins would be proved by His miraculous healing of the sick man. Jesus then spoke to the paralyzed man and commanded him to get up and pick up his mat and walk. From a human perspective, this was perfectly impossible, but Jesus had to show the religious leaders that He was indeed who He claimed to be, the incarnate Son of God who could indeed forgive sins.

It must be noted that in Jesus' mind and from a heavenly perspective, the primary concern was the man's spiritual wholeness through the forgiveness of his sins. The physical healing was an act of grace that proved the spiritual healing had indeed taken place, but true physical restoration only comes at Jesus' return on the Last Day. Do your students know any who are physically ill but are spiritually whole? What makes them whole?

4. The people's response (Mark 2:12). When Jesus commanded the paralyzed man to walk, the man did so immediately and publicly to the utter amazement of all the observers. The people in the crowd praised God for the miracle. No one had ever seen anything like this before. The scribes no doubt were stunned and baffled by the proof that walked before them. Ask your students what in their own lives has caused them to be amazed at God.

ILLUSTRATING THE LESSON

The paralyzed man's greatest need was not physical healing but spiritual healing. God's priority is always our spiritual relationship with Him.

GOD'S PRIORITY

SINS FORGIVEN!

SPIRITUAL HEALING

CONCLUDING THE LESSON

In our lesson this week we have talked about true wholeness. The paralyzed man's healing shows us that physical healing is important but that we cannot be truly whole without spiritual healing.

ANTICIPATING THE NEXT LESSON

Next week we will begin our final unit, considering how the exaltation of Jesus confirms His deity.

—A. Koshy Muthalaly.

PRACTICAL POINTS

1. In the daily course of life, we should look for opportunities to speak God's Word to others (Mark 2:1-2).
2. Our faith should not be shaken by any obstacle (vss. 3-4).
3. Faith itself is not an action, but it is always seen in our actions (vs. 5).
4. Spiritual truth cannot be grasped by the spiritually dead (Mark 2:6-7; cf. I Cor. 2:14).
5. We can fool *people,* but all our thoughts and motives are known by the Lord (Mark 2:8-9).
6. Critics have no answer for lives that have been changed by the Lord (vss. 10-12).

—*Jarl K. Waggoner.*

RESEARCH AND DISCUSSION

1. Do you see anything in Jesus' ministry at Capernaum that gives a pattern for us to follow (Mark 2:1-5)?
2. What made the faith of the men in verses 3-5 evident?
3. What did the men think their friend's greatest need was? What are the primary concerns of most people today?
4. How was the scribes' reasoning flawed (vss. 6-7)? What led them to their conclusions?
5. What effect should the Lord's knowledge of our thoughts have on us (vs. 8)?
6. Why is it significant that the Son (and not only the Father) has authority to forgive sins (vs. 10)?

—*Jarl K. Waggoner.*

ILLUSTRATED HIGH POINTS

Jesus saw their faith (Mark 2:5)

Early in His ministry, the Lord Jesus supplied a powerful illustration of what might be called wholeness healing. In dealing with the paralyzed man, Jesus addressed the man's need for both physical and spiritual healing. First, seeing the faith of this man and those who carried him, Jesus pronounced the man's sins forgiven. It was not until later that the Lord told him to take up his bed and walk.

The proper priority of helping people with their spiritual needs is clearly indicated. In our dealings with those whom we desire to bring to Christ, we must always have at the forefront of our minds the ultimate purpose—the basic need of all humans to have healing for their souls.

Reasoning in their hearts (vs. 6)

Where I live, a counseling establishment advertises holistic healing services. A staff member informed me that their activities include mainly clinical psychology and hypnotherapy. They claim that their procedures help people involved in drug abuse, alcoholism, and marriage problems. They also treat children who live in negative disciplinary situations.

The organization's director has a Ph.D. All the other workers are licensed mental health professionals. I eventually found out that all of the staff members considered themselves Christians and defined a person as having a body, soul, and spirit. However, they avoided mention of Jesus during therapy.

Their brand of therapy may have a place in helping people with mental and physiological difficulties. However, for truly holistic healing, there is only one source—Jesus Christ, who came that we might have abundant life (John 10:10).

—*P. Fredrick Fogle.*

Golden Text Illuminated

"But that ye may know that the Son of man hath power on earth to forgive sins, (he saith to the sick of the palsy,) I say unto thee, Arise, and take up thy bed, and go thy way into thine house" (Mark 2:10-11).

Cult leaders and false religions are proliferating all over the world. Many "spiritual leaders" falsely claim to know the way to God or to have the ability to forgive sins. One cynical book I read even suggested that starting a religion could be a great way to make money!

In this passage, the Pharisees think that Jesus is guilty of blasphemy and of leading people astray. They rightly knew that only God has the authority to forgive sins, but because they missed Jesus' identity, they assumed He was blaspheming when He told the man with palsy that his sins were forgiven.

Jesus responds before they even have time to voice their thoughts out loud. His ability to read their hearts like this should have been a hint to them of His true power and identity! He does not dispute their belief that only God can forgive sins—they were right to think that. However, they were wrong to assume that He was blaspheming, because they were wrong in their assumption that He was a mere man. He was a man, but He was in fact God incarnate, and although He had stepped into history and become a man, He still had full authority to forgive sins.

It is easy to *tell* someone that their sins are forgiven. But how can they verify whether you are telling the truth or not? The Pharisees thought Jesus was making false, empty promises, but Jesus wanted those around Him to know that He was no false prophet. He really did have the power to forgive sins. While a religious con artist might successfully lie about the forgiveness of sins, it is much harder to tell a paralytic to walk. Everyone will immediately know if you are a fraud.

Jesus healed the man with palsy in a sudden and miraculous display of divine power. His action demonstrated conclusively that just as He had the ability to heal the man's body, so He also had the ability to forgive his soul.

God does not owe people who disbelieve in Him miraculous evidence of His power, and He may not always provide it. But time and again we see Him choosing to do so: In Exodus 4, He gives Moses signs to show the people. In Judges 6, He gives Gideon signs. The prophets repeatedly foretell events before they happen, and there are many other signs recorded in the Bible.

God provided signs so that people would believe in Him, and likewise in this passage, Jesus heals the man so that those around would recognize His divine power and believe in His authority to forgive sins. On an even grander scale than this miracle, Jesus would later be declared the Son of God by His resurrection (cf. Rom. 1:4).

The Pharisees were right that only God can forgive sins. Jesus healed the man to show that He could indeed forgive sins, and thus to also show that He was God. No other religious leader can say this. Indeed, the founders of many other religions—men such as Buddha and Muhammad—will not even claim to be God. As God, Jesus has the authority to forgive sins, and there is salvation in no other name (cf. Acts 4:12). We should rejoice that Jesus has the authority to both heal our bodies and save our souls!

—*Tom Greene.*

Heart of the Lesson

People often focus on short-term concerns. They are anxious about everyday needs, such as food, clothes, and homes. While there is nothing wrong with taking care of those things, life consists of much more than everyday matters.

Our text tells of a man whom Jesus healed. Even more, though, the man became completely whole.

1. A strong faith (Mark 2:1-5). As Jesus was preaching to a crowd in a house in Capernaum, a paralyzed man was brought there by four friends. They had faith that Jesus could heal him. The four men realized the house was too crowded for them to get in, so they carried their friend up to the flat roof. They tore away the mud and thatching of the roof and lowered the man down through the ceiling, probably using ropes. It must have been an unpleasant surprise to have dirt and grass falling down on people's heads while Jesus was preaching!

Jesus readily recognized the faith of the man and his friends. He told the man that his sins were forgiven. Jesus was thinking long-term instead of focusing on the man's more obvious short-term need for healing.

2. The challenge of unbelief (Mark 2:6-9). The religious leaders in the crowd were eager to trap Jesus. Amazingly, the Lord knew their thoughts and answered their unbelief aloud. He asked whether it was more difficult to forgive the man's sin or to heal him.

Either one would be impossible unless Jesus was truly God. The scribes and Pharisees were ready to call Jesus a blasphemer because He claimed to be able to forgive sins. They knew that only God can do that; however, they did not believe Jesus was God.

The Jewish religious leaders must have wondered whether Jesus would be able to heal the man so that he could walk again. They had heard about the miracles Jesus had done in other towns.

It was hard for their hardened hearts to believe that Jesus could do either one of these miracles—heal the man or forgive his sin. Sadly, there are many people today who have this same problem of unbelief. They do not believe Jesus is truly God. They think they cannot trust Him for salvation because He is not quite "up to the job." They have pictured Him as far too small—certainly not the true picture of God!

3. Healed to complete wholeness (Mark 2:10-12). Jesus, the Son of God, did and still does have the authority to forgive sins. He can also heal anyone He chooses to heal. In this case Jesus did a miracle people could see so that they could know about the miracle of forgiveness that they could not see. The man's cure was instantaneous. He got up and walked. There was no getting around it. He was healed!

The crowd responded with amazement. They glorified God for such a great miracle, yet the inward miracle of the forgiveness of sin was much more important than physical healing. The man's changed life was a long-term change, making a difference for all eternity.

God can heal anyone He chooses, but He knows what is best. He knows it is much more important to be whole spiritually than to be whole physically.

God's long-term view encompasses all eternity. Those who love and follow God will live with Him forever. Those who choose to stay away from God and reject His gift of salvation will live without Him eternally.

—*Judy Carlsen.*

World Missions

The vast nation of Brazil has been a fertile field for the gospel for decades. From 1970 to 2010, the Protestant Christian population grew from 5 percent of the overall population to 22 percent ("Brazil's Changing Religious Landscape," www.pewresearch.org). The figures are impressive, but how do Christians reach such a large country? The answer is, one at a time.

Joaquim, called Joa, was a high school senior. He was headed for a legal career, but to be considered well-educated, it was necessary to master the English language. At the same time, two Brazil Gospel Fellowship missionaries were pioneering a new work at Joa's home city of Maceio. Patrick and his partner, Jerry, ached to start a new church in that city. In order to make contacts, the young missionaries signed on as English teachers.

Joa was assigned to the class taught by Patrick, a 1984 graduate of Calvary Bible College.

It was a slow start to reach a city of 800,000 people, but the classroom relationships warmed. At the end of the semester, Joaquim and three other young Brazilians were invited to the home of Patrick and his wife, Rachel, for games, food, and a Bible study. It was so enjoyable that Joa went back again and again. It was in those gatherings that he came to know Christ as his Saviour.

Joa went on to law school. He spent his spare time participating in the new Maceio church. From the very first, he wanted to teach God's Word. He concluded that law was not for him, and he headed for Calvary Bible College in Kansas City. Joa finished the course of study there and remained to attend seminary. He married soon after, with plans to return to Brazil with

the glorious message that "the Son of man hath power . . . to forgive sins" (Mark 2:10).

The story of Joa represents what missions should do. In bringing Christ's gospel to young men and young women who have their lives before them, we continue the advancement of the gospel message. Young Brazilians like Joa do not have to have a passport or visa to reach other Brazilians; they are citizens. They do not have to acquire the language in order to reach the populace. They are ready to serve.

In the early 1800s, most of the evangelical missionaries came from the British Isles. In the last half of that century, the premier missionary-sending country was the United States. In the twentieth century, Christians from the former British colonies of Canada, Australia, and New Zealand, along with American believers, staffed the major share of the world's missionary force.

Perhaps the greatest surge in missionary service took place right after World War II. Many young Christians who had served in the armed forces took up the burden of reaching the lost for Christ.

There was another movement for service after the much-publicized deaths of the missionaries in Ecuador in 1956 at the hands of the Aucas. By some estimates, one million men and women felt the call of God upon their lives as a result. Many of those did not make it into missionary service, but it was an exciting time in mission history.

Most of the postwar missionaries are now beyond the age of service. Now the productive fields for missionaries are in the nations that were reached in the past. Joa is representative of that movement.

—Lyle P. Murphy.

The Jewish Aspect

First-century Jews did not take sin lightly. They were very much aware of the reality and offensiveness of personal sin.

Extrabiblical writings such as the Prayer of Manasseh reveal that the people recognized the sin in their lives and understood that sin was universal. Many other sources reflect both an awareness of sin and the need for forgiveness. The Thanksgiving Hymns, part of the Dead Sea Scrolls from Qumran, reflect the understanding that all people are born in sin and remain in sin until they die.

While some Jewish views on sin were accurate, there was also a misunderstanding of the relationship between sin and physical ailments. Physical infirmities were viewed as punishment from God for specific sins. Logically, then, if such sins were forgiven, physical healing and restoration would result. Since God had given the punishment, only God could forgive the sin and remove the punishment. It was clearly understood that in any case only God could forgive sin.

Against such a backdrop, the Bible presents one of the most dramatic pieces of evidence for Jesus' identity in this week's lesson text.

Jesus asked His critics whether healing or forgiveness was easier to accomplish. On the one hand, it was easier to utter the words about forgiveness because that was unprovable. Healing, however, required physical evidence. On the other hand, pronouncing forgiveness was an action only God could actually do.

When Jesus pronounced the man forgiven, He was identifying Himself with God. If He could not prove His next words about healing, His claim to forgive sin could be dismissed. Jesus was not validating the connection between sin and physical infirmity, but He was demonstrating that He had power over both.

Jesus' actions produced an unspoken accusation of blasphemy from the scribes. The scribes were the experts in the Law. To become a scribe required several years of intense study. After proving his competence, a Jewish man could become a scribe at age thirty. Scribes who excelled in their knowledge of the Law were sometimes given the title "rabbi."

In time, the title "rabbi" would be given only to scribes. In Jesus' day, this was in transition and it was also given to some untrained yet knowledgeable leaders, such as Jesus. This contrast itself created jealousy and scorn on the part of the scribes toward Jesus.

The Law provided no allowance for anyone to declare forgiveness of sins. Offerings could be made for sin. Priests could examine and declare lepers ceremonially clean and offer sacrifices for atonement. Only God, however, could actually forgive sin. To make a pronouncement of forgiveness was to take the place and privilege of God and thus to speak blasphemy.

Based on Numbers 15:22-31, anyone committing blasphemy unintentionally could be atoned for. Anyone who committed blasphemy intentionally was to be executed (cf. Lev. 24:11-16).

If Jesus had not provided the evidence of His ability to forgive sin, He would have been open to the charge of blasphemy. Through His demonstration of power, He again proved His identity. He proved that He was more than human; He was God incarnate. Rather than acknowledge the truth, however, the scribes chose to accuse Him of blasphemy.

—Carter Corbrey.

Guiding the Superintendent

The program ministry of the twenty-first-century church is becoming increasingly complex. As my wife and I sat in church reading and listening to the annual report of our church's youth ministry, we were amazed at how diverse and complex it was. When I first started my pastoral ministry over twenty-five years ago, the method for reaching young people for Christ was much simpler.

It is appropriate for the body of Christ to be flexible and creative in developing methods to reach the masses with the gospel. But while doing so, it is imperative that the church not lose its focus on its main message—the forgiveness of sin based on the shed blood of Jesus Christ.

In this week's lesson text, Mark was led by the Holy Spirit to record an incident in the life of Christ that involved the healing of a paralytic. The healing was wonderful, but the main emphasis of the incident is the fact that the paralytic's sins were forgiven.

DEVOTIONAL OUTLINE

1. Act of faith (Mark 2:1-5). After Jesus had spent some time ministering in Galilee, He returned to the city of Capernaum. Many came to be in His presence, and He offered the people what they needed most—the preaching of God's Word.

While Jesus was preaching, four men brought a paralytic to Him to be healed. Their unusual act of faith (climbing to the roof and lowering the man through it into Jesus' presence) caused Jesus to make an unexpected public announcement—the paralytic's sins had been forgiven!

2. Spiritual authority (Mark 2:6-12). Jesus' announcement caused "certain of the scribes" to become inwardly agitated over what they were hearing. Their conclusion was that Jesus had just committed blasphemy, for only God could forgive sin. Jesus immediately made known their internal grumblings and challenged their skeptical conclusion. He then demonstrated His deity and spiritual authority to forgive sin by publicly healing the paralytic.

Following his instantaneous healing, the man got up and set out on his way home. All the people who had witnessed the miracle, including the scribes, were amazed at what they had seen and responded by giving glory to God.

AGE-GROUP EMPHASES

Children: The hearts and minds of children are capable of receiving the truth that God loves them and wants to forgive their sin. Encourage your teachers to use this week's lesson text to help their children know that Jesus truly has the power to take away their sin and takes delight in receiving their praise.

Youths: Even while they are challenging authority, young people long for someone to unconditionally love them and offer them forgiveness. Encourage your teachers to remind their students that only one person has provided convincing proof that He can offer them what they desperately seek—Jesus Christ.

Adults: Many adults have determined to lead spiritually "safe" lives. They truly believe that risky acts of faith are reserved for a younger spiritual generation. Use this week's lesson text to remind your adult students that Jesus delights in people who take unusual risks of faith—no matter how old they are!

—*Thomas R. Chmura.*

SCRIPTURE LESSON TEXT

HEB. 1:1 God, who at sundry times and in divers manners spake in time past unto the fathers by the prophets,

2 Hath in these last days spoken unto us by *his* Son, whom he hath appointed heir of all things, by whom also he made the worlds;

3 Who being the brightness of *his* glory, and the express image of his person, and upholding all things by the word of his power, when he had by himself purged our sins, sat down on the right hand of the Majesty on high;

4 Being made so much better than the angels, as he hath by inheritance obtained a more excellent name than they.

5 For unto which of the angels said he at any time, Thou art my Son, this day have I begotten thee? And again, I will be to him a Father, and he shall be to me a Son?

6 And again, when he bringeth in the firstbegotten into the world, he saith, And let all the angels of God worship him.

7 And of the angels he saith, Who maketh his angels spirits, and his ministers a flame of fire.

8 But unto the Son *he saith,* Thy throne, O God, *is* for ever and ever: a sceptre of righteousness *is* the sceptre of thy kingdom.

9 Thou hast loved righteousness, and hated iniquity; therefore God, *even* thy God, hath anointed thee with the oil of gladness above thy fellows.

NOTES

The Son Greater than Angels

Lesson Text: Hebrews 1:1-9

Related Scriptures: Psalm 2:1-12; Matthew 3:13-17; Hebrews 1:13—2:9

TIME: probably A.D. 60s   PLACE: unknown

GOLDEN TEXT—"God, who at sundry times and in divers manners spake in time past unto the fathers by the prophets, hath in these last days spoken unto us by his Son" (Hebrews 1:1-2).

Introduction

Much is unknown about the book of Hebrews, including who wrote it. While many like to believe the apostle Paul was the author, there are significant differences from his other letters that leave this open to question. Was it written only to Jewish believers or to Gentile ones as well?

While it is stimulating to discuss these questions academically, it is more important to focus on the message of the book. It appears from the context that some Jews who had become believers were frightened about the possibility of opposition and persecution and were considering a return to their former practices of Judaism.

There was much more to be gained in following Christ than in returning to Judaism. A key word for this book is the word "better." The author repeatedly pointed out various comparisons between Christ and Jewish teachings and rituals. In every comparison Jesus is superior.

LESSON OUTLINE

I. JESUS' IDENTITY AND DEEDS—Heb. 1:1-3

II. JESUS' SUPERIORITY TO THE ANGELS—Heb. 1:4-9

Exposition: Verse by Verse

JESUS' IDENTITY AND DEEDS

HEB. 1:1 God, who at sundry times and in divers manners spake in time past unto the fathers by the prophets,

2 Hath in these last days spoken unto us by his Son, whom he hath appointed heir of all things, by whom also he made the worlds;

3 Who being the brightness of his glory, and the express image of his person, and upholding all things by the word of his power, when he had

by himself purged our sins, sat down on the right hand of the Majesty on high;

Speaking through Him (Heb. 1:1-2). {The author of Hebrews began by stating that prior to his time, God had spoken through His prophets many times and in various ways. In contrast to that, God had now spoken through His Son.}^Q1 The writer thus divided time into "before Christ" when God sent His message through prophets, and "since Christ," when the word of His Son fulfills all previous prophecies.

"Sundry times" (vs. 1) means God spoke in many portions, giving His message in fragments. Each book of the Old Testament contains part of God's total message, but no one book contains everything. When the portions of His message are put together, a more complete picture of His plan emerges. "Divers manners" refers to the way God spoke through a variety of avenues, such as people, visions, dreams, incidents, and object lessons. An examination of men such as Joseph, Moses, Joshua, Ezekiel, Isaiah, and Jeremiah reveals this.

Notice how the author distinguished the past and present by saying God spoke in the past "unto the fathers" (vs. 1) but has "in these last days spoken unto us" (vs. 2). Everything God wanted Israel's forefathers to know was given to them through the Old Testament prophets. The arrival of Jesus on earth ushered in a new era in which God's message came directly through the divine Son Himself. {The Greek text has no definite article before "Son." The absence of an article puts the emphasis on the qualitative difference between the prophets and the Son. The word of Jesus is what all the Old Testament prophets looked forward to.}^Q2

Verses 1-4 serve as a prologue for the epistle. "These verses comprise one majestic sentence in the Greek text and read like the opening of a formal Greek oration rather than the customary 'greetings' of a letter" (Ryrie, ed., *Ryrie Study Bible,* Moody). In the sentence seven clear statements are made about the Son through whom God spoke. The first two are in verse 2.

First, God has appointed His Son as the Heir of all things. Hebrews 2:8 says, "Thou hast put all things in subjection under his feet. For in that he put all in subjection under him, he left nothing that is not put under him. But now we see not yet all things put under him." Jesus is ultimately going to receive all dominion that is due Him. Second, it was through Jesus that God created the universe. {The Greek word for "worlds" (1:2) also means "ages." Jesus has made and managed everything in creation throughout history.}^Q3

Exalting Him (Heb. 1:3). The other five statements about Christ are in this verse. He is next referred to as the "brightness," or radiance, of God's glory. God's "glory" is the brilliant radiance that emanates from Him. The "brightness" of that glory describes a beaming or flashing forth.

As the Word made flesh, Jesus is the radiant glory of God, which marks Him as divine. {He is not merely a reflection of God's glory; rather, His is an inherent glory similar to that of the sun's rays.}^Q4 While the sun is the source of brilliance, each ray contains the same brilliance as found in the source. Though the analogy is not perfect, in a similar manner, Jesus is the brightness of God's glory. For a better understanding of this brilliance, read John's description of the glory of the resurrected Christ in Revelation 1.

Next, Jesus is "the express image of his [God's] person." This phrase too is found nowhere else in the New Testament. {It means to be an exact representation, similar to the imprint of an object made by a seal. Jesus is the visible expression of God's invisible being.}[Q5] In Matthew 22:15-22, we read of Jesus being asked about paying taxes. He responded by asking whose image was on the coins. Anyone looking at a coin easily recognized Caesar. It was a clear representation of him. Likewise, anyone looking at Jesus sees God.

Fifth, Jesus upholds all things "by the word of his power" (Heb. 1:3). That is, He is the one sustaining, maintaining, and directing the course of the universe. He is not like the mythological Atlas, holding up the earth. Rather, He actively sustains and guides that which is in constant motion. The laws of nature operate under the command of Jesus Christ.

Sixth, He, by Himself, has "purged our sins." Titus 2:14 says He "gave himself for us, that he might redeem us from all iniquity, and purify unto himself a peculiar people, zealous of good works." It was His substitutionary death that accomplished this redemption.

{Seventh, He "sat down on the right hand of the Majesty on high" (Heb. 1:3), because the work of redemption was done.}[Q6] He is our great High Priest. Unlike the Levitical priests, whose work was never done, He could sit down in the place of honor and authority.

JESUS' SUPERIORITY TO THE ANGELS

4 Being made so much better than the angels, as he hath by inheritance obtained a more excellent name than they.

5 For unto which of the angels said he at any time, Thou art my Son, this day have I begotten thee? And again, I will be to him a Father, and he shall be to me a Son?

6 And again, when he bringeth in the firstbegotten into the world, he saith, And let all the angels of God worship him.

7 And of the angels he saith, Who maketh his angels spirits, and his ministers a flame of fire.

8 But unto the Son he saith, Thy throne, O God, is for ever and ever: a sceptre of righteousness is the sceptre of thy kingdom.

9 Thou hast loved righteousness, and hated iniquity; therefore God, even thy God, hath anointed thee with the oil of gladness above thy fellows.

Jesus is God's Son (Heb. 1:4-5). When Jesus had purged our sins and sat down at the right hand of God, He was "made" (that is, "became") much better than the angels. We must not confuse this with the fact that God the Son has always been superior to the angels throughout eternity. The inference is that for a time He was made lower than the angels in regard to His human nature, as explained in Hebrews 2:7, 9. After completing His work on earth, He was exalted, no longer only as God, but now as the God-Man.

For the first of thirteen times, the author uses the word "better" to reveal the superiority of Christ. {In some of the early churches, certain false teachers taught that God was to be approached through angels. Some even considered Jesus to be nothing more than the highest of the angels.}[Q7] One Jewish sect in Qumran went so far as to believe that Michael the archangel rivaled the Messiah in his authority. The writer of Hebrews was correcting these false ideas.

The superiority of Christ over angels is said to come from the fact that "he hath by inheritance obtained a more excellent name than they" (1:4).

In order to understand the idea of Christ's "inheritance," we need to read this verse together with verse 5, which indicates the promises of Psalm 2 apply to Jesus. Because Jesus is the eternal Son (cf. Ps. 2:7; Heb. 1:5), God promised from eternity past to give Him the nations as His "inheritance" (Ps. 2:8). The fulfillment of that promise came through Christ's purging of sins by His blood (Heb. 1:3), by which people from every nation have been redeemed (cf. Rev. 5:9). As a result, Jesus has obtained a "name" higher than the angels. Paul seems to make this same argument in Philippians 2:8-11.

{The name Jesus has is "Son" (Heb. 1:5), the only begotten Son of God. No angel is ever addressed that way. Angels are God's ministers who do His bidding, but they have never been and never will be exalted to the position of Son.}[Q8]

When Jesus paid for our redemption by His death and then came back to life again and ascended to heaven to sit down at the right hand of God, He proved once and for all that He was, and always has been, the Son of God. The author of Hebrews then uses seven Old Testament quotes to show the superiority of Jesus over angels, five of which appear in our lesson text.

Quoting from Psalm 2:7, he begins by asking this question: "For unto which of the angels said he at any time, Thou art my Son, this day have I begotten thee?" The implied answer is obvious. God never addressed any angel and called him His Son. Jesus Christ is the only being ever addressed this way. In the context of Psalm 2, the nations are plotting against God's Anointed One. In response, God laughs from the heavens because His Son's victory over their brazen but futile rebellion is certain.

As if to clarify further, the author also quotes II Samuel 7:14, where God specifically said He was the Father of David's seed and would establish his kingdom forever (cf. vss. 11-13). In this passage, there was to be an immediate fulfillment in Solomon but an ultimate fulfillment in Christ.

Angels are God's servants (Heb. 1:6-7). The exact words of the third quote cannot be found in the Old Testament, but the idea is in Psalm 97:7 and in the Septuagint's Greek rendering of Deuteronomy 32:43. Psalm 97:7 says, "Worship him, all ye gods." The Septuagint translates "gods" as "angels," which helps us understand how this verse would have been understood in a first-century Jewish context. Psalm 97 is a royal psalm portraying God's rule over the earth. While the primary emphasis is on the worship of God the Father, the Son is so closely related that He deserves the same worship.

The word "again" in Hebrews 1:6 suggests that the author has in mind the worship of Christ at His second advent. We could thus render the verse, "when He again brings His firstbegotten into the world." The title "firstbegotten" speaks of Jesus' rank above all others, not of a temporal birth. Paul used the same term in Colossians 1:15, where he said Jesus "is the image of the invisible God, the firstborn of every creature."

So what do angels do? The fourth quote (Heb. 1:7) is from Psalm 104:4, which refers to angels as "spirits" and "a flaming fire." The word translated "spirits" can refer to a current of air, a breath, or wind. This verse gives us insight into the nature and purpose of angels. They are compared to the natural elements of wind and fire, both of which accomplish God's bidding. These metaphors tell us that the angels are created beings that provide useful service to God.

Hebrews 1:14 further clarifies the messenger duties of angels. {They have been sent forth to assist us, indicating that their role is very different from that of the Son, who is to be worshipped by them.}[Q9] The angels come to where we are in order to help us in whatever ways we need them. God is using them in the daily operation of His universe and in the care of His children. As His servants, they carry out His orders. Of course, the Son is even more intimately involved in our lives than angels are, but only the Son remains exalted at the right hand of the Father.

Jesus is enthroned (Heb. 1:8-9). The fifth Old Testament quote is from Psalm 45:6-7. Psalm 45 is both a royal and a messianic psalm. In it the future glorious reign of Christ is portrayed. By quoting from that psalm, the author of Hebrews applied everything in it to the Messiah, who is going to have an eternal throne from which He will reign. Reference to a throne that will last forever and ever indicates that His kingdom will be a never-ending one. No angel will ever have either a throne or a kingdom.

It is extremely significant that in this quote, Jesus is addressed as "God" (Ps. 45:6; Heb. 1:8). It is an indication of His status and rank, for this address confirms His deity. As deity, He is far above human beings as well as angels, who, along with us, are created beings. Psalm 148:5 says, "Let them praise the name of the Lord: for he commanded, and they were created." The context reveals that the angels were created along with the sun, moon, and stars. They are not, therefore, eternal, as is the Son.

Living in the world today should make us long for the coming kingdom, for it is described as a kingdom ruled by righteousness. A reign characterized by righteousness is unknown today. Many countries suffer under oppressive dictatorships, and even the world's best political systems have no shortage of corruption. Mention of a scepter reminds us of Esther, who was accepted by the king when he held out the scepter upon her unexpected arrival (Esth. 5:2). It is a symbol of authority. Under Jesus' rule, everything will be righteous.

{Lawlessness will no longer be tolerated or present, for the righteous King loves righteousness and hates lawlessness. Gladness will characterize His rule.}Q10 Perhaps most interesting: the King will have more gladness than all of us! No angel can ever hope to assume the role given to the Son. He is, and always will be, superior to all of them. The last two quotes in the chapter come from Psalms 102 and 110, further stating His superiority.

This revealing text should be an inspiration for trust for every believer. What God says about His Son, our Saviour, exalts Him to a position far above every being in creation.

—*Keith E. Eggert.*

QUESTIONS

1. How did God speak to His people in the past, and how does that differ from how He speaks now?

2. What is the significance of "Son" (Heb. 1:2) as it appears in the original wording?

3. What is included in the fact that Christ created the "worlds"?

4. What is meant by the fact that Jesus is "the brightness of [God's] glory" (vs. 3)?

5. What does it mean that Jesus is "the express image of [God's] person" (vs. 3)?

6. What did Jesus do after completing the payment for our sins?

7. Why was it important for the first-century readers of Hebrews to understand Jesus' superiority over angels?

8. What name proves His superiority, and how do the angels compare with what this name tells us?

9. What is the role of angels, and how does that differentiate them from the Son?

10. How is Jesus' kingdom described?

—*Keith E. Eggert.*

Preparing to Teach the Lesson

This week we begin a new unit in which we will see the deity of Jesus confirmed by His exaltation at the right hand of the Father. In today's lesson, the writer to the Hebrews affirms the ultimate superiority of Christ as God's perfect self-revelation.

TODAY'S AIM

Facts: to set forth Christ as God's ultimate revelation of Himself.

Principle: to establish the divine identity of Jesus Christ.

Application: to give students a deeper and richer appreciation of who Jesus Christ is.

INTRODUCING THE LESSON

The idea of television can be traced back to the nineteenth century. By the 1930s, some experimental television broadcasting was being done. Some can remember what television was like in its early days. To those seeing the grainy, black-and-white images for the first time, television was practically a miracle.

Through the years, television technology has advanced greatly. The sharp, clear, color images of today can hardly be compared to the fuzzy images of years ago.

In Old Testament times, God revealed Himself through His chosen vessels, the inspired prophets. Those revelations served their intended purpose. It was only in Jesus, however, that God's ultimate self-revelation came. This week's lesson explores that revelation.

DEVELOPING THE LESSON

1. Christ, the revelation of God (Heb. 1:1-2). Discuss how God revealed Himself to His people throughout the Old Testament era. Ask the class for exam-

ples. Read I Peter 1:10-12. The prophets were God's mouthpieces, revealing information on the nature of God and alluding to the coming Messiah.

What are "these last days" (Heb. 1:2)? The last days began with the first advent of Jesus Christ. God has spoken to us in these last days through His Son. Refer the class to John 1:1, which refers to the Son as "the Word." As words communicate ideas from one mind to another, so God's Son communicates the very essence of God to people. Refer to Colossians 1:15 and 19.

Discuss the concept of the Son being declared "heir of all things" (Heb. 1:2). What does that mean? As William G. MacDonald wrote, it "means that the universe belongs to Him by divine appointment and He will soon reign over it" (*Believer's Bible Commentary,* Thomas Nelson).

Christ's role in Creation is reaffirmed in Hebrews 1:2. Refer to John 1:3 and Colossians 1:16. Read Genesis 1:1, which states that "God created." Our lesson text affirms that God created through the agency of the Son.

2. Christ's divine attributes (Heb. 1:3a). Christ is "the brightness of his glory." Discuss the implications of that statement. It is hard to find a stronger way of saying that Christ is indeed God. Read II Corinthians 4:6. Remind the class how the glory of God was revealed on Mount Sinai (Ex. 19:16-18). Christ shares in that divine glory.

Focus next on Christ as "the express image of his person." MacDonald stated that "the Lord Jesus is the exact image of God's essential being." Explain this in light of the fact that God is spirit. Everything that the invisible God wanted to reveal of Himself, He revealed through the visible Christ.

What did the author of Hebrews mean

when he noted that Christ is "upholding all things by the word of his power"? Refer to Colossians 1:17. He not only created the universe but also sustains it.

3. Christ's completed work (Heb. 1:3*b*). Christ "purged our sins." Refer to John 1:29. Remind the class that Jesus dealt with our sins by dying on the cross to pay the full penalty for them. Note that "purged" is in the past tense. Jesus' work in regard to sin is a finished work. His sacrifice for sin was a one-time event. Read Romans 8:1.

What is the significance of Christ sitting down after His work of redemption was done? He sat down because there was no more that had to be done. Read Colossians 3:1.

4. Christ's superiority (Heb. 1:4-9). The word "angel" also means "messenger." Angels are God's messengers. Christ is God Himself. There is no comparison between the Creator (Christ) and the created (angels). Christ is far superior. Discuss what it means that the Son has a "more excellent name" than the angels.

Note that verse 5 is a quote from Psalm 2:7. In what sense was the eternal Christ "begotten"? Remind students that the Second Person of the Godhead had no point of beginning (cf. John 1:1). The point of the verse is Christ's identity as Son, not the timing of His Sonship.

Angels are never to be worshipped. They worship. Read Luke 2:13-14. What does the fact that angels worship Christ prove?

Hebrews 1:8-9 is a quote from Psalm 45:6-7. The Son is referred to as God, thus reaffirming the unmistakable deity of Christ. Reference to the Son's eternal throne also supports the idea of His deity.

Note that the King "loved righteousness, and hated iniquity" (Heb. 1:9). This characterized Jesus' time on earth. Read Hebrews 4:15. Refer also to I John 1:5, which speaks of the light of God's righteousness.

Who are "thy fellows" (Heb. 1:9)? They are those who are Christ's companions and share with Him (cf. 3:1, 14). In that sense, all Christians are His companions.

ILLUSTRATING THE LESSON

God has revealed Himself through His Son. Jesus is the visible representation of the invisible God, who is spirit.

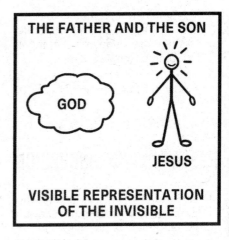

THE FATHER AND THE SON

GOD

JESUS

VISIBLE REPRESENTATION OF THE INVISIBLE

CONCLUDING THE LESSON

God has indeed spoken through His Son. The Son, who shares the divine attributes of the Father, reveals the invisible God in visible form. This week's lesson has reaffirmed the deity of Christ and has demonstrated Him to be far superior to all His creation, including the angels. The realization of who Christ Jesus actually is should cause us to humble ourselves before Him in sincere worship and praise.

ANTICIPATING THE NEXT LESSON

In next week's lesson we will look at Revelation 5, which gives us a picture of what the worship of Jesus is like in heaven.

—*Bruce A. Tanner.*

PRACTICAL POINTS

1. We should not expect God to speak to us the same way He did to people in Old Testament times (Heb. 1:1).
2. Never accept any teaching if it disagrees with what Jesus taught (vss. 2-4).
3. Our worship must be directed to the three Persons of the Trinity alone (Heb. 1:5).
4. It is never enough that we respect Jesus as a great man. The Father has commanded even the angels to worship Him (vss. 6-8).
5. Like our Lord, we should love righteousness and hate iniquity (vs. 9).

—Ralph Woodworth.

RESEARCH AND DISCUSSION

1. Why did God use a variety of ways to speak to people in the Old Testament (Heb 1:1)?
2. Why does God keep speaking to people who repeatedly shun everything He says?
3. Does God continue to speak to people today outside of the Bible? If so, in what ways might that look different today than it did before Christ?
4. What was different about the way God spoke through His Son from the way He spoke through the prophets (vs. 2)?
5. In what ways is Christ superior to the angels (vss. 4-9)?
6. Since angels are mentioned so frequently in the Bible, why do we see so little evidence of them in the world today?

—Ralph Woodworth.

ILLUSTRATED HIGH POINTS

Spoken unto us by his Son (Heb. 1:2)

In the Bible, God most often used human messengers to make Himself known to people. He sent His greatest message by way of His own Son.

It was not a message about a local event. It was, rather, the whole mind and heart of a loving Father expressed in everything said and done by His Son.

Purged our sins (vs. 3)

After seventeen years of marriage, Marianne left Larry because of some unspecified wrong he had done. She went to stay with her parents. After sending five dozen roses and getting no response, Larry took out a full-page ad costing $17,000. It read "I can only hope you will give me a chance to prove my unending love for you." It produced no immediate results.

When it comes to our relationship with God, we all have sinned. No amount of money or extravagant effort to demonstrate our regret can change that. Thankfully, God has chosen to offer us forgiveness through His Son.

Thy kingdom (vs. 8)

In April 2001, in the midst of Arab-Israeli conflict, a motorcade carrying the security service chief of Gaza came under fire from Israeli troops. The frightened official called for help to Yasir Arafat on his car phone. Arafat, in turn, called the U.S. ambassador, who then called the U.S. secretary of state, Colin Powell. Powell then phoned Ariel Sharon, the Israeli prime minister, who ordered the shooting to stop immediately. It did.

In a similar way, believers have a connection to the ultimate power in the universe. However, there is no need to go up the chain of command. We need only pray in Jesus' name.

—Ted Simonson.

Golden Text Illuminated

"God, who at sundry times and in divers manners spake in time past unto the fathers by the prophets, hath in these last days spoken unto us by his Son" (Hebrews 1:1-2).

Jesus came into the world to redeem us, but He also came to reveal the Father to us. To view Jesus is to see God, for He was and remains the very image of God. Our Lord revealed the Father in both His words and His works.

Before Jesus came and revealed the Father, the Spirit also revealed the Son to the world by means of words, the words of His prophets. At various times in the preceding generations, God had raised up prophets, through whom He addressed the Israelites concerning sin and the need for a right relationship with Him. Prophets were those who both proclaimed the word of God and foretold events to come. The former was usually the more prominent feature of their ministries, but each prophet also foretold a coming Messiah who would rescue God's people from sin.

As for the "sundry times" in which God spoke by means of prophets, these usually came when the spiritual climate of Israel was at a very low point. A prophet then was very much like a revivalist or even an evangelist (perhaps a combination of the two). If a person reads the Old Testament prophets in their historical setting as found in Kings and Chronicles, he will see that God's people were usually committing spiritual harlotry, turning away from God.

God also spoke through His prophets in a variety of "manners." The one we are probably most familiar with is direct verbal prophecy, often introduced by the phrase "Thus saith the Lord" (cf. Isa. 45). But He also revealed Himself through visions (cf. Ezek. 8), laments of His prophets (as in Lamentations), and signs or object lessons (cf. Ezek. 4). He even spoke through the life circumstances of His prophets (cf. Jonah 1:17; Matt. 12:39-40) and the history of Israel (cf. Hos. 11:1; Matt. 2:13-15).

The author of Hebrews was saying that although God spoke in many ways at many times in the past, He had in the writer's own recent past spoken to His people by means of His Son. The One prophesied had come and by means of His works and His words had spoken clearly to a nation that was far from Him.

Jesus spoke in various manners too. He spoke by His sinless life, by His sterling character, by His kindness and mercy, by His miracles, and by His teaching, just to name a few. Jesus' teaching was distinct, clear, forceful (see Matthew 5:20 and similar verses in that chapter), and challenging. He made it clear who He was and invited people to believe in Him. He affirmed the prophets of old and gave new teaching designed to lead people into the truth.

By hearing Jesus, people could see themselves and their sins more clearly. They could see how to escape coming the judgment by placing faith and trust in Jesus. They could know the gospel, repent of their former life, have their sins purged by the blood of Christ, enter the kingdom of God, and enjoy the abundant life Jesus promised.

For those in the first century, as well as for us in the twenty-first century, the application is the same. We have the testimony of the Son of God Himself. What else can God say? Who else can He send? There is no one greater than the Son of God.

—Darrell W. McKay.

Heart of the Lesson

The author of the book of Hebrews is unknown. There are those who believe it was written by the apostle Paul. Most would agree that the superiority of Jesus Christ is the main topic of the book of Hebrews. Jesus is superior to the Mosaic Law, the prophets, and the priesthood. The Mosaic Law was instrumental in helping the Jews become aware of their sins, but it was not able to make them righteous. Jesus, who came to fulfill the Law, is able to make the believer righteous.

The Old Testament prophets spoke for God and told people what they needed to do, but the prophets could not provide salvation for them. Salvation is provided only through Jesus Christ. The priests could offer a sacrifice to atone for sin, but they could not take away anyone's sin. Sacrifices offered by the priests had to be continually repeated both for themselves and for God's people. Jesus' onetime, supreme sacrifice is sufficient for the past, present, and future. He will never again have to sacrifice His life.

The word "better" is found numerous times throughout the book of Hebrews. Compared to all other alternatives, Jesus offers a "better" way. He offers a "better hope" (7:19), a "better testament" (vs. 22), a "better covenant," "better promises" (8:6), and a "better resurrection" (11:35).

This week's lesson will help us further our knowledge concerning Jesus' superiority and supremacy.

1. Jesus' supremacy over the prophets (Heb. 1:1-3). It is a privilege to receive God's truth, regardless of the means by which it comes. It has always been imperative for God's people to hear and obey His words. God spoke to the prophets in dreams, by signs, and in visions. They were responsible for sharing God's messages with His people.

Jesus is far superior to the prophets. Whereas the prophets proclaimed God's word, Jesus is that Word. Jesus is the only begotten Son of God. He is the eternal Heir of all things. Jesus has power and dominion over all creation. Every prophetic word recorded in the Old Testament is fulfilled in Jesus Christ, either at His first coming or His second coming. "All the promises of God in him are yea, and in him Amen" (II Cor. 1:20).

2. Jesus' supremacy over the angels (Heb. 1:4-9). Many people have been inspired by the thought of having a guardian angel. It gives them a feeling of protection. But Jesus is much greater than any of the angels. Our needs are fulfilled through Jesus Christ alone.

Names often have significant meanings. Jesus' name means "Saviour." He is the Saviour of the world. His excellent name and position of power are above all others, including those of angels. We are privileged to be able o call upon the name of Jesus. This is invaluable, especially in troubling situations. The things we do and say are done to glorify the name of Jesus.

Many prayers are offered in the name of Jesus. We cannot pray in the name of angels and expect to be heard. It is the name of Jesus alone that we proclaim as we take the gospel to the nations (cf. I Cor. 1:23). Demons have been cast out by the name of Jesus. Sick people have been healed in the precious name of Jesus.

Jesus is exalted above the angels. He has rights and privileges that no one else has. Jesus is King and will reign forever. Everyone shall bow down to worship Him, including the angels. Jesus is Lord!

—*Arletta Merritts*

World Missions

A missionary has to be convinced that the One in him is greater than the enemy who is in the world. That enemy is Satan, aided by his demons.

The passage before us delineates unequivocally the superiority of Jesus to any and all angelic beings, fallen or unfallen. It is this superior One whom we serve and upon whose help we depend to accomplish our missionary task.

Although false gods have no real existence in themselves (cf. I Cor. 8:4), the Bible equates the worship of false gods with the worship of demons (Deut. 32:17; I Cor. 10:19-20). These demons are certainly powerful. They can overcome us when we labor in the flesh, but they cannot overcome us when we go in the power of the Spirit of God. That same Spirit, the Spirit of Jesus Christ (Phil. 1:19), is the one who is in us. Through Him Jesus is with us "even unto the end of the world" (Matt. 28:20).

If the worship of Allah, Krishna, Vishnu, and others is connected with demonic activity, we can engage in spiritual warfare by presenting Christ and His Word as better in every way than these false gods. Neither the Koran nor the Vedas compare with the Bible in beauty and accuracy of language, truth about the way of salvation, wisdom for living, or consistency of thought.

The Bible bears the stamp of truth. No angelic being can inspire a book as the Holy Spirit can. God has indeed spoken by His Son, and it has been recorded for us.

The missionary's success does not depend on his own personality or strength of persuasion. The simple preaching of the Bible (indeed, even the reading of the Bible) convinces and convicts. God speaks through His Word. The task then becomes translation of this Word into the local language. The gospel worker strives to give the sense of God's Word and cause his hearers to understand (cf. Neh. 8:8). When that happens, Jesus speaks from the pages. The preacher may explain, but his expositions are just to reveal the meaning of the text, not to add to it.

Humanitarian aid may be given to bring people to the point where they can listen to the preaching without distraction. Such aid gains an audience for the Word of God. However, the mission that neglects the preaching in order to provide only social help makes a grave mistake. This so-called language of love does not state the salvation message openly. Only the Bible does that. God has spoken by His Son, and that message is embodied in the written Word.

Some minimize the written Word to promote modern prophecies, healings, visions, and deliverances. This is wrong. God has chosen preaching, that is, the explaining of His revealed Word, as the means to convey the message of salvation (cf. Rom. 10:13-15). Satan can imitate sign miracles (cf. Rev. 13:13-14) but not the Word. He can imitate charismatic personalities (cf. vss. 3-4), but not the written Word.

Performances are often put in place of the written Word, but salvation is never the result of a performance. Actors can never replace preaching. No actor can adequately portray the gospel message. God's Spirit convicts of sin, taking the written or spoken word and confirming it to the hearts of the hearers. We must depend on this. Without it we may get a reaction such as amazement, but not the repentance that we seek.

People are not saved by applauding the Lord but by recognizing Him as their Saviour, the Son of God.

—Philip J. Lesko.

The Jewish Aspect

The idea that God spoke to the fathers by means of the prophets was central to the Judaism of the first century. It is still central in Orthodox Judaism today.

At the time Hebrews was written, the Jewish communities in Israel and in the nations believed in the writings of Moses and the prophets. There is much evidence that what we now call the Old Testament was regarded as the inspired Word of God.

For example, the Dead Sea Scrolls, preserved by a community of Essene Jews living near the Dead Sea, include copies of many parts of the Old Testament. Individual books were written separately on scrolls; some smaller books were joined together. Because of the age of the scrolls, most are in fragments as small as pennies. Much of the library is now lost; yet even with just the fragments of the scrolls that remain, all of the books of the Old Testament are represented except one! These Jewish scribes made copies of the Old Testament books because they revered them as Scripture.

Another evidence of the Jewish view of the Scriptures is found in the writings of Flavius Josephus. Josephus was a Jewish historian who was captured by the Romans. His book *Against Apion* was written around A.D. 100. In it he said, "For we have not an innumerable multitude of books among us, disagreeing from and contradicting one another [as the Greeks have] but only twenty-two books" (Whiston, trans., *The New Complete Works of Josephus,* Kregel).

It might seem that something is wrong with Josephus's number, since our Old Testament contains thirty-nine books. But in Jewish scrolls, some books were combined: I and II Samuel, I and II Kings, I and II Chronicles, Ezra-Nehemiah, the twelve Minor Prophets, and possibly Jeremiah-Lamentations. When we take this into account, Josephus likely had in mind the same canon of Scripture that we recognize as the Old Testament.

The writer of Hebrews was thus expressing classic Jewish doctrine when he wrote of the prophets speaking to the fathers. The divinely inspired Scriptures had revealed God to man.

The rabbis are very keen about the grace of God in choosing to reveal Himself to Israel. So precious to the rabbis is God's revelation that they said, "Three precious gifts did the Holy One, blessed be He, bestow upon Israel, and all of them He gave only through the medium of suffering: they are the Torah, the land of Israel, and the world to come" (Cohen, *Everyman's Talmud,* Schocken). The rabbis believed in the inspiration of every word and letter of Scripture: "'He hath despised the word of the Lord' (Num. 15:31)—this refers to one who says the Torah is not from heaven, and even to one who admits that the Torah is from heaven except a single verse which the Holy One, blessed be He, did not utter but Moses said it of his own accord" (Cohen).

The writer of Hebrews said that while God had revealed Himself to the fathers by means of the prophets, He has in these days revealed Himself to us in Jesus (cf. 1:2). If the words of God's prophets were precious to His people, how much more should His Son be precious to us?

The doctrine of God's self-revelation climaxes in the appearance of Jesus, the God-Man. Words reveal a great deal about God, but the living, breathing God-Man reveals even more. How revolutionary a thought it was for the Jews to hear that Jesus is greater than the Torah!

—*Derek Leman.*

Guiding the Superintendent

Jesus told His disciples, "He that hath seen me hath seen the Father" (John 14:9). In this lesson we find God the Father confirming that truth about His Son. Hebrews 1 is God's testimony of who Jesus Christ really is. Our lesson text identifies four key facts about the identity of Jesus Christ: He is the Messiah, He is God's Son, He is God Himself, and He is the Sovereign of the universe.

DEVOTIONAL OUTLINE

1. Jesus Christ is the Messiah (Heb. 1:1-3). Throughout the history of Israel, the people were told to look for their Messiah. By the time Jesus Christ arrived on the scene, anticipation of the Messiah was at a fever pitch.

The word "Messiah" means "anointed." In the New Testament, the word "Christ" has the same meaning. To speak of Jesus as the Christ was to identify Him as the prophesied Messiah. In the days of the Old Testament, the offices of prophet, priest, and king were commonly conferred on individuals by anointing.

In the first three verses of Hebrews, God identified His Son as holding all three offices. As prophet, He came as God's final message or revelation to mankind (vss. 1-2). As priest, He was the one who "purged our sins" (vs. 3). As king, He is seated on the throne in heaven, indicating that He has finished the work of salvation and has begun His reign as head of the church (cf. Col. 1:18).

2. He is the Son of God (Heb. 1:4-9). In these verses God stated three great truths about who Jesus Christ is. Note that this section contains a series of quotes from the Old Testament. The point the author of Hebrews was making is that the deity of Jesus Christ is clearly taught in the Old Testament.

The first quotation emphasizes that Jesus Christ is God's Son (vs. 5). It is important to remember that here "son" does not indicate birth but relationship. The relationship between God the Father and Jesus, the Son, is eternal. As Paul explained, this fact was declared to the world by the resurrection (Acts 13:32-33).

Second, Jesus Christ is identified as divine, for He receives the worship of the angels. God is the only object of angelic worship; therefore, Jesus Christ is God.

Finally, while the angels are merely God's servants, Jesus Christ is the Sovereign of the universe. He rules over the entire eternal kingdom.

AGE-GROUP EMPHASES

Children: Part of the growing-up process is learning the meaning of different words. This process carries over into the children's church experience. Help them learn what the name "Christ" really means.

Youths: Many teens are enamored of the supernatural, including angels. This lesson focuses on how Jesus Christ and angels compare. Help them understand that while both are supernatural, Jesus Christ is infinitely superior to the angels. They also need to learn where the angels fit in God's overall redemptive program.

Adults: This lesson is rich with information about the identity of Jesus Christ. Pick a few of the facts that are important to you, and have the students reflect on the significance of these facts for their daily lives. For example, how does Jesus Christ sovereignly direct their lives?

—Martin R. Dahlquist.

SCRIPTURE LESSON TEXT

REV. 5:6 And I beheld, and, lo, in the midst of the throne and of the four beasts, and in the midst of the elders, stood a Lamb as it had been slain, having seven horns and seven eyes, which are the seven Spirits of God sent forth into all the earth.

7 And he came and took the book out of the right hand of him that sat upon the throne.

8 And when he had taken the book, the four beasts and four *and* twenty elders fell down before the Lamb, having every one of them harps, and golden vials full of odours, which are the prayers of saints.

9 And they sung a new song, saying, Thou art worthy to take the book, and to open the seals thereof: for thou wast slain, and hast redeemed us to God by thy blood out of every kindred, and tongue, and people, and nation;

10 And hast made us unto our God kings and priests: and we shall reign on the earth.

11 And I beheld, and I heard the voice of many angels round about the throne and the beasts and the elders: and the number of them was ten thousand times ten thousand, and thousands of thousands;

12 Saying with a loud voice, Worthy is the Lamb that was slain to receive power, and riches, and wisdom, and strength, and honour, and glory, and blessing.

13 And every creature which is in heaven, and on the earth, and under the earth, and such as are in the sea, and all that are in them, heard I saying, Blessing, and honour, and glory, and power, *be* unto him that sitteth upon the throne, and unto the Lamb for ever and ever.

14 And the four beasts said, Amen. And the four *and* twenty elders fell down and worshipped him that liveth for ever and ever.

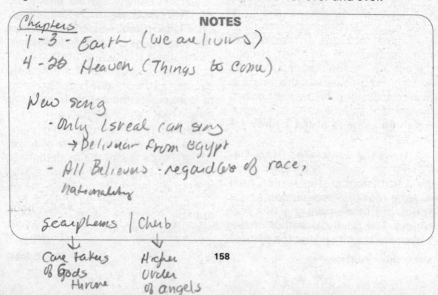

NOTES

Chapters
1-3 - Earth (we are livins)
4-20 Heaven (Things to come).

New song
- Only Isreal can sing
  → Delivence from Egypt
- All Believers - regardless of race, nationality

Seaiphems / Cherb
↓   ↓
Care takers   Higher
of Gods   Order
Throne   of angels

158

The Lamb Worthy of Worship

Lesson Text: Revelation 5:6-14

Related Scriptures: John 1:29-34; Revelation 20:1-6

TIME: about A.D. 96   PLACE: from Patmos

GOLDEN TEXT—"Worthy is the Lamb that was slain to receive power, and riches, and wisdom, and strength, and honour, and glory, and blessing" (Revelation 5:12).

Introduction

The word "forever" is a big part of our Christian vocabulary. We speak of the Lord who has lived and shall live forever, and we rejoice in the fact that we shall live forever in heaven.

We know that the word "forever" means "without end," or "eternal," but many of us do not take enough time to ponder the concept of the word "forever." Though we can never grasp its meaning fully, we would do well to meditate regularly on this important truth.

The Triune God has lived forever. He had no beginning. There never was a time when He did not exist. We cannot ask where God came from or how or when He began. Our finite minds cannot grasp this truth. Looking ahead, we know that all of us who believe and trust the Lord will worship the Lord forever and ever! We will never cease to worship Him. Lead your students in this study to capture a small part of this eternal worship.

LESSON OUTLINE

I. THE LAMB IN THE MIDST OF THE THRONE—Rev. 5:6-7

II. THE WORSHIP AROUND THE THRONE—Rev. 5:8-14

Exposition: Verse by Verse

THE LAMB IN THE MIDST OF THE THRONE

REV. 5:6 And I beheld, and, lo, in the midst of the throne and of the four beasts, and in the midst of the elders, stood a Lamb as it had been slain, having seven horns and seven eyes, which are the seven Spirits of God sent forth into all the earth.

7 And he came and took the book out of the right hand of him that sat upon the throne.

The Lamb's description (Rev. 5:6). In Revelation 4, we were introduced to the throne room in heaven where John saw God the Father on the throne (vs. 2), surrounded by four creatures and twenty-four elders. We also saw God the Holy Spirit represented in the seven lamps of fire (vs. 5). In the first five verses of Revelation 5, we read about an event in this throne room that prepares us for the appearance of God the Son. In the Father's right hand is "a book written within and on the backside, sealed with seven seals" (vs. 1).

This book was probably in the form of a scroll. The seven seals were most likely not all on the outside of the rolled scroll. Rather, every time the scroll was rolled once, a seal was put on it to hold it. Thus, when a person unrolled the scroll, he had to break the seals one by one.

What was written in the book? We are not told, but some have thought it was the terms to a deed, similar to what is described in Jeremiah 32:7-15. {If this is the case, perhaps this book is the title deed to the universe.}[Q1] The universal worship in the last part of Revelation 5 would certainly support that idea.

We must also connect this book with Revelation 6, 7, and 8, where we learn that the Lamb unrolled the scroll and opened each of the seven seals, which brought judgments on the earth. The fact that the book had seven seals reminds us of God's perfection, even in judgment. Ezekiel was handed a similar scroll when God sent him to warn Israel about their impending exile (2:9—3:3). Christ's opening of the scroll is thus a fulfillment of Ezekiel's ministry.

John then saw a "strong angel" who asked this question: "Who is worthy to open the book, and to loose the seals thereof?" (Rev. 5:2). We are not told the identity of the "strong angel," but it may be Gabriel since his name means "God is my strength." The answer immediately came back that no one in the universe ("no man in heaven, nor in earth, neither under the earth") was able to open the book or even to look inside of it (vs. 3).

Evidently, the heavenly worshippers, especially John, were concerned that no one was able to open the seals and look in the book. That is why John wept bitterly when no one was found who could open it.

Why were John and the others so concerned that no one was able to open the book? If the book is the title deed to the universe, then perhaps they recognized that earth's history was coming to a point of culmination and that they did not know who would sovereignly control everything.

At that point one of the elders around God's throne said, "Weep not: behold, the Lion of the tribe of Juda, the Root of David, hath prevailed to open the book, and to loose the seven seals thereof" (vs. 5). The elder informed John that Christ had already gained the right to open the book and break its seals, so John did not need to continue weeping.

We know that the elder was speaking about none other than the Lord Jesus Christ (cf. Gen. 49:8-10; Isa. 11:1). In Revelation 5:6-14, we learn more about the Lord Jesus and what He will do.

John then saw the Lord Jesus Christ standing in the throne room in the midst of the four living creatures ("beasts") and twenty-four elders. The fact that He is standing shows His victory over death and His readiness to take the book. The living creatures are probably angels (cf. Ezek. 10:20), and the twenty-four elders likely represent the redeemed of the church.

Revelation 5:6 describes Jesus as "a Lamb as it had been slain." {This description brings to mind Jesus' work as the Passover Lamb who was sacrificed for us (Isa. 53:7; John 1:29).}[Q2] When John saw the Lord Jesus, he could tell He had been slain because He still bore the marks of His crucifixion.

Interestingly, John first described Jesus as a lion, and now he describes Him as a lamb. Perhaps the analogy to a lamb refers to His first coming in meekness and His role as a lion to His second coming in power.

John wrote that the Lord Jesus had seven horns and seven eyes. Animals use their horns to exert strength and power, so the horns probably represent Jesus' authority and power. The seven eyes are described as being the seven "Spirits of God" that He had sent out into every part of the earth. This phrase, also used in Revelation 4:5, probably points to the Holy Spirit in His sevenfold character (cf. Isa. 11:2) or to the Holy Spirit as pictured in the lampstand with seven lamps (Zech. 4:1-10). The number seven represents perfection, showing the Spirit's perfection.

{Here we have the Triune God in His full display. God the Father is seated on the throne with the book in His right hand. God the Son is standing in the midst of this scene as the Lamb who was slain for our sins. God the Holy Spirit is represented through the seven eyes of the Lamb.}[Q3] No wonder the worshippers were overawed by the scene!

The Lamb's triumph (Rev. 5:7). This section concludes with Jesus' triumphal act of receiving the book from the hand of God the Father. The action shows that the Lord Jesus is indeed worthy to take the book and open its seals. {As we will see in verse 9, His work of redemption on the cross is the reason He is worthy to do this.}[Q4] He is the Creator and Owner of the universe,

and He will direct the course of the events that are described in the book of Revelation.

THE WORSHIP AROUND THE THRONE

8 And when he had taken the book, the four beasts and four and twenty elders fell down before the Lamb, having every one of them harps, and golden vials full of odours, which are the prayers of saints.

9 And they sung a new song, saying, Thou art worthy to take the book, and to open the seals thereof: for thou wast slain, and hast redeemed us to God by thy blood out of every kindred, and tongue, and people, and nation;

10 And hast made us unto our God kings and priests: and we shall reign on the earth.

11 And I beheld, and I heard the voice of many angels round about the throne and the beasts and the elders: and the number of them was ten thousand times ten thousand, and thousands of thousands;

12 Saying with a loud voice, Worthy is the Lamb that was slain to receive power, and riches, and wisdom, and strength, and honour, and glory, and blessing.

13 And every creature which is in heaven, and on the earth, and under the earth, and such as are in the sea, and all that are in them, heard I saying, Blessing, and honour, and glory, and power, be unto him that sitteth upon the throne, and unto the Lamb for ever and ever.

14 And the four beasts said, Amen. And the four and twenty elders fell down and worshipped him that liveth for ever and ever.

The worshippers—beasts and elders (Rev. 5:8). Revelation 5:8-14 describes three groups of worshippers and their acclamation of praise to the

Lamb. In verses 8-10, we find the first group of worshippers and their song of praise. When Jesus Christ had taken the book, showing His authority and ownership, the four living creatures ("beasts") and the twenty-four elders fell down before Him. They had in their hands harps and "golden vials full of odours," meaning golden bowls full of incense.

The harp was used in Old Testament times to accompany vocal praise to God (cf. I Chr. 25:6) and, sometimes, prophetic statements (cf. I Sam. 10:5). Perhaps this dual purpose is in view here as the worshippers praise God and note the fulfillment of prophecies.

{Revelation 5:8 states that the bowls of incense are the prayers of the saints. These prayers, wafting up to God like incense, may be the prayers believers have prayed through the ages concerning the culmination of God's redemptive plan.}[Q5]

Their worship (Rev. 5:9-10). The elders sang a new song of worship to the Lamb. (The worship song uses the word "us," so likely the elders, not the creatures, are the ones who sing this song since the elders, not angels, are the ones who were redeemed.) Their song highlighted three aspects of Christ's life and work.

{The first aspect is His worthiness. "Thou art worthy to take the book, and to open the seals thereof" (vs. 9). The second is His worldwide redemption. "For thou wast slain, and hast redeemed us to God by thy blood out of every kindred, and tongue, and people, and nation." The third is His elevation of believers. "And hast made us unto our God kings and priests: and we shall reign on the earth" (vs. 10).}[Q6]

The worshippers—angels (Rev. 5:11). Accompanying the creatures and elders is a second group of worshippers—an innumerable host of angels. {The phrase "ten thousand times ten thousand, and thousands of thousands" is not meant to be a mathematical equation; rather, it is meant to convey a number beyond calculation (cf. Heb. 12:22).}[Q7]

Their worship (Rev. 5:12). The angels then offer their praise to the Lord. They speak "with a loud voice" because of the majesty of the Lamb. Like the worshippers in verses 9 and 10, they highlight the Lamb's worthiness and crucifixion and exclaim what He is worthy of receiving: power, riches, wisdom, strength, honor, glory, and blessing. This sevenfold ascription of praise is a good model for us to follow as we worship the Lord.

The worshippers—every creature (Rev. 5:13a). The worship scene reaches a crescendo as "every creature which is in heaven, and on the earth, and under the earth, and such as are in the sea, and all that are in them" join the throng around the throne. {In essence, this description says that everyone and everything in the universe will join in praising the Lamb.}[Q8] Apparently, even the land and sea animals will participate in this worship.

Their worship (Rev. 5:13b-14). In this grand finale of praise, all living beings, which includes all of us, offer to the Lamb blessing, honor, glory, and power. This group adds a new thought in their worship—the eternal nature of the worship of Christ. Our worship of the Saviour will not be an occasional experience, but we will gather around His throne through all eternity to worship the Lamb who redeemed us.

The worship scene comes to a conclusion as the four living creatures bow and say "amen" and the elders fall down to worship the Lamb. John

162

closes this section with a clear expression of the eternality of Christ. He is the one who lives forever and ever. {Our worship of Christ will go on for all eternity because Jesus Christ will live forever.}[Q9]

We have looked at the different parts of this great chapter, but let us step back now to see some of the lessons about worship.

First, true worship is about the Lord Himself, not about us. Some worship today tries to bring in human elements and focuses too much on what we do or what benefits we may gain. Revelation 5 shows that Jesus Christ is the sole object of worship. All we can do is fall before Him.

Second, true worship is about giving, not getting. Sometimes we hear people say, "I did not get much out of the service this morning." Getting is not the point of worship. Rather, we come to give something—we give the Lord our heartfelt worship.

{Third, true worship places a great emphasis on Christ's death.}[Q10] Look back through the words of Revelation 5 to see how many times John referred to Christ's death: "A Lamb as it had been slain" (vs. 6), "For thou wast slain, and hast redeemed us to God by thy blood" (vs. 9), and "Worthy is the Lamb that was slain" (vs. 12). In our singing, praying, and preaching, let us exalt the crucified Christ.

Fourth, true worship ascribes to the Lamb what He deserves—power, riches, wisdom, strength, honor, glory, and blessing. In our prayers, our singing, and even in personal conversations, let us tell the Lord that He is indeed worthy of all these ascriptions of praise. He never tires to hear these words from our lips.

Fifth, this chapter gives us insight into music used in worship. True worship music extols the death of Christ, His marvelous attributes, and expressions of His great worth. Music based on the expressions of worship in this chapter and other chapters of the Bible leads us to the throne room of God.

Sixth, true worship will be our eternal activity. We do not know all that we will do in heaven someday, but we do know that our time will be filled with regular and unending worship and praise for the Lamb. Such heavenly worship is possible because Jesus Christ, the Lamb, lives forever.

The truths of Revelation 5 should lead us to more meaningful private worship times and more expressive corporate worship with our church family.

—Don Anderson.

QUESTIONS

1. What might have been contained in the book with the seven seals?
2. Why did Jesus Christ appear in the form of a lamb in John's vision?
3. How do we see the three Persons of the Triune God in this chapter?
4. Why is Jesus worthy to take the book and open its seals?
5. What is the significance of the golden bowls?
6. What three aspects of Christ's work are highlighted in the elders' song?
7. How many angels are involved in worshipping the Lamb?
8. How extensive or widespread is the worship of the Lamb?
9. How does Christ's eternal nature impact our worship?
10. What aspect of Christ's work should be the emphasis of our worship?

—Don Anderson.

Preparing to Teach the Lesson

We are to be praising God and honoring Him every day of our lives, and we will continue to do so throughout all eternity. God does not need our praise, since He is perfect and has no needs, but we certainly have a deep-seated need within our souls to praise Him.

The most wonderful thing we can have in our lives is a right relationship with God. It is not possible for a human being to be fulfilled without this, for we would always have a "God-shaped void" in our inner being. Without the new birth through Jesus Christ, we are dead spiritually and incapable of knowing or responding to God, incapable of being rightly related to Him or to our fellow human beings. To be a born-again person, to have all our sins confessed to Him and forsaken, and to be yielded to His Holy Spirit puts us in the right place spiritually, mentally, and emotionally.

TODAY'S AIM

Facts: to gain insight into the heavenly worship of the Lamb.

Principle: to understand the implications of that heavenly worship for our worship here and now.

Application: to make it a daily practice to honor and praise God and the Lamb of God above all else.

INTRODUCING THE LESSON

In Revelation 4 God is declared worthy to receive glory and honor and power because He created everything for His own pleasure. When we see all that mankind has done with what God has given us, we might wonder what God's plan could possibly be for a creation that dishonors Him so continually.

We are thankful for all those who honor Him and are walking with Him, but there are many people in this world who seem bent on being as wicked and sinful as possible. So in chapter 5, we are doubly heartened to see that it will all be resolved to the point where God is given all praise and honor, and everything is made right. The plans and purposes of God will be carried out to His complete satisfaction, and it will be to our great blessing.

DEVELOPING THE LESSON

1. The Lamb is worthy (Rev. 5:6-7). In the first five verses of this chapter, we see that a highly important book, or scroll, is in the hand of God on His throne. The question comes from an anonymous "strong angel" (vs. 2) asking who is worthy to open this very important document. No man is found worthy.

In our society, we hold in high regard people who accomplish great things. We give degrees to those who achieve much in our schools of higher education. We praise and honor those who contribute to humanity through medicine, inventions, art, and science. We applaud the selfless dedication of missionaries and servants of humanity in difficult places. While it is all well and good that we do this, no human being is really capable or worthy to initiate the things that are in the hand of God alone. The great mysteries of life, death, the future, sin, righteousness, and judgment to come cannot be completely understood by any of us. Much less can we do anything about them.

2. The Lamb is worshipped (Rev. 5:8-10). When the Lamb in John's vision proves worthy and takes the book, this triggers worship of the Lamb by the four beasts and the twenty-four elders. The Lamb was slain and has redeemed the elders and a countless host from all humanity by His blood. He has elevated them to be kings and priests who will reign on the earth.

Worthy of note are the golden vials full of the prayers of the saints. Our "unanswered" prayers that we offered according to the will of God have not been forgotten. They have been presented before the throne of God and will yet be answered.

3. The great multitude (Rev. 5:11-14). The great multitude includes the representatives of every redeemed person (the elders), many angels, the four beasts, and everything in creation. Tens of thousands of angels speak our golden text: "Worthy is the Lamb that was slain to receive power, and riches, and wisdom, and strength, and honour, and glory, and blessing" (vs. 12). This sevenfold blessing, denoting fullness and completeness, is in response to the Lamb's perfections—seven horns, which represent all power, and seven eyes, which represent all vision or knowledge (vs. 6). We learn later that the scroll contains prophecies of God's judgment on sin. Right up to the end, we see God's justice, mercy, and forgiveness for all who trust Him.

We then see every creature in heaven and earth echoing this same praise and honor "for ever and ever" (Rev. 5:13). The four beasts say, "Amen" (vs. 14), which means "so be it." All those who thus bless God are being and will be blessed themselves. The appropriate answer of our hearts to this revelation is praise and worship. Much of worship is saying back to God, from our hearts, what we know to be true of Him. We thank Him for all that He is and does. We acknowledge Him in all His perfections and the glorious things we know to be true about Him. We will have all eternity to revel and bask in all His perfections. It will be fulfilling and exciting and rewarding beyond our highest expectations.

ILLUSTRATING THE LESSON

The Lamb of God, Jesus Christ, is worthy of our praise forever.

WORTHY IS THE LAMB

AMEN

CONCLUDING THE LESSON

We have read the verses and tried to see what has been so carefully written for us, but we must admit it is still beyond us and our experience. However, if we continue to walk in the light of this revelation and continue to praise God and the Lamb, we can come into a fuller understanding of it. We know that for the child of God, through faith in Christ, all will come out well—very well. Our prayers are presented at God's throne, and He will answer them.

Nothing is a surprise to God. He has made arrangements for everything from your salvation to your ultimate blessing. Bless and honor Him now while you have opportunity, because in so doing you anticipate the worship of the Lamb in heaven.

ANTICIPATING THE NEXT LESSON

Next week we will conclude our series on the deity of Christ by looking at another description of Him in Revelation, this time as the "Beginning and the End" (chap. 22).

—Brian D. Doud.

PRACTICAL POINTS

1. Jesus died on earth so that we can live in heaven with Him (Rev. 5:6).
2. Jesus is the only person with the power to redeem mankind (vss. 7- 8).
3. The blood of Jesus has the power to save people of every nation (vs. 9).
4. As believers, we become royalty through the grace of God, and we reign with Him (vs. 10).
5. All living creatures in heaven and earth must worship Jesus (vss. 11-13).
6. Jesus is worthy of eternal praise (vs. 14).

—Valante M. Grant.

RESEARCH AND DISCUSSION

1. How can Jesus be both the Good Shepherd and the Lamb of God? Discuss.
2. What does the number seven signify throughout the Bible? How does it relate to the description of the Lamb (Rev. 5:6)?
3. How does Jesus' death, burial, and resurrection affect eternity for believers?
4. Compare and contrast the humble beginning of Jesus' life on earth with the glory and majesty of His return.
5. What can we learn from the fact that the Lord God Almighty humbled Himself to the point of death for our sake (cf. Phil. 2:1-11)?
6. As believers, how can we honor the Lord with the praise that He is worthy of while we are still on earth?

—Valante M. Grant.

ILLUSTRATED HIGH POINTS

Out of every . . . nation (Rev. 5:9)

In his book *Be Victorious* (Cook), Warren W. Wiersbe repeated the story of a man who happened to come to a missions conference. During the offering, he told the usher, "'I don't believe in missions!' 'Then take something out,' said the usher, 'It's for the heathen.'"

Thankfully, many others have faithfully gone out to reach the lost.

Shall reign on the earth (vs. 10)

From time to time, some of the world's leading scientists review what they call the Doomsday Clock and try to calculate how close the world is to total destruction due to climate change, the proliferation of nuclear weapons arsenals, and other issues. Recently, they calculated that it was still resting on "100 seconds to midnight."

Yes, there is doom in the future due to God's judgment, but Christians look forward to a future of blessings with Christ when He returns to set up His kingdom. Believers are confident that God is in control of the world.

Ten thousand (vs. 11)

Some seventy years ago, we thought one thousand was a big number. Then it was one million, which later became one billion. Now our government spends money in the trillions. Will our grandchildren be facing government spending of one quadrillion (one thousand trillion)?

In Bible times, the greatest number was the "myriad" (translated as "ten thousand"). But even when that number was multiplied by itself, it did not exhaust the number of heavenly angels. There were still thousands more. John saw a seemingly infinite number praising the Lamb.

—Ted Simonson.

Golden Text Illuminated

"Worthy is the Lamb that was slain to receive power, and riches, and wisdom, and strength, and honour, and glory, and blessing" (Revelation 5:12).

Have you ever gone to a sports game and felt the crowd erupt around you in wild celebration? Believe it or not, the fans of a few teams have caused small-scale earthquakes! But the angels in this chapter number far more than the largest stadium in the world could hold, and the celebration is far greater than any ever seen. At the center of it all is Jesus, the Lamb of God. Jesus is proclaimed here to be worthy of seven things; let's look at each.

First, He is worthy of power. Elsewhere, Jesus is described as "the power of God" (I Cor 1:24) and we know "all things were created by him, and for him: and he is before all things, and by him all things consist" (Col 1:16-17). During His life on earth, He accepted human limitations and weakness, but He does not need to be given power He never had; He possessed it all in eternity past.

Second, He is worthy of riches. As the Creator of all, He had all riches. But when He became a man, He "became poor, that ye through his poverty might be rich." (II Cor 8:9). He gave up riches, trading heaven's courts to be born in a stable, and He is worthy to receive these riches back again.

Third, He is worthy of wisdom. In Jesus "are hid all the treasures of wisdom and knowledge" (Col 2:3). But Luke tells us that as a child, "Jesus increased in wisdom and stature" (Luke 2:52). We may wonder how He was able to grow in wisdom, since He had all wisdom before His birth. During His incarnation, as a man He somehow set this aside, although He clearly had access to supernatural knowledge (cf. Matt. 17:27; John 4:18). This is hard to understand, but we can all agree that Jesus, "the wisdom of God" (I Cor. 1:24), is worthy of all wisdom.

Fourth, He is worthy of strength. Jesus is mighty, "upholding all things by the word of his power" (Heb. 1:3). When He became a man, Jesus accepted our weaknesses: "We have not an high priest which cannot be touched with the feeling of our infirmities; but was in all points tempted like as we are, yet without sin" (Heb. 4:15). Being sinless, He is worthy of receiving back all strength.

That He would choose to lay so much aside and suffer is amazing! Jesus is worthy of honor, glory, and blessing. These three things are distinct, but closely related.

After His death, "we see Jesus, who was made a little lower than the angels for the suffering of death, crowned with glory and honour" (Heb. 2:9). He "humbled himself, and became obedient unto death, even the death of the cross. Wherefore God also hath highly exalted him, and given him a name which is above every name: That at the name of Jesus every knee should bow, of things in heaven, and things in earth, and things under the earth; And that every tongue should confess that Jesus Christ is Lord, to the glory of God the Father" (Phil. 2:9-11). The only proper response to His perfect life and death is worship.

That is exactly what we see in Revelation: angels, humanity, and even animals rejoicing, celebrating, and joyfully praising Jesus, who temporarily accepted weakness. Now He is worthy to receive back forever all power, riches, wisdom, strength, honor, glory, and blessing!

—*Tom Greene.*

Heart of the Lesson

I joined an oratorio society my freshman year of college. Twice a year, this massive choir, comprising all music majors and other musical students, performed a major oratorio such as Handel's *Messiah*. Singing with several hundred voices was exhilarating. But our lesson describes a choir too big to number as it praised Jesus, the Lamb.

1. The Lamb receives the scroll (Rev. 5:6-7). John had entered God's throne room as part of his vision and saw an angel searching for someone worthy to open a scroll that revealed the world's destiny. Finally, John saw the only one in all the universe who was found worthy to open the scroll: Jesus the Lamb, who still bore the marks of His crucifixion. He had seven horns, representing His majestic power, and seven eyes, showing He was all-seeing and all-knowing.

The Lamb took the scroll from the right hand of God the Father as He sat on His throne. The Lamb was worthy; the Father relinquished the scroll.

2. Worshippers sing a new song (Rev. 5:8-10). Immediately, the twenty-four elders and four living creatures surrounding God's throne fell down before the Lamb to worship Him. The elders had harps and golden bowls of incense. The incense signified the prayers of the saints. God views His people's prayers as a fragrant offering to Him—a pleasing expression of trust.

The elders and living creatures began to sing a new song, a new composition especially for this occasion. Did they break out in glorious harmony as they praised the Lamb? Perhaps. But what mattered most was their words. They proclaimed Jesus as worthy to take the scroll and to open its seals because of His death on the cross.

He was worthy not just because of His death but because of what His death accomplished. The singers praised Him for redeeming people from every kindred, language, people, and nation on earth. His death united this diverse group into God's kingdom of priests, enabling them to approach God personally and to bring the good news of Jesus to everyone on earth. These redeemed persons had a glorious future of reigning on the earth.

3. Angels join the praise (Rev. 5:11-12). Suddenly John heard the voices of angels around the throne praising the Lamb. He was at a loss to describe the number of angels he heard: "ten thousand times ten thousand, and thousands of thousands." Millions of angels proclaimed, "Worthy is the Lamb," along with the elders and living creatures.

They sang that the Lamb was worthy to receive power, riches, wisdom, strength, honor, glory, and blessing.

4. The universe worships the Lamb (Rev. 5:13-14). Then the biggest round of praise ever heard began. Every creature in heaven, every creature on the earth, and every creature under the earth praised God and the Lamb. All living creatures ascribed to God the Father and to Jesus the Son blessing, honor, glory, and power forever and ever. All of nature and all created beings joined in worship.

The worship ended with the four living creatures saying, "Amen." Then the elders fell down in worship before God the Father and the Lamb.

We, the redeemed, can embrace the words of heaven to praise God and the Lamb. Sing your praise, write it, say it, pray it, think it. The Lamb is worthy of our praise.

—*Ann Staatz.*

World Missions

"If God is good and loves people, why doesn't He come down and stop this evil?" The question came from a woman at an event on fighting human trafficking. Others have asked similar questions throughout the ages.

If God has all power, why does He let bad things happen?

Why does God not put an end to world poverty and suffering?

And most significantly, if God has all power and wisdom and strength and honor, why are there still people who have never heard the gospel?

Sometimes when Jesus was asked a question, He replied with another question that led deeper into the heart of the matter. Let us consider this from a heavenly perspective.

Perhaps instead of questioning God, who we know is holy and good, we should question ourselves. Has God not commanded us to go and make disciples of all the nations (Matt. 28:19)? Has He not promised that our mission is safeguarded by His own universal power (vs. 18)? Has He not said He will be with us on this mission (vs. 20)? Then what are we doing to obey?

Over two billion people in the world claim to be Christians. If even one third of those two billion are true believers and each believer took the gospel to ten different people, we could reach the world in just one generation. Not everyone would respond in faith, but the world would be reached and be radically changed.

Furthermore, if God's people truly obeyed the instructions in Scripture, imagine how the statistics might change regarding world poverty, despair, orphans on the street, crime, exploitation, and the other evils in our world today.

Jesus Himself said God sent Him to "heal the brokenhearted, to preach deliverance to the captives" (Luke 4:18). If we truly long to follow Him and to be like Him, we will care about what He cares about. We will do what He commanded us to do (cf. John 14:15).

The problem is not that God does not have power. The problem is not even that He does not have a plan. He does have a plan, and as we see in Revelation 5, that plan will one day come to its perfect completion. And He gives us the privilege of being part of the fulfillment of His plan. But many of God's people are not obeying. Why?

We love ourselves more than we love our neighbor. And that means we also love ourselves more than we love God (cf. I John 3:17).

If He says go, give, and pray, do we come up with reasons why it is impossible or unreasonable or too much to ask?

William Wilberforce, the well-known member of British parliament, who spent most of his adult life fighting slavery, said, "If there is no passionate love for Christ at the center of everything, we will only jingle and jangle our way across the world, merely making a noise as we go."

John Stott said, "We must be global Christians with a global vision because our God is a global God."

Instead of asking God why He does not do something, perhaps we should ask what *we* are to do in His name.

As one pastor concludes, we only have three options when it comes to global missions: "Go, send, or disobey." Either bring the gospel to unreached nations or support those who do in whatever way you can. Otherwise, you will be disobedient to God's command.

—*Kimberly Rae.*

The Jewish Aspect

On October 6, 1973, during the holiday of Yom Kippur, Egypt and Syria invaded Israel's territories. Because it was Yom Kippur, many of the Israeli soldiers had been given leave. The size of the attacking armies was large, and Israel's army was small, so initially the foreign armies made rapid advances. However, within a week, Israel had driven back the enemy forces.

This week's lesson deals with the throne of God. On the holiday of Yom Kippur, the Jews believe that God moves from His throne of justice—where He is believed to be seated on Rosh Hashanah—to the throne of compassion. The Jewish person believes that on this day God hears his prayers and accepts his repentance.

Yom Kippur, also known as the Day of Atonement, falls on the tenth of Tishri, the seventh month in the Jewish calendar. Usually this holiday occurs in September. Jews consider Yom Kippur the holiest and most important day of the year.

Yom Kippur brings to a close the ten days of repentance that begin with Rosh Hashanah, the Festival of Trumpets. Rosh Hashanah, Yom Kippur, and the days in between are called the Days of Awe. The holiday of Rosh Hashanah begins the Days of Awe and lasts two days. Yom Kippur ends the Days of Awe and lasts one day.

Jews believe that at the end of Yom Kippur, the gates of heaven are closed. If a person is to have his name sealed in the book of life for the year, it must be written in the book by that day.

Yom Kippur rituals take place primarily in the synagogue. Jews observe a twenty-five-hour fast and follow certain traditions. Prayer is an important element in the holiday.

When the temple stood, there were elaborate ceremonies and sacrifices on Yom Kippur based on Leviticus 16. One of the most interesting parts of the ancient ceremony involved two sacrificial goats.

At the prescribed time, two goats would be made ready for the ceremony. The high priest would place two golden tablets in an urn. On one tablet were the words, "For YHWH" (the Lord). On the other were the words, "For Azazel" (the scapegoat). The high priest would shuffle the tablets and withdraw them one at a time. He would put "For YHWH" on one goat and "For Azazel" on the other. If "For YHWH" came out in the high priest's right hand, it was considered a good omen. If "For YHWH" came out in his left hand, it was considered a bad omen.

After slaughtering a bull, the high priest would gather its blood in a basin. Then he would fill the Holy of Holies with smoke from incense and sprinkle the bull's blood on the mercy seat.

Next he would move to the eastern side of the courtyard and slaughter the "For YHWH" goat. He would then enter the Holy of Holies and sprinkle this blood on the mercy seat as well.

After finishing all the requirements, the high priest would begin the symbolic process of transferring the sins of the people to the Azazel goat. This goat, known as the scapegoat, would be led to a high cliff and pushed over the edge—an expansion on the original command in Leviticus 16:21-22. This act signified the sins of the people being carried off forever. In Revelation 5, we see that Christ alone has fulfilled the requirements of the scapegoat and redeemed His people from their sins.

—*Robin Fitzgerald.*

Guiding the Superintendent

Revelation 4 and 5 gives us a detailed description of John's great heavenly experience. In a vision, John was transported from his island exile to the very throne room of heaven. In chapter 4, his attention was quickly drawn to the Person sitting on the throne.

The reader soon learns this is God Himself. With deep reverence, He was worshipped as the Creator by the heavenly beings assembled around the throne. In chapter 5, the attention is drawn to Jesus Christ.

DEVOTIONAL OUTLINE

1. The Lamb described (Rev. 5:6). Using symbolic language, John describes Jesus Christ. He was like a lamb that was slain. The Lamb had seven horns and seven eyes. Encircled by the four living creatures and twenty-four elders, the Lamb stood near the throne.

A threefold description identifies this special Lamb as none other than Jesus Christ. First, the Lamb was seen "as it had been slain." Slaughtered lambs were often seen in the markets of the day, but this one was alive. This could be none other than Jesus Christ.

Second, the Lamb had seven horns, not two as a normal lamb would. Horns in Revelation are usually a picture of strength (cf. Rev. 12:3; 13:1).

Third, the Lamb had seven eyes. This is a picture of the all-seeing, all-watching God.

2. The Lamb worshipped by all heaven (Rev. 5:7-14). Displaying the same passion with which they worshipped God chapter 4, the living creatures and elders also worshipped the Lamb here, with instrumental music (harps) and incense, representing the prayers of the saints (cf. Ps. 141:2).

They sang a new song that extolled the worthiness of the Lamb to take the book from the One who sat on the throne, because He was slain and has redeemed people from all ethnic groups. They completed their new song by exclaiming the future reign of this great multitude of people.

Next John saw and heard such a large assembly of angels that they could not be numbered. To the worship vocabulary found in Revelation 4:11, four new words are added (5:12). It was customary to bring a valuable gift ("riches") when visiting an ancient sovereign. "Wisdom" focuses on knowledge and judgment. "Strength" emphasizes the personal nature of Christ's power. "Blessing," meaning praise, ascends from those worshipping the Lamb.

Almost like a zoom lens, the view pulls back so that the reader sees and hears all creation praising the Lamb (vss. 13-14). They cannot stop their worship. John heard them saying, "Blessing, and honour, and glory, and power, be unto him that sitteth upon the throne, and unto the Lamb." The four creatures joined this choir with shouts of "Amen."

Revelation 5 ends with the entire universe voicing praise to the Father and the Son. A great anthem of praise resounded throughout heaven. The Lamb is indeed worthy of all our worship.

AGE-GROUP EMPHASES

Children: This is a great lesson to teach children about how one should worship Jesus Christ.

Youths: Revelation 5 contains one of the most detailed descriptions of Jesus Christ. What can your teens learn about Jesus from this chapter?

Adults: To aid your adults in worship, help them distinguish the meanings of the seven worship words found in Revelation 5:12.

—*Martin R. Dahlquist.*

SCRIPTURE LESSON TEXT

REV. 22:6 And he said unto me, These sayings *are* faithful and true: and the Lord God of the holy prophets sent his angel to shew unto his servants the things which must shortly be done.

7 Behold, I come quickly: blessed *is* he that keepeth the sayings of the prophecy of this book.

8 And I John saw these things, and heard *them.* And when I had heard and seen, I fell down to worship before the feet of the angel which shewed me these things.

9 Then saith he unto me, See *thou do it* not: for I am thy fellowservant, and of thy brethren the prophets, and of them which keep the sayings of this book: worship God.

10 And he saith unto me, Seal not the sayings of the prophecy of this book: for the time is at hand.

12 And, behold, I come quickly; and my reward *is* with me, to give every man according as his work shall be.

13 I am Alpha and Omega, the beginning and the end, the first and the last.

16 I Jesus have sent mine angel to testify unto you these things in the churches. I am the root and the offspring of David, *and* the bright and morning star.

17 And the Spirit and the bride say, Come. And let him that heareth say, Come. And let him that is athirst come. And whosoever will, let him take the water of life freely.

18 For I testify unto every man that heareth the words of the prophecy of this book, If any man shall add unto these things, God shall add unto him the plagues that are written in this book:

19 And if any man shall take away from the words of the book of this prophecy, God shall take away his part out of the book of life, and out of the holy city, and *from* the things which are written in this book.

20 He which testifieth these things saith, Surely I come quickly. Amen. Even so, come, Lord Jesus.

21 The grace of our Lord Jesus Christ *be* with you all. Amen.

NOTES

The Alpha and Omega

Lesson Text: Revelation 22:6-10, 12-13, 16-21

Related Scriptures: John 7:37-39; Revelation 1:4-11; 21:9—22:5

TIME: about A.D. 96   PLACE: from Patmos

GOLDEN TEXT—"He which testifieth these things saith, Surely I come quickly. Amen. Even so, come, Lord Jesus" (Revelation 22:20).

Introduction

Someone once said that the theme of the Old Testament is that Christ is coming, while the theme of the New Testament is that Christ is coming again.

To be sure, much is said in both Testaments concerning the coming of the Lord. Regarding the first coming of Christ, "we have also a more sure word of prophecy" (II Pet. 1:19), for those events have already occurred. But concerning the Second Coming, we wait in confident expectation, knowing that Christ will be faithful to His promise to return.

All true Christians believe that He will "appear the second time" (Heb. 9:28). We must be careful, however, to avoid the dangerous practice of attempting to ascertain the precise date. Concerning this, our Lord was crystal clear: "Of that day and that hour knoweth no man, no, not the angels which are in heaven, neither the Son, but the Father" (Mark 13:32).

LESSON OUTLINE

I. **WORSHIP ADMONISHED—** Rev. 22:6-10

II. **WORKS AFFIRMED—** Rev. 22:12-13

III. **WARNING ANNOUNCED—** Rev. 22:16-21

Exposition: Verse by Verse

WORSHIP ADMONISHED

REV. 22:6 And he said unto me, These sayings are faithful and true: and the Lord God of the holy prophets sent his angel to shew unto his servants the things which must shortly be done.

7 Behold, I come quickly: blessed is he that keepeth the sayings of the prophecy of this book.

8 And I John saw these things, and heard them. And when I had heard and seen, I fell down to worship before the feet of the angel which shewed me these things.

9 Then saith he unto me, See thou do it not: for I am thy fellowservant, and of thy brethren the prophets, and of them which keep the sayings of this book: worship God.

10 And he saith unto me, Seal not the sayings of the prophecy of this book: for the time is at hand.

Faithful Saviour (Rev. 22:6-7). Our lesson text picks up right after John saw the New Jerusalem descending from heaven to be God's dwelling place with man. Already John learned that this was to be a place where no death, sorrow, crying, or pain exists (21:4). Because this city has been prepared for the redeemed, all evildoers will suffer the fate of being cast into the lake of fire, "which is the second death" (vs. 8).

The glorious city was then described by John (vss. 10-27). As in the original Paradise (Eden), the "tree of life" (22:2) grows in the New Jerusalem. Man will no longer be under the curse of sin and death (vs. 3), and he will be privileged to look upon the face of God (vs. 4). John's vision was about to come to an end, however. Final words were about to be given to the apostle and his readers.

Revelation 22:6 begins something like an epilogue to the Apocalypse. {Earlier the speaker was identified as one of the seven angels who had the seven bowls of wrath to be poured out upon the earth (21:9). Now, however, the speaker seems to be Jesus Himself (22:7), though some suggest that the angel was merely relaying the words of the Lord, since John fell at the feet of the angel (vs. 8).}[Q1] That a precise identification of the speaker is not made should not trouble us, though, especially when we remember that from the very beginning this is the "Revelation of Jesus Christ" (1:1) given to John through an angel. "The difficulty of identifying speakers is only superficial because ultimately we hear the voice of Christ, whether echoed by the angel or recorded by the prophet" (Mounce, *The Book of Revelation,* Eerdmans).

Whatever the case, the one speaking to John reminded him, "These sayings are faithful and true" (22:6). They could not be otherwise, for Christ is "the faithful and true witness" (3:14) and the conquering King known as "Faithful and True" (19:11).

Ultimately, the message that John received was from the "Lord God of the holy prophets" (22:6). Receiving this prophetic message from the Lord put John in a long line of others who had received similar messages by divine inspiration. At the very beginning, John was told that this was "prophecy" (1:3), and he is identified as one of God's "servants the prophets" (10:7).

Since we are living nearly two thousand years after John originally received these visions, some find it puzzling that he was told that what he saw were "things which must shortly be done" (22:6). Our understanding of time is relative, though. When we are late for an appointment, standing a few minutes in a grocery line may seem long. But when compared with the length our whole life, it is a very short time. Likewise, to live to be a hundred may seem like a long life, but compared to Methuselah (Gen. 5:27), it would be brief!

From the standpoint of the eternal God, time is insignificant, since He operates from a different realm altogether. In response to those who mock believers because the Second Coming has not yet occurred, the apostle Peter said, "But, beloved, be not ignorant of this one thing, that one day is with the Lord as a thousand years, and a thousand years as one day" (II Pet. 3:8). Peter is using figurative language to make His point, but by that calculation, we could say that only two "days" have passed from God's perspective since the writing of Revelation.

The Lord Jesus' declaration "Behold, I come quickly" (Rev. 22:7) should not be seen as an erroneous prophecy. As Peter pointed out, one of the reasons for the seeming postponement of the Lord's return has to do with His patience toward the human race. He is "not willing that any should perish, but that all should come to repentance" (II Pet. 3:9).

More important than trying to discern God's timetable regarding prophetic events is being faithful to His teachings—hence the blessing upon those who keep the words of the prophecy found in Revelation (22:7).

Fellow servant (Rev. 22:8-10). John then reminded his readers that he was writing about things he had both seen and heard. "His literary product is not the result of any flight of imagination" (Mounce).

As he had done previously (19:10), John fell in worship at the feet of the revealing angel. Once again, John was told not to worship the angel. "Its repetition may have been occasioned by John's desire emphatically to repudiate tendencies to angel worship among the churches known to him. Colossians 2:18 attests the existence in his day of such a propensity among some Christians in Asia Minor" (Beasley-Murray, *Revelation,* Eerdmans).

{Significantly, the angel reminded John that he was only a fellow servant of the apostle, other prophets, and all those who are faithful to the teachings of the "Revelation of Jesus Christ" (Rev. 1:1).}Q2 {Our faithfulness is confirmed by doing precisely what the angel told John to do: "worship God" (22:9)!}Q3

"Do you believe what the angel told John? That not only these words, but God's Word in its entirety, is trustworthy and true? That all the things described in His Word *must* take place, if for no other reason than because God said so? If you have not done so before, would you make the decision at this moment to *believe* God's Word? You may not understand everything in it, but take it by faith as the truth because it is *God's Word,* and He does not lie" (Lotz, *The Vision of His Glory,* Word).

For John to be told "Seal not the sayings of the prophecy of this book" (vs.

10) was quite the opposite of what was usually done in Jewish apocalyptic literature (cf. Dan. 12:4). {The reason for this was that the time was at hand. That is, the fulfillment of the Apocalypse was imminent.}Q4

Again, we must be reminded that God's timetable is different from ours; we should not try to second-guess God regarding His eternal plans and purposes. {"The end is always near in the sense that each successive Christian generation may be the last" (Mounce). We must therefore be ready for the return of the Lord.}Q5 As Paul said, "But of the times and the seasons, brethren, ye have no need that I write unto you. For yourselves know perfectly that the day of the Lord so cometh as a thief in the night" (I Thess. 5:1-2).

WORKS AFFIRMED

12 And, behold, I come quickly; and my reward is with me, to give every man according as his work shall be.

13 I am Alpha and Omega, the beginning and the end, the first and the last.

Again the Lord declared, "Behold, I come quickly," thus affirming once again that "the time is at hand" (vs. 10). As the prophet Amos put it, "Prepare to meet thy God" (4:12).

{While works do not save (Eph. 2:8-9), they are nevertheless the basis of judgment. With regard to the lost, their works condemn them (Rev. 20:12-13). With regard to the saved, though, works are both the fruit of faith (Eph. 2:10; Jas. 2:14-26) and the basis of eternal rewards (I Cor. 3:10-15).}Q6 "The final judgments of both the wicked and the righteous will be judgments of works. This is the joyous expectation of those who are faithful and the fear of those who have not been faithful" (Walvoord and Zuck, eds., *The Bible Knowledge Commentary,* Victor). Works are not the means of salvation but the result! And God graciously rewards those works that He Himself has worked in us (cf. Phil. 2:12-13).

In Revelation 1:8 and 21:6 God is identified as "Alpha and Omega," the first and last letters of the Greek alphabet. Christ now describes Himself in the same way, using the designations "the beginning and the end, the first and the last" (22:13), which were used previously of the Son of God (cf. 1:17; 2:8).

In light of the fact that the Father and the Son are one (John 10:30; 14:9-11), it should not be surprising that these designations would be used interchangeably. "Christ is before all Creation and He will continue to exist after the present creation is destroyed. He is the Eternal One" (Walvoord and Zuck).

WARNING ANNOUNCED

16 I Jesus have sent mine angel to testify unto you these things in the churches. I am the root and the offspring of David, and the bright and morning star.

17 And the Spirit and the bride say, Come. And let him that heareth say, Come. And let him that is athirst come. And whosoever will, let him take the water of life freely.

18 For I testify unto every man that heareth the words of the prophecy of this book, If any man shall add unto these things, God shall add unto him the plagues that are written in this book:

19 And if any man shall take away from the words of the book of this prophecy, God shall take away his part out of the book of life, and out of the holy city, and from the things which are written in this book.

20 He which testifieth these things saith, Surely I come quickly. Amen. Even so, come, Lord Jesus.

21 The grace of our Lord Jesus Christ be with you all. Amen.

Invitation (Rev. 22:16-17). After an admonition to be obedient (vs. 14) and a warning about the disobedient being excluded from the New Jerusalem (vs. 15), the reader is reminded that Jesus Himself is the Author of the Apocalypse. Although He used an angel as an intermediary and spokesman, the true message came from the Son of God Himself (1:1).

We are also reminded that the original message of Revelation was given to the seven churches of Asia (cf. 1:11). While they were the first recipients, they were certainly not the last. What was revealed to these early Christians continues to have relevance for us today, especially as we approach the end of the age. While no one knows when the end of time will occur, world conditions are such that we may be living on the very brink of the fulfillment of the things John saw in these visions.

{By identifying Himself as "the root and the offspring of David" (22:16), Christ was claiming the promise of Isaiah 11:1: "There shall come forth a rod out of the stem of Jesse, and a Branch shall grow out of his roots."}[Q7] Earlier in Revelation, Christ was identified as "the Root of David" (5:5).

That the Messiah would be a descendant of David is clearly taught in Scripture. The angel told Mary, "He shall be great, and shall be called the Son of the Highest: and the Lord God shall give unto him the throne of his father David: and he shall reign over the house of Jacob for ever; and of his kingdom there shall be no end" (Luke 1:32-33). These promises were now coming to complete fruition.

Christ also referred to Himself as "the bright and morning star" (Rev. 22:16). A prophecy in Numbers 24:17 states, "There shall come a Star out of Jacob, and a Sceptre shall rise out of Israel." {"The star was a familiar symbol in Jewish writings for the expected Davidic king . . . The morning star is a promise that the long night of tribulation is all but over and that the new eschatological day is about to dawn" (Mounce).}^{Q8}

Revelation 22:17 consists of four invitations. Some see the first two invitations directed to Christ for His return and the latter two as invitations to the world. Others, however, see all four invitations as directed toward the world.

Obviously, the "Spirit" is the Holy Spirit and the "bride" the church of Christ. {Those who have responded to the Spirit's call and become a part of the body of Christ (I Cor. 12:13) must now extend this invitation to others. The redeemed have had their spiritual thirst quenched by the "living water" (John 4:10), and they must invite others to "take the water of life freely" (Rev. 22:17). Far from excluding any who desire to come, the invitation is to "whosoever will."}^{Q9}

Admonition (Rev. 22:18-21). As the Apocalypse draws to a close, there is a strong warning not to tamper with the message that has been revealed to the apostle. Similar warnings are given elsewhere in Scripture (Deut. 4:2; 12:32; Josh. 1:7; Prov. 30:5-6; Gal. 1:6-9).

"These verses . . . are primarily a strong warning to false prophets not to alter the sense of John's prophecy in this book, either textually or in its moral and theological teaching (cf. 1 Cor. 16:22). {So severe is the danger he is warning against that John says that those who teach contrary to the message of Revelation will not only forfeit any right to salvation in the Holy City but will have visited on them the divine judgments ('plagues') inflicted on the beast worshipers"}^{Q10} (Barker and Kohlenberger, eds., *Expositor's Bible Commentary,* Zondervan).

Because of this warning given at the end of Revelation, some have been fearful of any attempt to interpret or understand the book. This warning, however, was not given to keep people away from the study of Revelation but to remind them of the seriousness of tampering with God's Word. Indeed, there is a blessing pronounced upon all those who read, hear, and keep these prophetic words (Rev. 1:3).

The Son of God again affirms that His return is near (22:20). With great anticipation, John and all the faithful pray, "Even so, come, Lord Jesus." "Redemptive history remains incomplete until Christ returns. It is for the final act in the great drama of redemption that the church waits with longing" (Mounce).

Similar to the final words of several New Testament epistles (I Cor. 16:23; Gal. 6:18; Phil. 4:23), John offered a final benediction for his readers: "The grace of our Lord Jesus Christ be with you all. Amen."

—*John Alva Owston.*

QUESTIONS

1. Who do we find speaking in this week's Scripture text?
2. How did the angel describe himself to John?
3. Why must we worship only God?
4. Why was John told not to seal the prophecy?
5. How might we understand the Lord's promise to "come quickly" (Rev. 22:7) in light of the length of time since the promise was made?
6. What role do works play in the final judgment?
7. Why did Christ identify Himself as "the root and the offspring of David" (vs. 16)?
8. Why is Christ called "the bright and morning star"?
9. Who offers the great invitation? Who is invited?
10. What strong warning is given about altering the message of Revelation?

—*John Alva Owston.*

Preparing to Teach the Lesson

This lesson is based on texts that conclude the revelation of God to men in His holy Word. Although the central message is the coming of the Lord Jesus Christ, other themes are present as well. One is that an angel should never be worshipped, for worship belongs to God alone. Another is that Christ will come to give both the righteous and the wicked what they deserve. A third is that nothing is to be added to or taken away from the book of divine prophecy.

TODAY'S AIM

Facts: to elaborate on several subjects in the conclusion of the book of prophetic revelation given to the apostle John.

Principle: to realize that the promise of Christ's second coming is fully dependable and should be awaited with keen anticipation.

Application: to be daily reminded that the sure hope of the return of Christ ought to help believers deal with difficult situations as they arise.

INTRODUCING THE LESSON

Various individuals have different ways of reading a book. Some like to start at the beginning, progress through it methodically, and finish with the ending. Others take a peek at the end before they begin. Still others may scan through the book quickly before going back to read it thoroughly.

The book of Revelation is obviously easier to understand in its opening and closing chapters. Those in the middle are loaded with imagery and symbolism requiring careful interpretation. As we come to concluding remarks in the book, we are thankful for the simplicity of their wording. No matter how we read the book, we may be thankful for how it ends.

DEVELOPING THE LESSON

1. Angel's comments (Rev. 22:6-7). The angel speaking to John was first mentioned in 21:9. He now stated that all he had said about the New Jerusalem was faithful and true (reliable and genuine). The same God who had inspired the holy prophets of old had sent His angel at this time to show His servants what would shortly come to pass.

Verse 7 has the angel quoting from Christ, who said that He would come quickly. Your students may wonder how the intervening two thousand-plus years could be considered a short time. Have them turn to II Peter 3:8 to be reminded that a thousand years is as a day to the Lord.

The angel then said that reading the prophecy of the book had to be supported by keeping its sayings. Knowledge demands action.

2. Angel's rebuke (Rev. 22:8-10). John was so impressed by the angel's comments that he fell down at his feet to worship him. This drew a prompt rebuke from the angel. He declared himself to be merely a fellow servant of God's prophets and of those who keep God's Word.

With just two terse words, the angel instructed John to "worship God." The implication was that God alone deserves worship. Have your students look at Colossians 2:18—"Let no man beguile you of your reward in a voluntary humility and worshipping of angels, intruding into those things which he hath not seen, vainly puffed up by his fleshly mind." God is the only one who should impress us to the point of worship.

3. Rewards dispensed (Rev. 22:12-13). Considering what is said in verse 11, we know Christ will come and dispense blessing on the righteous (cf. Rom. 14:10-13; I Cor. 3:12-15) and judgment on the wicked (cf. Rev. 20:11-15). We must not confuse the reward for believers' good works with the free gift of salvation. Salvation is by grace through faith alone (Eph. 2:8-9), but the fruit of our faith is good works, which God generously rewards even though the works, too, are His own doing (cf. Phil 2:13).

Revelation 1:8 and 22:13 both refer to Christ as Alpha and Omega, the beginning and the end. These letters of the Greek alphabet symbolize His eternality.

4. Invitation given (Rev. 22:16-17). Jesus identified Himself as a descendant of King David, as prophets had foretold. He called Himself the morning star, which precedes the sunrise. The Holy Spirit and the bride of Christ invite all who hear and thirst for the water of eternal life to come.

5. Warning given (Rev. 22:18-19). A solemn warning is given to avoid adding anything to the prophetic book. Anyone guilty could suffer the plagues described in the book. Anyone taking anything away from the book could have his name deleted from the book of life and be denied entrance into the holy city, the New Jerusalem.

6. Last promise and prayer (Rev. 22:20-21). The Bible ends with the promise of the Lord Jesus to come back to the earth quickly. Despite the years, the Saviour's return is imminent. John's response to the promise was "Amen [so be it]. Even so, come, Lord Jesus."

Verse 21 is a brief benediction addressed by John to his readers, trusting that the grace of the Lord Jesus Christ would rest upon them.

ILLUSTRATING THE LESSON

There is a great deal of conversation about when Jesus will return and the order of events. Regardless, the illustration points to the blessed hope of the believer. The blessed hope is that Jesus will return. Everything else will pale in significance to that truth. Prepare yourself spiritually for that return.

CONCLUDING THE LESSON

At some points in church history the doctrine of Christ's second coming was downplayed. Thankfully, it is now receiving much attention. No one has the right to set dates for prophetic fulfillments, but many conditions in our world would indicate that the time is growing ripe for the coming of the Prince of Peace.

Discuss with your class such things as nuclear destructive power, rampant secularism, declining morality, and worldwide terrorism. Does hope of Christ's return give you and your students optimism and a reason to persevere?

ANTICIPATING THE NEXT LESSON

Next week we will begin a new quarter that highlights the way God worked through women and young people in the Bible. The series will begin with the creation of woman in Genesis 2:18-25.

—*Gordon Talbot.*

PRACTICAL POINTS

1. If we desire God's blessing, we must scrupulously heed His Word (Rev. 22:6-7).
2. Faithful servants deserve honor but not worship (vss. 8-10).
3. We should strive for justice now but recognize that perfect justice awaits Christ's return (vss. 12-13).
4. The promise of Christ's coming should move us to present the gospel to all (vss. 16-17).
5. We must be on guard against any distortion of God's Word (vss. 18-19).
6. Christians should be joyously anticipating Christ's return, not dreading it (vss. 20-21).

—Jarl K. Waggoner.

RESEARCH AND DISCUSSION

1. Why did Jesus say three times in this passage "I come quickly" (Rev. 22:7, 12, 20)? What practical point was He conveying with this emphasis?
2. How did the revelation of future events affect John (vss. 8-9)? Why? What effect should prophecies of Christ's return have on us?
3. Does verse 12 indicate that there will be various degrees of punishment for the unsaved (cf. Matt. 11:20-24; 23:14; Rom. 2:5-6; Jas. 3:1)?
4. What implications does Revelation 22:17 have for our motivation and methods in evangelism?
5. What safeguards can we establish to keep us and our church from falling prey to the errors described in verses 18-19?

—Jarl K. Waggoner.

ILLUSTRATED HIGH POINTS

I come quickly (Rev. 22:7, 12, 20)

Recently I ordered something from a merchant in another state. I was eager to receive the package and expected it to arrive quickly. I drove to town to check our post office box for several days in a row, but to no avail.

One afternoon as I was working in my study, I was startled to hear the loud engine of a delivery truck pull into our driveway. I was unaware of the truck's presence until it was just in front of the house. The driver was at our door almost as quickly as I was. Without warning, he had arrived with my package.

The Greek word used in Revelation to describe Jesus' coming can be translated as either "soon" or "quickly." Jesus warned that His return will be sudden. Many will be taken by surprise.

Written in this book (vss. 18, 19)

God's Word is the perfect and complete revelation that contains all we need to know for salvation. In His Word we find the record of the past, man's need for redemption, the way of redemption in Christ, the knowledge of future events, and the culmination of God's plan for humanity. To alter this revelation in any way is to hide essential information we need.

Prescription drugs contain warning labels. The side effects caused by some drugs could be injurious or even fatal. If a warning label is tampered with, there may be serious consequences. For example, a person with specific allergies could experience a fatal reaction, unaware that the drug contains certain elements.

Changing the words of the Bible would be changing the message God inspired for mankind. Such a change could be spiritually fatal for many people.

—Carter Corbrey.

Golden Text Illuminated

"He which testifieth these things saith, Surely I come quickly. Amen. Even so, come, Lord Jesus" (Revelation 22:20).

The blessed hope for God's people is His return. The apostle John records Jesus' beautiful word picture of this wonderful promise. "Let not your heart be troubled: ye believe in God, believe also in me. In my Father's house are many mansions: if it were not so, I would have told you. I go to prepare a place for you. And if I go and prepare a place for you, I will come again, and receive you unto myself; that where I am, there ye may be also" (John 14:1-3).

Down through the years, Christians have taken great comfort in the promise of the Lord's return. Since the day Christ ascended to heaven, believers have been looking for His return.

Christ spoke often concerning His coming. The disciples, upon hearing Jesus tell of the destruction of the beautiful temple in Jerusalem, came to Him as He sat upon the Mount of Olives. They had an excellent view of the temple in all its splendor. Because of their confusion, they wanted to ask Jesus an important question. They asked, "Tell us, when shall these things be? and what shall be the sign of thy coming, and of the end of the world?" (Matt. 24:3).

Jesus then proceeded to give what is known as the Olivet Discourse. In it He spoke of His coming. "But of that day and hour knoweth no man, no, not the angels of heaven, but my Father only" (Matt. 24:36). Continuing to speak of His coming, He taught the importance of being ready for that glorious event. "Watch therefore, for ye know neither the day nor the hour wherein the Son of man cometh" (25:13).

We should live expecting Christ's coming at any time. His imminent return is sufficient reason to live every day to the fullest for Him. Wonderful sermons have been preached and heart-stirring songs have been written regarding that blessed event.

The apostle Paul, in his first letter to the Thessalonian Christians, wrote about the believers' blessed hope: "For the Lord himself shall descend from heaven with a shout, with the voice of the archangel, and with the trump of God: and the dead in Christ shall rise first: then we which are alive and remain shall be caught up together with them in the clouds, to meet the Lord in the air: and so shall we ever be with the Lord" (4:16-17).

The subject of Christ's coming is one that challenges God's people to live holy lives. In his epistle to the believers at Colossae, the apostle Paul wrote, "Set your affection on things above, not on things on the earth. For ye are dead, and your life is hid with Christ in God. When Christ, who is our life, shall appear, then shall ye also appear with him in glory" (3:2-4).

We are told to love Christ's appearing. Paul wrote to Timothy, "I have fought a good fight, I have finished my course, I have kept the faith: henceforth there is laid up for me a crown of righteousness, which the Lord, the righteous judge, shall give me at that day: and not to me only, but unto all them also that love his appearing" (II Tim. 4:7-8). God's people should not only look for His appearing but also love His appearing. The Bible tells us to do both.

—*V. Ben Kendrick.*

Heart of the Lesson

The church has its hope centered on the imminent return of Jesus. Without that hope the church would not be different from any other social organization. What makes the church unique is that we believe in a risen Saviour who is coming back to take the church to enjoy all He has been preparing for them through the ages. The church today ought to live with its "eye on the sky" every day, looking in eagerness for its Master's return.

1. Jesus is coming soon (Rev. 22:6-10). God who spoke through the prophets has now sent His angel to declare that which must soon come to pass in our day. John heard Jesus say that He was coming soon and that those who obey the instructions in the scroll will be blessed. John was so overwhelmed that he bowed down to worship the angel. The angel stopped him and said that he ought to worship God, for he was a creation just as John was. Only God is worthy of worship. All those who do what is written on the scroll are to worship God also. It was then that the angel told John that the scroll was to stay open and not be rolled up, for the time had come for the things that were written in it to pass.

We must remember that the time for the coming of our Lord is near. Jesus has reminded us in no uncertain terms that He is coming quickly and that we need to be prepared and ready for His return.

2. When Jesus comes (Rev. 22:12-13). As a church, we often take this matter lightly. But here again, we have been adequately warned about the things that will happen. All who stand before Him will receive rewards for what they have done while on the earth. Jesus said that He was the Alpha and the Omega, the beginning and the end.

This meant that He had the authority to give rewards, for there is none greater in all the universe.

3. The world must be told (Rev. 22:16-21). The church is called not only to be ready for the Master's coming but also to tell others so that everyone else is ready when Jesus is here.

The message that Jesus had for God's people on earth through the angel was simple yet profound. Jesus was the shoot from the root of David. He was the descendant of David from what appeared to be cut down. He was also going to sit on the throne of David in the end times, which was absolute proof of His messiahship before the world. Jesus also called Himself the bright and morning star. This star was the final star before dawn, symbolic of the Messiah who is the true light in the world.

Then John tells us that the Holy Spirit and the church, the bride of Christ, welcome Him to come. They need Him. Those who are thirsty need the Redeemer. Everyone is welcome to receive Jesus. The water of life is given freely, and the world will be satisfied.

The words declared on the scroll are sacred. They are not to be added to or taken away from, for the words are God's. Terrible punishments, like those mentioned in the scroll, await those who distort the message of the book by adding to or taking away from the judgments of God. The inheritance in the holy city and one's part in the book of life will be taken away from such people.

Jesus reminds us that He is coming quickly. In the meantime, we are to tell the world the message of Christ and help them get ready. Most of all, we live by His grace.

—A. Koshy Muthalaly.

World Missions

In certain circumstances a person might be quite certain that because one thing has happened, a second thing will also happen. It is called waiting for the other shoe to drop. So it should be for Christians everywhere. Because Christ's first coming is history and because He has promised to return, we wait for the Second Coming.

The testimony of the church over the centuries is that Christ could come back at any time. It is called the imminent return of Christ. It is something we have read about and are taught, and it is something that could happen today. It is this great truth that should govern what we do and what we say. Our lives should reflect not only that our faith is placed in Christ but also that we expect Him at any moment.

Think of the various problems we get into simply because we forget the promise of His return. We can sometimes adopt the same logic as those who scoff about the Lord's return (cf. II Pet. 3:3-4). Because many centuries have gone by since the promise was given and He has not appeared, some are assuming it will not be today (or ever), and they do things they would otherwise not do if they really believed He might come soon.

Relationships are allowed to deteriorate, unwarranted separations and divorces happen, immorality is committed, thefts take place—the list could be greatly extended—all because some do not believe Jesus could come back at any time.

Something else that suffers is the church's missionary endeavor. Affluence, apathy, and apostasy plague the church in general in Western countries. Missionaries come home because of a lack of financial support. They come home because they do not get along with one another. They come home for other reasons too—some more legitimate than others. But whatever the reason, in the end the work of missions suffers.

We need to revisit basic doctrine and commit ourselves to the conviction that the Bible is the Word of God; therefore, it is true from Genesis to Revelation. Since it is true, the promise our Lord made to come back—a promise reiterated by others in the Scriptures—is still in effect, and it could happen today. We must keep that possibility in mind and live accordingly.

The other great truth to remember is that our Lord has rewards to give out to faithful servants. He is coming soon, and His reward is with Him to give to His own according to their work. What is it we would want to be doing when Christ comes back?

There are a number of very basic questions we need to ask ourselves in light of His promise to come back. Do we really believe He will come back? Do we really believe it could be at any moment? Do we believe that how we have lived up to the time of His coming will make a difference? Do we believe He has rewards to give His faithful workers? Do we want to hear Him say, "Well done" (cf. Matt. 25:21, 23)? If we knew Jesus was coming back later today, who would we contact to urge to receive Christ as Saviour? If we knew Christ was coming back in five years, would that affect our giving to support missionaries on the field? Would we increase support to Bible schools or Bible distribution organizations?

Spend some time making a list of things you would do today if Jesus were coming back tomorrow.

—*Darrell W. McKay.*

The Jewish Aspect

As John concluded Revelation, he issued an invitation. His words surely struck a familiar chord in the minds of his Jewish readers: "And the Spirit and the bride say, Come. And let him that heareth say, Come. And let him that is athirst come. And whosoever will, let him take the water of life freely" (22:17).

John's invitation to "come" has its roots firmly embedded in the Old Testament. From God's invitation to Noah to "come thou and all thy house into the ark" (Gen. 7:1) to His call to Israel to "come now, and let us reason together" (Isa. 1:18), the invitation to "come" shows the heart of God to His people.

The most specific passage that comes to mind, however, is Isaiah 55:1-2. That text and Revelation 22:17 have numerous parallels, including the emphasis on spiritual water.

The threefold use of the verb "come" in both passages is also remarkable. Motyer observed that each use of the verb in Isaiah "highlights a distinct aspect of what is offered" (*The Prophecy of Isaiah,* InterVarsity).

Motyer elaborated on this by observing that the first "come" "highlights the existence of need and the adequacy of the provision of water for the thirsty." The second "come" "highlights the poverty of the needy one," since he has no money. The third "come" "highlights the richness . . . as well as the freeness of the commodity," since it includes wine and milk. John's words have the same threefold emphasis.

The prophet Isaiah issued his call to "every one," parallel to John's "whosoever." The Jews commonly thought that God's redemptive plan was limited to the nation of Israel. Isaiah's call, however, was extended to the "nations that knew not" God (vs. 5), that is, the Gentile nations. He "issues a sweeping invitation: every thirsty person is invited to come to the water" (Oswalt, *The Book of Isaiah, Chapters 40—66,* Eerdmans).

This invitation to receive spiritual water reflects Isaiah's earlier words—"For I will pour water upon him that is thirsty, and floods upon the dry ground" (Isa. 44:3)—and the words of David—"My soul thirsteth for thee, my flesh longeth for thee in a dry and thirsty land, where no water is" (Ps. 63:1).

The fullness of God's salvation is found in Isaiah's passage and is indicated in John's use of the word "freely." Not only is spiritual water offered, but so are "wine and milk" (Isa. 55:1). "Water" represents the prime necessity of life and thus pictures the blessings of salvation. "Wine" represents that which brings gladness and joy to life (Ps. 104:15), and "milk" symbolizes that which nourishes life (Josh. 5:6). These elements of a completed salvation are purchased "freely" (Rev. 22:17), "without money and without price" (Isa. 55:1), because the price was paid by the Messiah (cf. chap. 53), our coming Lord Jesus (cf. Rev. 22:20).

Horatius Bonar wrote "I Heard the Voice of Jesus Say" in 1846. The second stanza echoes Revelation 22:17:

I heard the voice of Jesus say,
"Behold, I freely give
The living water; thirsty one,
Stoop down, and drink, and live."
I came to Jesus, and I drank
Of that life-giving stream;
My thirst was quenched, my soul revived,
And now I live in Him.

—*R. Larry Overstreet.*

Guiding the Superintendent

As believers, when we begin to contemplate the Lord's imminent return, we cannot help desiring to live a life that pleases Him. As our faith grows, so does our assurance that Christ will accept us into His eternal bliss. Christ will return. He is coming back for His bride, the church, which will be without spot or wrinkle. We will return with Him and rest with Him in that place of heavenly peace. What a glorious climax to a life dedicated to kingdom building! Will you be ready when Jesus comes?

DEVOTIONAL OUTLINE

1. God knows the time (Rev. 22:6-10). John had been given the special privilege of being taken to heaven to receive a divine message for believers. He faithfully recorded what he heard and saw. His message is trustworthy, and there is a blessing for those who attend to its truths.

John was overwhelmed by the experience and began to bow down to worship the angel who had been his guide during the vision. Immediately he was admonished to get up, since his guide was actually a fellow servant.

Revelation 22:10 reads, "Seal not the sayings of the prophecy of this book: for the time is at hand." Daniel, however, was told, "Shut up the words, and seal the book, even to the time of the end" (Dan. 12:4). There is an obvious contrast in these two commands, but the common theme is time. At the time of Daniel's prophecy, the "time of the end" had not yet come, but for John the final judgment was imminent, so he was not to fail to make the message known.

2. God crowns our faith (Rev. 22:12-13, 16-17). Everything has a price, but not everything has a reward. Having faith in the One who is omnipotent, possesses all authority, and is from everlasting to everlasting has its own reward. Christ announces with boldness that He is both the "root" and the "offspring" of King David. Those who believe that Jesus is indeed the Christ, the Son of the living God, shall be rewarded with a crown of life. It strengthens our faith to be reminded of all that God is. The Spirit and the church welcome and embrace us. How refreshing it is to drink freely of the water of life!

3. God guards His Word (Rev. 22:18-21). It is imperative that we heed God's warning concerning the handling of His Word and the dangers of willfully perverting its teachings. Omissions are just as wrong as additions. Teachers must be careful to present the pure, unadulterated, life-giving word of truth, since they have a greater accountability to God (cf. Jas. 3:1).

AGE-GROUP EMPHASES

Children: Even a very young child can sense Mom's absence. Some experience separation anxiety and accept comfort only once she has returned. Encourage the children by reminding them that Jesus is coming back again.

Youths: Teens relate well to rewards. They need to know that the greatest reward we can receive is the one that Christ will bring with Him when He returns. That reward is, first and foremost, Christ Himself.

Adults: To be complacent and self-righteous is dangerous, particularly in light of Christ's inevitable and soon return. Challenge your adults to observe the Lord's admonitions to the church in Revelation 22.

—*Jane E. Campbell.*

sus calmed the storm, prompting the disciples to worship Him.

Even supernatural beings submit to the power and will of Jesus. In Mark 9:20, a father brought his demon-possessed son to Jesus for healing. When the demon saw Jesus, he threw the boy into convulsions, and the boy fell to the ground. Jesus' disciples had already tried to cast out the demon but could not do so because of their lack of faith. Jesus, being God, has none of the disciples' limitations. He rebuked the demon, commanding that he leave the boy and never return. The demon left the boy in obedience to Jesus' voice (vs. 26).

Not only is Jesus greater than the demons, but He is also greater than the angels. Angels are powerful beings. They are God's messengers and servants for many important tasks. But Jesus, our mighty God, is better than the angels as He has a better name: Son (Heb. 1:4). It is the Son who will sit on God's throne, not angels. All of God's angels worship the Son without reservation (vs. 6).

Angels recognize the many excellent attributes possessed by Jesus as part of their worship of Him. They praise Him as the lamb that was slain to pay for our sins, by ascribing to Him power, wisdom, strength, and glory (Rev. 5:12). Angels recognize that only Jesus, being God, is worthy of worship. When the apostle John falls at the feet of an angel to worship him, the angel tells him that he must not do that—the angel is only a servant. Only God is worthy of worship (Rev. 22:8–9).

Jesus asserts that He is God by many indisputable proofs. As God, He is worthy of our worship and complete obedience. Let us praise Him for His goodness toward us!

Jesus: Worthy of Our Obedient Faith

GLENN WEAVER

According to many people, faith means little more than hoping something will come to pass. But genuine biblical faith has an object: trust in Jesus Christ. The concept of faith frequently appears in the Bible, using the synonyms "belief," "trust," and "faith" to get the idea across.

To trust in Jesus requires allegiance to Him and His Word. He is God, the King of kings, the Alpha and the Omega. Some people view Him as a man who died a long time ago. But He is the living Saviour, mighty and active in this world. His Word is trustworthy and honorable, and to obey it results in godly living. To have biblical faith results in loyalty and obedience to Jesus.

Jesus sought to convey to a crowd that belief needs to result in obedience. He explained that true disciples continue following His word (John 8:31). But they misplaced the object of their faith. They believed that merely because they were descendants of Abraham, they followed God faithfully. Jesus promised them freedom from sin if they followed Him; instead, they sought to kill Him because they did not want to follow His words (vss. 34–37).

Again Jesus sought to convince the crowd to follow His teaching. He explained that those who follow His word would conquer death (vs. 51). The crowd responded by claiming that Jesus had a demon. The group claimed to follow God, but Jesus asserted they did not know God (vss. 54–55).

Faith is an important element when Jesus heals people. When Jesus healed the sick woman who touched His garment, He explained that her faith had made her well (Luke 8:48). On His way to Jairus's house, Jesus was told that He was no longer needed; Jairus's daughter had died. Jesus encouraged Jairus to have faith. His daughter would be well (vs. 50).

At a later time, Jesus impressed the same lesson on Martha when her brother Lazarus died. When Jesus met her at the tomb, He responded to her lack of faith by reminding her of what He said earlier—she would see God's glory if she had faith (John 11:40). Jesus prayed to God audibly so that bystanders would believe that the Father sent Him, then He commanded Lazarus to come out of the grave (vss. 41–43). Lazarus walked out of the tomb in obedience.

There were examples of faith and lack of faith at Jesus' crucifixion (Luke 23:33–49). The Jewish rulers, Roman soldiers, and one of the crucified criminals taunted Jesus. They said that if He was the Christ, He should save Himself. But the other crucified criminal expressed his faith in Jesus. He knew that Jesus was innocent of the charges against Him. Jesus promised that the man would be with Him in paradise because of his faith (vs. 43).

The crucifixion tested the disciples' faith. Mary Magdalene and other women went to the tomb to anoint Jesus' body with spices, but they found the tomb empty (Luke 24:1–10). Two men in shining garments told them that Jesus was alive. The women went to the disciples and told them what they had seen and heard. The disciples refused to believe the women's report that Jesus had risen from the dead (vs. 11). But when Jesus appeared to the disciples, they believed He had risen (vs. 34).

The purpose of Jesus' miracles was to persuade people to believe in Him. The first miracle in Cana of Galilee occurred at a marriage feast (John 2:1–12). They ran out of wine, so Jesus turned water into the best wine. This miracle revealed Jesus' glory and led His disciples to trust in Him.

Later a man brought his demon-possessed son to Jesus' disciples (Mark 9:14–29). They could not cast out the demon, so the father brought the son to Jesus. Why were the disciples unable to cast out the demon? The father, the gathering crowd, and even the disciples were weak in their faith (vs. 19). Jesus would later tell His disciples that they could increase their spiritual strength through prayer and fasting (vs. 29).

The Jewish leaders had a different view of obedience than Jesus. They were concerned with the minutiae of the Old Testament law. But Jesus saw the bigger picture. He saw a man with a withered hand that needed healing. As the Lord of the Sabbath, He healed the man and did not violate the Sabbath (Luke 6:1–10). The leaders were furious; they saw Jesus' act of compassion as a violation of the Sabbath and discussed what they could do to Him (vs. 11).

Peter learned that faith in Christ is not a one-time event but a continual calling. Jesus sent His disciples across the Sea of Galilee in a boat while He went up a mountain to pray (Matt. 12:22–23). At nighttime, He walked across the sea to the boat. When Peter saw Jesus, he said he would like to walk to Him on the sea. At Jesus' bidding, Peter got out of the boat and walked toward Him. When the fierce winds and waves distracted Peter, he began to sink. As Jesus saved him from the water, He explained that Peter sank for lack of faith (vs. 31).

Faith often leads to action. Four men with a paralyzed friend heard that Jesus was in a house in Capernaum (Mark 2:1-3). They wanted Jesus to heal their friend, but the crowd was too large. They decided to remove a portion of the roof and lower their friend through it. When Jesus saw their faith, He healed the paralyzed man and forgave his sins (vss. 5, 11–12).

A life of faith is an active life. Faith in Christ leads us to pray for others and help them. At times faith may lead us into situations where we feel uncomfortable or unprepared. But we should not fear. Christ wants us to trust Him through difficult times. He will never fail us!

TOPICS FOR NEXT QUARTER

PARAGRAPHS ON
PLACES AND PEOPLE

CAPERNAUM

Capernaum was a village located on the north side of the Sea of Galilee, along a trade route between Damascus and Egypt. It was probably constructed in the second century B.C.

After leaving Nazareth, Jesus lived in Capernaum (Matt. 4:13-16). Peter, Andrew, James, and John were fishermen from the area (Mark 1:16-34). Matthew was also nearby when Jesus called him (Matt. 9:1, 9-13). Many events recorded in the Gospels happened here (Matt. 8:5-13; 14:34—15:20; 17:24-27).

Archaeologists have discovered graffiti-scratched ruins that might have been Peter's house. Basalt foundations have been found beneath a fourth-century synagogue—perhaps this was an older synagogue built by the Roman centurion (Luke 7:1-10).

THE TREE OF LIFE

The Bible begins with the creation of heaven and earth. Immediately afterward, humanity is put at the Garden of Eden, with a flowing river and the tree of life (Gen. 2:8-14). After the Fall, Satan's destruction is promised (Gen. 3:15). In Revelation, we see a mirror of this in the fulfillment of all that was meant to be. After Satan is fully defeated (20:7-10), we once again see the tree of life by the river (22:1-2). Some scholars think the tree of life has multiplied into many trees, explaining how it can stand on both sides of the river (cf. Ezek. 47:12).

By beginning and ending with the tree of life by the river, the Bible highlights the unity of history as a single story focused on Jesus, who declares: "I am Alpha and Omega, the beginning and the end, the first and the last" (Rev. 22:13).

THE WOMEN AT THE TOMB

Some skeptics claim to find contradictions between the Gospels in their lists of the women at the tomb, since not all the same names are given. But not naming someone is not the same as denying they were present. John only *names* Mary Magdalene, but he clearly knew she was not alone, since she says, "They have taken away the Lord out of the sepulchre, and we know not where they have laid him" (John 20:2).

Who were these women? Apart from the more famous Marys, here are a few: Salome was at the crucifixion and resurrection (Mark 15:40; 16:1). Tradition says she may be the mother of James and John. Her name could be a variation of *shalom*, meaning "peace." She may have had "Mary" in her name, which would make her one of three Marys!

Joanna was healed by Jesus and helped provide for Him (Luke 8:2-3, 24:10). She was also the wife of Herod's steward, which shows that Christianity had spread to high places.

THE AUTHOR OF HEBREWS

Who wrote the book of Hebrews? The short answer is, no one is sure. We know Hebrews was written before A.D. 96 because it is quoted by Clement of Rome at that time. It was almost certainly written before the destruction of the temple in A.D. 70 because the author warns against going back to the Jewish sacrificial system, which would have been impossible after that date.

Many prominent Christians in history have thought the author was Paul, but others object: Paul signs his letters, and Hebrews is anonymous. Scholars have suggested Barnabas, Luke, or others.

—Tom Greene.

Daily Bible Readings for Home Study and Worship

(Readings are for the week previous to the lesson topics.)

1.   March 3.   Jesus' Claim to Deity

M — Christ Is Truth. II John 1:2, 9-11.
T — Live as Jesus Did. I John 2:3-6.
W — Grateful Slaves to Righteousness. Rom. 6:15-23.
T — Death for Apostasy. Deut. 13:6-11.
F — Obedience by Faith. Heb. 11:8-12.
S — Your Father the Devil. John 8:39-47.
S — Before Abraham Was, I Am. John 8:31-38, 48-56, 58-59.

2.   March 10.   Jairus's Daughter and the Bleeding Woman

M — Healing a Suffering Woman. Mark 5:25-34.
T — Rules About the Discharge of Blood. Lev. 15:25-30.
W — Jairus's Daughter Brought Back to Life. Mark 5:21-24, 35-43.
T — Rules About Touching the Dead. Num.19:11-21.
F — Matthew's Account of the Restoration of Life. Matt. 9:18-19, 23-26.
S — Anointed with Power and the Holy Ghost. Acts 10:34-38.
S — Faith in Jesus' Power. Luke 8:40-56.

3.   March 17.   The Raising of Lazarus

M — Many Believe. John 10:39-42.
T — Friends of Jesus. Luke 10:38-42.
W — A Planned Delay. John 11:1-16.
T — I Am the Resurrection. John 11:17-27.
F — Plotting Against Jesus. John 11:45-57.
S — A Devoted Follower. John 12:1-8.
S — God's Glory Revealed. John 11:38-44.

4.   March 24.   The Crucifixion of Jesus

M — Lament of Forsakenness. Ps. 22:1-18.
T — Jesus Foretells His Death. Matt. 16:13-23; 17:22-23.
W — Disciples Will Be Scattered. Mark 14:27-31.
T — Jesus Before Pilate. Matt. 27:11-26.
F — Jesus Mocked by the Soldiers. Mark 15:15-20.
S — Weeping Daughters of Jerusalem. Luke 23:26-32.
S — Jesus Commits His Spirit to His Father. Luke 23:33-49.

5.   March 31.   The Resurrection of Jesus (Easter)

M — Jesus' Burial. Luke 23:50-56.
T — Disciples Find the Tomb Empty. John 20:1-10.
W — Mary Magdalene Meets the Risen Lord. John 20:11-18.
T — The False Report of the Roman Guards. Matt. 28:11-15.
F — Jesus Appears to Two Disciples. Luke 24:13-29.
S — Jesus Appears to All the Disciples. Luke 24:36-49.
S — The Empty Tomb. Luke 24:1-12, 30-35.

6.   April 7.   Jesus' First Miracle

M — Jesus Gains Followers. John 1:35-42.
T — More Follow Jesus. John 1:43-51.
W — A Roman Official Believes. John 4:46-54.
T — A Blind Man Sees and Believes. John 9:1-7, 35-38.
F — The Purpose of Signs. John 20:26-31.
S — Disciples Affirm Their Faith. John 6:66-69.
S — Water Turned to Wine. John 2:1-12.

7.   April 14.   Jesus' Authority over Demons

M — Authority Given to the Twelve. Matt. 10:1-15.
T — Sent Two by Two. Mark 6:7-13.
W — The Seventy Are Sent and Return. Luke 10:1, 17-20.
T — A Demoniac by the Sea of Galilee. Mark 5:1-13.
F — Go and Proclaim. Matt. 28:18-20.
S — Philip Casts Out Unclean Spirits. Acts 8:4-8.
S — Unclean Spirit Departs at Jesus' Command. Mark 9:14-29.

8.   April 21.   Healing on the Sabbath

M — Observing the Sabbath. Deut. 5:12-15.
T — David Given Consecrated Bread. I Sam. 21:1-6.
W — Disabled Man Healed on the Sabbath. John 5:1-16.
T — Sabbath Made for Man. Mark 2:23-28.
F — Compassion, Not Sacrifice. Matt. 12:1-8.
S — Opponents Humiliated. Luke 13:10-17.
S — Lord of the Sabbath. Luke 6:1-11.

9.   April 28.   Jesus' Mighty Power

M — Jesus Calms the Sea. Matt. 8:23-27.
T — Power over Demons. Mark 1:21-28.
W — Power over Living Things. Mark 11:12-23.
T — Power over the Waves. Luke 8:22-25.
F — Undeniable Power. Matt. 9:27-35.
S — Power over the Wind. Mark 6:45-51.
S — Jesus Walks on the Sea. Matt. 14:22-36.

10.   May 5.   Healing and Forgiveness

M — The Blessing of Forgiveness. Ps. 32:1-5.
T — Power to Forgive. Matt. 9:1-8.
W — Forgiveness and Redemption in the Lord. Ps. 130:1-8.
T — A Readiness to Forgive Sins. Luke 5:18-26.
F — The Power of the Righteous Man's Prayer. Jas. 5:13-18.
S — The Lord Forgives and Heals. Ps. 103:1-5.
S — Jesus Responds to Evidence of Faith. Mark 2:1-12.

11.   May 12.   The Son Greater than Angels

M — Crowned with Glory. Heb. 1:13—2:9.
T — Glory Forever. II Tim. 2:8-10.
W — The Image of God. II Cor. 4:1-6.
T — At the Right Hand of God. Acts 2:32-36.
F — God's Unique Son. Ps. 2:1-12.
S — God's Beloved Son. Matt. 3:13-17.
S — He Has Spoken by His Son. Heb. 1:1-10.

12.   May 19.   The Lamb Worthy of Worship

M — The Lamb of God. John 1:29-34.
T — Jesus Worshipped. Luke 24:50-53.
W — Worthy to Reign. Rev. 5:1-5.
T — Root of Jesse. Isa. 11:1-10.
F — Redeemed by His Shed Blood. I Pet. 1:17-21.
S — Reigning with Christ. Rev. 20:1-6.
S — The Lion Is the Lamb. Rev. 5:6-14.

13.   May 26.   The Alpha and Omega

M — The New Jerusalem. Rev. 21:9—22:5.
T — I Come Quickly. Rev. 3:7-13.
W — The Word of the Lord Stands Forever. Isa. 40:6-8.
T — Salvation Is Coming with His Reward. Isa. 62:10-12.
F — A Free Invitation. Isa. 55:1-13.
S — Let the Thirsty Come. John 7:37-39.
S — Come, Lord Jesus. Rev. 22:6-10, 12-13, 16-21.

REVIEW

Can you answer these questions?

Jesus Is God

UNIT I: Confirmed by Power over Death

March 3

Jesus' Claim to Deity

1. What did Jesus identify as the mark of a true disciple?
2. What does sin do to a person who is living apart from God?
3. What contrast did Jesus draw between Abraham and the Jews who opposed Him?
4. Why did Jesus say He was not seeking His own glory?
5. What are our only two options in responding to Jesus' claim to deity?

March 10

Jairus's Daughter and the Bleeding Woman

1. Why was it so surprising that Jesus asked who had touched Him?
2. What was it about the woman that caused Jesus to respond to her?
3. How did Jesus respond to the bad news about Jairus's daughter?
4. Over what two areas did Jesus demonstrate His authority here?
5. Why is it significant that Jesus refers to death as "sleep"?

March 17

The Raising of Lazarus

1. Why was Jesus angry as He approached the grave of Lazarus?
2. Why did Jesus pray before raising Lazarus?
3. Did the resurrection of Lazarus fulfill Jesus' desire to arouse faith in the onlookers? Explain

4. What was foreshadowed by Jesus' call for Lazarus to come forth?

March 24

The Crucifixion of Jesus

1. How did Jesus practice what He preached even when hanging on the cross?
2. How did the Jewish rulers mock Jesus' claim that He was the promised Messiah?
3. How did Jesus extend God's grace to the second criminal?
4. What miracle did God perform as Jesus hung on the cross?
5. What did the tearing of the veil symbolize?

March 31

The Resurrection of Jesus (Easter)

1. Why did the women come to the tomb?
2. How did the apostles at first react to the report of the women?
3. What was significant about the arrangement of the graveclothes in the tomb?
4. How did the apostles react to the arrival of the disciples from Emmaus?

UNIT II: Confirmed by Mighty Miracles

April 7

Jesus' First Miracle

1. What does Jesus' attendance of the wedding tell us about Him?
2. Why was the shortage of wine of such momentous concern?
3. Why did the servants' obedience to Jesus' instructions require faith?
4. What does John indicate was the purpose of Jesus' miracles (cf. 20:30-31)?
5. What response came from the disciples of Jesus? What response should come from us?

April 14

Jesus' Authority over Demons

1. What happened when the boy first saw Jesus?
2. What seemed to have happened to the father's faith? Why?
3. Why did Jesus say "If thou canst believe" (Mark 9:23) to the father?
4. How did Jesus explain the disciples' inability to succeed?

April 21

Healing on the Sabbath

1. Why did the Pharisees think Jesus' disciples were breaking the Sabbath law?
2. Did Jesus and His disciples actually violate God's Sabbath law? Explain.
3. What was Jesus' point in citing the example of David and the tabernacle bread?
4. What principle about obedience did Jesus teach through His question to the scribes and Pharisees?

April 28

Jesus' Mighty Power

1. Why did Jesus send the disciples ahead of Him?
2. What request did Peter make of Jesus? How did Jesus respond?
3. In what sense was Peter's faith "little" (Matt. 14:31)?
4. What happened as soon as Jesus and Peter reached the boat?
5. How did the disciples respond to what they had witnessed on the sea?

May 5

Healing and Forgiveness

1. What happened that interrupted Jesus' teaching?
2. What was so shocking about Jesus' first words to the paralytic?
3. What was the reaction of the religious leaders to Jesus' words?

4. What did Jesus call Himself, and what did this title convey?
5. What did Jesus intend to prove by healing the paralytic?

UNIT III: Confirmed by His Exaltation

May 12

The Son Greater than Angels

1. How did God speak to His people in the past, and how does that differ from how He speaks now?
2. What is meant by the fact that Jesus is "the brightness of [God's] glory" (Heb. 1:3)?
3. What does it mean that Jesus is "the express image of [God's] person" (vs. 3)?
4. What is the role of angels, and how does that differentiate them from the Son?
5. How is Jesus' kingdom described?

May 19

The Lamb Worthy of Worship

1. What might have been contained in the book with the seven seals?
2. How do we see the three Persons of the Triune God in this chapter?
3. Why is Jesus worthy to take the book and open its seals?
4. How extensive or widespread is the worship of the Lamb?

May 26

The Alpha and Omega

1. How did the angel describe himself to John?
2. Why was John told not to seal the prophecy?
3. How might we understand the Lord's promise to "come quickly" (Rev. 22:7) in light of the length of time since the promise was made?
4. What role do works play in the final judgment?
5. What strong warning is given about altering the message of Revelation?